Grammar and Lexicon: Interactions and Interfaces (GramLex 2016)

Osaka, Japan
11 December 2016

Editors:

Eva Hajicova
Igor Boguslavsky

ISBN: 978-1-5108-3318-0

Grammar and Lexicon: Interactions and Interfaces (GramLex 2016)

Osaka, Japan
11 December 2016

GramLex 2016

Grammar and Lexicon: Interactions and Interfaces

Proceedings of the Workshop

Eva Hajičová and Igor Boguslavsky (editors)

December 11, 2016
Osaka, Japan

Preface

The proposal to organize the workshop on **"Grammar and lexicon: interactions and interfaces"** was motivated by suggestions made by several participants at previous COLINGs, who expressed their concern that linguistic issues (as a part of the computational linguistics agenda) should be made more visible at future COLINGs. We share the feeling of these colleagues that it is time to enhance the linguistic dimension in the CL spectrum, as well as to strengthen the focus on explanatory rather than engineering aspects, and we decided to organize a workshop with a broad theme concerning the relations between GRAMMAR and LEXICON, but specifically focused on burning issues from that domain. This idea was met enthusiastically by many colleagues who are also feeling that our conferences are excessively biased towards mathematical and engineering approaches to the detriment of discovering and explaining linguistic facts and regularities. The workshop is aiming at bringing together both linguistically as well as computationally minded participants in order to think of fruitful mutual exploitation of each other's ideas. In the call for papers, we have tried to motivate the authors of the papers to bring in novel, maybe even controversial ideas rather than to repeat old practice.

Two types of contributions are included in the programme of the workshop and in these Proceedings: (a) presentations of invited **position statements** focused on particular issues of the broader topic, and (b) papers selected through an **Open Call** for papers with a regular reviewing procedure. This format allows for short presentations of leading scholars just setting the framework for the discussion in which all the participants will have space for their engagement. To ensure this, abstracts of the invited statements have been included on the workshop web page so that the prospective authors of submissions from the Open Call obtain well in advance a good orientation, and full versions of these position papers are included in the volume of workshop Proceedings, followed by full versions of the papers accepted for presentation during the review process.

We hope that the workshop will come out as a lively forum touching upon issues that might be of interest (and, possibly, an inspiration for application both in theory and in practice) for a broader research community with different background: linguistic, computational or natural language processing and that it will facilitate a focused discussion, which could involve even those in the audience who do not yet have research experience in the topic discussed.

We would like to thank the panelists for the help they have provided us in forming the shape and contents of the workshop, all authors for their careful preparation of camera ready versions of their papers and, last but not least, all the members of the reviewing committee for their efforts to make their reviews as detailed as possible and thus helped the authors to express their ideas and standpoints in a most comprehensible way.

Eva Hajičová
Igor Boguslavsky

Organisers of the Workshop

Eva Hajičová

Igor Boguslavsky

Workshop Proceedings Editor

Eduard Bejček

START Submission Management

Zdeňka Urešová

Table of Contents

Part I:

Invited Position Papers

Information structure, syntax, and pragmatics and other factors in resolving scope ambiguity

Valentina Apresjan

National Research University "Higher School of Economics"
20 Myasnitskaya Ulitsa, Moscow 101000, Russia
Vinogradov Russian Language Institute
Volkhonka 18/2, 119019 Moscow
`valentina.apresjan@gmail.com`

Abstract

The paper is a corpus study of the factors involved in disambiguating potential scope ambiguity in sentences with negation and universal quantifier, such as *I don't want talk to all these people*, which can alternatively mean 'I don't want to talk to any of these people' and 'I don't want to talk to some of these people'. The relevant factors are demonstrated to be largely different from those involved in disambiguating lexical polysemy. They include the syntactic function of the constituent containing *all* (subject, direct complement, adjunct), as well as the deepness of its embedding; the status of the main predicate and *all* with respect to the information structure of the utterance (topic vs. focus, given vs. new information); pragmatic implicatures pertaining to the situations described in the utterances.

1   Introduction

Scope ambiguity is a wide-spread phenomenon, which is fairly well described in the studies of semantics-syntax interface. However, in actual communication we rarely experience difficulties in assigning correct scope to operators in the contexts which allow potential ambiguity. Unlike lexical polysemy, which is more frequently resolved by semantic factors, i.e. semantic classes of collocates, one of the crucial factors in resolving scope ambiguity is pragmatics. Consider the adverb *accidentally*, which presupposes an action and asserts its non-intentionality; cf. *I didn't cut my finger accidentally* = 'I cut my finger [presupposition]; it was not intentional [assertion]'.

Accidentally can have wide scope readings as in (1), where it has scope over the verb and the modifier of time, and narrow scope readings as in (2) where it has scope only over the complement:

(1) *The house was accidentally [**burnt in 1947**]*

(2) *We accidentally planted [**potatoes**]*

Wide scope readings refer to purely accidental events and narrow scope readings denote mistaken intentional actions.

The readings are determined by pragmatics: *We accidentally planted [**potatoes**]* favors narrow scope, since in a plausible world, planting is deliberate; therefore, the mistake concerns only a certain aspect of this action. On a linguistic level, it means that the adverb *accidentally* affects only one argument of this verb (the object – the planting stock).

On the other hand, *The house was accidentally [**burnt in 1947**]* favors wide scope, since house-burning is normally unintentional; as for the possibility of a deliberate reading, an arson meant for a particular year is pragmatically implausible.

The discussion is mostly devoted to pragmatic and other factors that are at play in the interpretation of scope ambiguities in the combination of the universal quantifier *all* with negation. It is well-known, that in certain sentences with *all* and *not*, negation can have scope either over the verb, or over *all*, as in (1) and (2):

(3) *I did not [**see**] all these people* ≈ *I saw none of those people*
(*not* has scope over the verb)

Proceedings of the Workshop on Grammar and Lexicon: Interactions and Interfaces,
pages 1–6, Osaka, Japan, December 11 2016.

(4) *I did not see [**all**] these people* ≈ *I saw some of these people* (*not* has scope over the universal quantifier)

Thus, the surface structure with negation, a verb and a quantifier phrase *not V all X* can be interpreted as either as (5) or (6) depending on whether negation has scope over the verb or over the universal quantifier.

(5) *not V all X* = not [**V**] all X (of all Xs, it is true that they are not V)

(6) *not V all X* = not V [**all X**] (it is not true that all Xs are V = some Xs are V and some Xs are not V)

Yet cases where both interpretations are equally feasible are quite rare. In the majority of cases, context provides sufficient clues as to the choice of the intended reading; cf.

(7) *I don't believe all this bullshit he [**tells**] me* (≈ 'I don't believe anything of what he tells me', negation has scope over the VP)

(8) *I don't agree with [**all he says**] but many things sound reasonable* (≈ 'I agree with part of what he says', negation has scope over the quantifier phrase)

2   Methods and material

The paper employs corpus methods. The material comes from the parallel Russian-English and English-Russian corpus, which is a sub-corpus of the Russian National Corpus (ruscorpora.ru). It counts 24,675,890 words and comprises 19-21 century Russian and English literature (mostly novels), as well as a certain amount of periodicals, in translations. Parallel literary corpus has been chosen because there is plentiful context to verify the correctness of the reading, which is further facilitated by the presence of the translation or the original. The use of a parallel corpus also enables one to conduct a contrastive study of the factors involved in disambiguation. These factors have been found to be the same for Russian and English, although English sentences with scope ambiguity of this type are on the whole more typical of English than for Russian, which favors constituent negation.

The search query has been formulated as *not + v + all*, with the distances set at 3 words. All contexts that preclude ambiguous readings in principle, such as various idiomatic expressions (*not at all, all of it, at all costs, after all, all the more, not only…but also* etc.); combinations of *all* with numerals (*all four*), deeply embedded clauses (*They told them not to stop running until they got all the way back to Tokyo*) have been excluded from the search. Total useful results yielded 147 hits.

3   Results and discussion

The distribution of the interpretations is as follows:

- 82 readings where *not* has scope over the universal quantifier, such as *You haven't told me [all]* ≈ 'You have told me part of what you know'; *I haven't eaten [all] the apples she bought* 'I have eaten some of the apples that she bought';

- 58 readings where *not* has scope over the matrix verb or another constituent, such as *I don't [give a heck] about all these idiots* ≈ 'I don't give a heck about any of these idiots'; *I didn't come all the way from Alabama [to hear you say that]* ≈ 'I came all the way from Alabama for another reason';

- 7 ambiguous readings.

As appears from these data, the actual ambiguity is indeed rather rare, though the distribution of the interpretations is not exactly balanced. Contexts when the universal quantifier does not fall into the scope of negation are less frequent, and can therefore be assumed more marked in terms of semantic, pragmatic, syntactic and communicative conditions.

4 Factors at play in scope disambiguation

The following factors appear to be relevant in the choice of interpretation:

- **Information structure** of the utterance, namely whether *all* is in the topic or in the focus;

- **Semantic structure** of the utterance, namely, whether the universal quantifier is presupposed;

- **Syntactic structure** of the utterance, namely whether there is a "competing" constituent that can "attract" negation in lieu of the universal quantifier;

- **Conventional implicatures**, namely what are the normal pragmatic expectations in the situations that are introduced by verbs and quantifier phrases.

Besides the factors listed above, there are some basic syntactic considerations that affect the possible readings; they are listed below.

If *all* is part of the **subject**, it usually requires constituent negation rather than sentence negation. Sentences like (9) are considerably less frequent that phrases like (10).

(9) ?*All Russians are not gloomy*

(10) *Not all Russians are gloomy* (V. Nabokov, Pale Fire)

So, it seems to be that the universal quantifier has to be to the right of negation in order to be able to fall into its scope.
And in that case, it is most easily affected by negation if it is a **direct complement** to the syntactically negated verb, as in (11):

(11) *He didn't like all his students* 'He liked only some of his students'

If *all* is part of the the **adjunct**, it is less accessible to negation, since certain adjuncts can move around more freely and can be fronted and topicalized, so (12) is more likely to be interpreted with negation scoping over the verb:

(12) *He didn't talk to me all this time* ≈ *All this time, He didn't talk to me*
'The entire time, he didn't talk to me'

Also, if the constituent containing *all* is **deeply embedded**, it prevents negation from affecting the universal quantifier:

(13) *"Well…" and here Clyde hesitated and stumbled, quite as if he had not been instructed as to all this beforehand* (Theodore Dreiser, An American Tragedy) ≈ 'He had been instructed as to all this beforehand, but hesitated and stumbled as though he hadn't'

On the whole, *all* is most flexible as part of direct complements and adjuncts and in this syntactic function allows, in principle, both scope interpretations. The factors influencing these interpretations are examined below.

5 Information structure of the utterance

5.1 Both *all* and the matrix verb are part of the Topic

When both *all* and the matrix verb are part of the Topic, they are normally presupposed, and not asserted, and therefore, do not fall under negation; cf. discussion in Hajičova (1973). Thus, in the utterances where the universal quantifier *all* and the matrix verb are in the topic, negation has scope over the remaining constituent, usually the verbal adjunct:

(14) *I have not said all this* | [***in order to annoy you***]

In (9), the fact of saying certain things (*I have said all this*) is Topic, and the purpose of this speech act (*not in order to annoy you*) is Focus. Negation, as a typical focalizing component, does not affect the topic part, and therefore, *all* and the matrix verb remain presupposed and outside of the scope of the negative operator. Syntactically, adding a constituent that can "attract" negation helps create conditions for this type of information structure and interpretation. Negation shifts both from the universal quantifier and from the matrix verb to the purposive adjunct. Compare (14) with (15) which can only be interpreted as 'I have said some things but not all', where *all* is in the Focus and negated:

(15) *I have not said* | [***all***]

In the absence of a contracted proposition *in order to annoy you* a non-negated quantifier reading is not available.

A subtype of sentences with this information structure are phrases with another universal quantifier which creates a target for constituent negation. In sentences like (16) and (17) both the verb and the *all*-phrase are in the topic and the negated quantifier forms a contrastive focus.

(16) She had not [**ONCE**] [contrastive Focus] thought of him all the morning [Topic] [Leo Tolstoy. Anna Karenina (parts 5-8) (Constance Garnett, 1911)]

(17) And not [**a CREATURE**] [contrastive Focus] coming near us all the evening! [Topic] [Jane Austen. Persuasion (1816)]

5.2 *All* is given information, the matrix verb is new information[1]

In this type of sentences, *all* constitutes given information, although it is usually part of the Focus, along with the verb; it is presupposed and does not fall into the scope of negation. However, the matrix verb, which is either non-factive or is placed in a non-veridical context (Giannakidou 1998) constitutes new information and is not presupposed. Therefore, negation has scope over the matrix verb, but not over the universal quantifier:

(18) I'm not [**going**] all the way to Huntingdon to celebrate the ruby wedding of two people I have spoken to once for eight seconds since I was three (Helen Fielding, Bridget Jones's Diary (1996)] ≈ 'All the way to Huntington to celebrate the ruby wedding… [given information, presupposition]; I am not going [new information, assertion]' ≈ 'I am not going to Huntington at all for the ruby wedding'

The choice between interpretation in phrases like (18), on the one hand, and (19), on the other, frequently depends on the sentence type. Veridical contexts, like (19), license the factual interpretation

---

[1] For this type of sentences, it is more meaningful to distinguish between given information and new information. Universal quantifier *all* is given, it belongs to the background knowledge, and the verb is new. As for Topic-Focus structure, because sentences in this type are usually non-veridical, they tend to consist entirely of focalized information; cf. *I don't know what to do with all this food* (information about the food is presented as known to the listener, yet it forms part of the focus together with the verb).

of the verb, which is conducive to its placement in the presupposition and topic. Non-veridical contexts, like (18), license the non-factual interpretation of the verb, which inhibits its placement in the presupposition and topic. If the context in (18) were changed to veridical, as in (19), the entire semantic and informational structure would be changed; cf.

(19) I have not come all the way to Huntingdon [Topic] // [**to celebrate the ruby wedding of two people I have spoken to once for eight seconds since I was three**] [Focus] ≈ 'I have come all the way to Huntington, but not for the purpose of celebrating the ruby wedding'

5.3 *All* is in the Focus, the matrix verb is part of the Topic

In this type of sentences, the matrix verb and the rest of the sentence are in the topic, while *all* forms a contrastive focus. The verb is presupposed and does not fall into the scope of negation, whereas *all* is asserted and becomes target for negation, attaining the interpretation 'some'. Consider the following sentences:

(20) The right rim of the casket had not fallen [**ALL**] [contrastive Focus] the way to the floor and was still propped partially on its supports [Dan Brown. Angels and Demons (2000)] ['The rim had fallen part of the way']

(21) They could not watch [**ALL**] [contrastive Focus] places [**ALWAYS**] [contrastive Focus] [Isaac Asimov. The Gods Themselves (1972)] ['They watched some places some of the time, or all places some of the time, or some places all of the time']

This type of information structure is fairly frequent. It can be explained by the existence of pragmatic implicatures shared by the speaker and the hearer that allow the speaker to rely on this common background to draw contrast between the natural expectations and the actual situation. Some of these implicatures are considered in the section below.

6   Pragmatic implicatures

While in some cases the likelihood of a particular scope interpretation is determined by syntactic or information structure of an utterance, sometimes these considerations are overridden by pragmatic factors, most frequently by conventional pragmatic implicatures. An interesting case of pragmatic implicatures is provided by time expressions. The following examples demonstrate a certain pragmatic difference which determines different scope interpretations:

(22) *I haven't [**slept**] all night* ['The whole night, I haven't slept']

(23) *I haven't slept [**all**] day* ['I slept only part of the day']

There are different conventional implicatures concerning night and day, and they involve different pragmatic expectations: people usually sleep the greater part of the night, and do not sleep at all during the day. Saying that one did not sleep part of the night would not be particularly informative because people often sleep only the bigger part of the night, but not the whole night. This is proved by sentences like *I slept the whole night today*, stating this as a somewhat unusual occurrence. Thus, *sleeping the whole night* (very good night sleep) and *not sleeping the whole night* (total insomnia) are both noteworthy occurrences.

As for (23), it also describes an unusual situation, but it sets a different pragmatic context. It cannot be interpreted as (22), meaning that the speaker had day insomnia; since during the daytime people are expected to be active, an emphatic statement of their inability to sleep during this time would be pragmatically uninformative, thus violating Gricean maxims. The only way it can be plausibly interpreted is as a disproval of the interlocutor's conjecture that the speaker has slept all day, with the background knowledge that the speaker has slept at least some time during the day. Therefore, *all* is necessarily focused and emphasized and thus becomes available for negation.

To generalize, in context when *all* is part of a time expression, the interpretation is determined by pragmatic factors. Sleepless nights constitute a substantial part of this context type, with only negated verb readings available. As for the remaining contexts, for negated verb readings, the pragmatic implicature is as follows:

(24) It is unusual when there is no action V at all during the entire time period T, but also unusual if action V takes the entire time period T

Consider phrases like *He had not [**thought**] of her all evening; Her bed [**had**] not [**been made**] all day, They [**had**] not [**spoken**] all day* to illustrate this type of implicature and the consequent scope reading.

For negated quantifier readings, the pragmatic implicature is as follows:

(25) It is normal that action V is taking place during some of the time period T

Consider phrases like *The concert couldn't have detained you [**all**] this time, I don't want to be explaining myself [**all**] the time, I simply cannot work [**all**] the time* to illustrate this type of implicature and the consequent scope reading.

7   Conclusion

To conclude, the scope of negation over universal quantifier is determined by a range of factors. The preliminary "sifting" of contests shows the syntactic function of the constituent containing *all* to be the factor influencing scope interpretation. The next level of analysis demonstrates the role of information structure in selecting the plausible reading. Finally, in a variety of contexts scope disambiguation is triggered by conventional pragmatic implicatures.

Acknowledgments

This paper was funded by the grant of the Russian Scientific Fund, project 16-18-02054.

References

Giannakidou, A. 1998. *Polarity Sensitivity as (Non)veridical Dependency.* John Benjamins, Amsterdam-Philadelphia.

Hajičova, E. 1973. *Topic, Focus and Generative Semantics.* Kronberg/Taunus: Scriptor.

Multiword Expressions at the Grammar-Lexicon Interface

Timothy Baldwin
Dept of Computing and Information Systems,
The University of Melbourne
`tb@ldwin.net`

Abstract

In this talk, I will outline a range of challenges presented by multiword expressions in terms of (lexicalist) precision grammar engineering, and different strategies for accommodating those challenges, in an attempt to strike the right balance in terms of generalisation and over- and under-generation.

Proceedings of the Workshop on Grammar and Lexicon: Interactions and Interfaces,
page 7, Osaka, Japan, December 11 2016.

Microsyntactic Phenomena as a Computational Linguistics Issue

Leonid Iomdin

A.A.Kharkevich Institute for Information Transmission Problems,
Russian Academy of Sciences, Moscow, Russia

iomdin@gmail.com

Abstract

Microsyntactic linguistic units, such as syntactic idioms and non-standard syntactic constructions, are poorly represented in linguistic resources, mostly because the former are elements occupying an intermediate position between the lexicon and the grammar and the latter are too specific to be routinely tackled by general grammars. Consequently, many such units produce substantial gaps in systems intended to solve sophisticated computational linguistics tasks, such as parsing, deep semantic analysis, question answering, machine translation, or text generation. They also present obstacles for applying advanced techniques to these tasks, such as machine learning. The paper discusses an approach aimed at bridging such gaps, focusing on the development of monolingual and multilingual corpora where microsyntactic units are to be tagged.

1   Introduction

This work is largely based on the theory of microsyntax developed by the author over the last 15 years (see e.g. L.L.Iomdin 2013, 2014, 2015). In this theory, which has much in common with construction grammar (Fillmore 1988, Goldberg 1995, Rakhilina 2010) two main groups of linguistic units are distinguished: lexically oriented syntactic idioms and lexically independent non-standard syntactic constructions. Throughout the paper, I will be mostly concerned with syntactic idioms, which means that the concepts "microsyntactic units" and "syntactic idioms" are basically synonymous.

Microsyntactic linguistic units, such as syntactic idioms and non-standard syntactic constructions,[1] are poorly represented in linguistic resources, mostly because the former occupy an intermediate position between the lexicon and the grammar and the latter are too specific to be routinely tackled by general grammars. Consequently, many such units produce substantial gaps in systems intended to solve sophisticated computational linguistics tasks, such as parsing, deep semantic analysis, question answering, machine translation, or text generation. They also present obstacles for applying advanced techniques to these tasks, such as machine learning. I will discuss an approach aimed at bridging such gaps, focusing on the development of monolingual and multilingual corpora where microsyntactic units are to be tagged.

One of the difficult issues in dealing with microsyntactic units is the fact that, in many cases, they are extremely difficult to identify, discriminate between, and even nominate adequately. This happens because such units may have an intricate set of senses. In addition, a microsyntactic unit may be homonymous with a free word sequence so that it is unclear which of the two occurs in a given text. To illustrate this assertion, let us consider the English polysemous microsyntactic unit *all the same,* which may (1) refer to something happening despite some fact, as in *She was kind, but all the same she terrified me, or* (2) denote an indifference: *It is all the same to me whether you stay or go.* It is not always easy to choose between the two readings, and the task is even more difficult for an NLP system. On top of this, these two interpretations of the idiom have to compete with word sequences of *all, the* and *same* occurring in sentences like *Men are all the same* or *If all the cells in our body have the same DNA, then why aren't they all the same cell?,* which have nothing to do with the idiom.

Proceedings of the Workshop on Grammar and Lexicon: Interactions and Interfaces,
pages 8–17, Osaka, Japan, December 11 2016.

In what follows, I will focus on Russian, where such idiomatic units are numerous and extremely varied. The situation is especially typical for units formed with functional words: pronouns, adverbs, particles, prepositions, and conjunctions.

By way of illustration, let us look at some instructive microsyntactic elements which require special attention and in-depth research.

(a) ***Tot že*** is a two-word adjective meaning "identical", as in (1). This phrasemic unit is homonymous with a sequence including the pronominal adjective (as in (2a)) or noun (as in (2b)) ***tot*** 'that', used anaphorically, followed by the discourse particle *že* (with the meaning close to 'as concerns'), cf.

(1) *Ja čital **tot že** rasskaz, čto i ty* 'I read the same story as you did' vs.

(2a) *Prišlos' kupit' novyj xolodil'nik – **tot že** slomalsja* lit. 'One had to buy a new fridge: as far as that one (= the old fridge) is concerned, it broke down' ('One had to buy a new fridge because the old one had broken down');

(2b) *Ja pozval druga v kino, tot **že** predložil pojti na futbol* lit. 'I invited my friend to the movies, as for him, he proposed to go to football' (I invited my friend to the movies but he suggested that we should go to a football game').

(b) a two-word phrasemic adjectival quantifier ***ni odin*** *'not a single one'* (3), which may be homonymous with a random juxtaposition of a member of the two-part coordinating conjunction *ni.. ni* 'neither… nor' and the numeral *odin* 'one' (4):
(3) *V komnate ne bylo ni odnogo čeloveka* 'There was not a single person in the room' vs.

(4) *"Irka ne žalela dlja Nataši ni duxov, ni odnogo iz svoix ženixov, no eto nikogda ničem ne končalos'* (Victoria Tokareva) *'Ira did not hesitate to spare Natasha her perfume, or one of her suitors, but that never brought any result'* (the story goes that Ira was willing to agree that one of her suitors should court her friend Natasha instead of her).

In this paper, we will investigate two polysemous microsyntactic units of Russian – *v silu* and *kak by*[2] – in order to find out with what other entities or groups of entities they come into contact. This task will be largely solved by corpus techniques.

2   Microsyntactic Markup in the SynTagRus Corpus

It is well known that lexically annotated text corpora are extremely helpful in lexical ambiguity resolution, especially in computational linguistics tasks. Lexical annotation means that polysemous words occurring in the corpus (ideally, all such words) are tagged for concrete lexical senses, specified by some lexicographic resource, be it a traditional explanatory dictionary or an electronic thesaurus like WordNet. Such lexically annotated corpora play a crucial role in word sense disambiguation (WSD) tasks. These tasks are normally solved by machine learning techniques, which are rapidly developing and improving. Research work in this area performed in varied paradigms for a multitude of languages is immense; recent papers, to cite but a few, include a comprehensive review by Navigly 2009, a paper by Moro et al. 2014, and newest research involving neural networks presented by Dayu Yuan et al. 2016.

It is to be added that text corpora, fully or at least partially tagged for lexical senses, are extremely helpful in disambiguation tasks within theoretical semantics and lexicography not necessarily directly related to computational linguistics or automatic text processing (see e.g. B.Iomdin 2014, B.Iomdin et al. 2016, Lopukhin and Lopukhina 2016).

We may regret that text corpora tagged for senses of «normal» words are not large enough, but they do exist and thus are at researchers' disposal. In contrast, to the best of my knowledge, there have been no resources so far to offer texts annotated for phraseological units of any types, including of course syntactic idioms. We have endeavored to mend the situation by introducing microsyntactic markup in the deeply annotated corpus of Russian texts, SynTagRus. This corpus, created in the Laboratory of Computational Linguistics of A.A.Kharkevich Institute of Information Transmission

---

[2] We are not glossing the microsyntactic units here because of their polysemy: they will be glossed later when individual senses are discussed.

Problems of the Russian Academy of Sciences in Moscow, contains several types of annotation: morphological, syntactic (in the form of dependency trees), lexico-functional, elliptic, and anaphoric annotation. (For details, see e.g. Dyachenko et al. 2015, where the current state of SynTagRus is presented.)

Microsyntactic annotation of the corpus is far from being an easy task. An important reason for that is the fact that no comprehensive, or even representative, list of microsyntactic units in general, and syntactic idioms in particular, is available to researchers. This is true of any language, including Russian. To overcome this deficiency, we resorted to two different strategies of tagging corpus sentences for microsyntactic elements:

1) continuous examination of a text aimed at finding all candidates to microsyntactic elements;

2) preliminary search for linear strings or syntactic subtrees composed of such words about which we have had previous knowledge or reasonable conjecture that they form, or may form, microsyntactic units. To give a few examples, these are strings or subtrees like *vse ravno* 'all the same', *kak budto* 'as though', *kol' skoro* 'since; as long as', *razve čto* 'if only, except that', *poka čto* 'so far; for the time being', *tol'ko liš'* 'nothing but; as soon as', *malo li* 'all sorts of things'; *vo čto by to ni stalo* 'at any cost; whatever happens', *ni razu* 'not once', *to i delo* 'over and over again', *čert znaet + interrogative word* 'devil knows (what, where,…)' etc.[3]

Understandably, in both cases only manual annotation of text for microsyntactic elements was possible: even its partial automation is a matter of the future (see however the discussion at the end of Section 3 below).

As a result of continuous scrutiny and targeted search of the material, we were able to obtain a draft version of microsyntactic markup of the corpus, which was later processed in detail. A thorough analysis of post-processed results revealed that the number of microsyntactic elements occurring in the text is quite considerable. In numerous texts, as many as 25% of sentences contain at least one microsyntactic element.

Fig. 1 below represents a connected fragment of a randomly chosen text of the corpus, which was annotated according to the first strategy. It is easy to see that, out of 30 sentences, 6 sentences contain syntactic idioms, whilst one sentence features two such idioms: adverbials *po idee* 'in theory; at face value' and *v pervyju očered'* 'primarily; first and foremost. '

---

[3] In order to avoid extended discussion, which could lead us far from the main topic, we list only one or two English equivalents for all microsyntactic units cited. Interestingly, in all of these cases Russian microsyntactic units correspond to multiword English microsyntactic units which we use as glosses. It can thus be hypothesized that the number and composition of microsyntactic phenomena in various languages are commensurable.

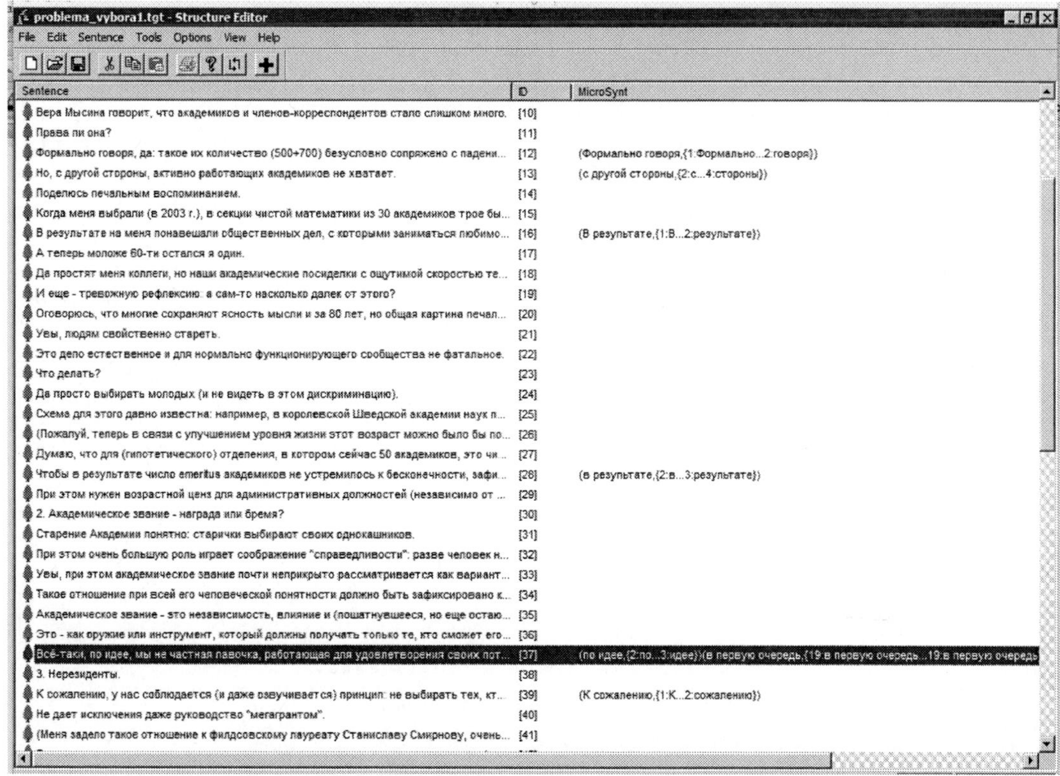

Fig. 1. Annotation of a SynTagRus text with microsyntactic elements.

We will now concentrate on the second strategy of microsyntactic annotation and consider two specific examples, represented in Sections 3 and 4, respectively.

3   A polysemous microsyntactic unit *v silu* and its context

Fig. 2 represent a subcorpus fragment in which syntactic structures of each sentence contains a binary subtree consisting of the preposition *v* '≅ in' and the noun *sila* '≅ force' in the accusative case, singular number, dominated by the preposition *v*.[4] The whole SynTagRus corpus (amounting to 1,000,000 words today) was found to contain 86 such sentences.

The annotation of this fragment performed by linguist experts revealed that the majority of these sentences (in all, 57 of them) contain a compound preposition *v silu* 'because of; by virtue of'[5], as in the sentence

(5) ***V silu*** *specifiki Moskvy daže takie obščepriznannye kriterii, kak mestopoloženie doma i cena kvadratnogo metra, nel'zja sčitat' osnovnymi.* 'By virtue of the specific character of Moscow, even such generally recognized criteria as the location of the house and the price of a square meter cannot be considered to be the main ones'.

Six sentences contain a very different microsyntactic unit, which could reasonably be named «v takuju-to silu» 'to such and such extent', as in

(6) *Eto govorit o tom, čto my ne spravljaemsja s potokom našix doxodov, ne v sostojanii **v polnuju silu** aktivizirovat' biznes.* 'This says that we are not coping with the flow of our incomes, are unable to activate the business in full swing'.

---

4 It must be noted that the syntactic formalism underlying the syntactic annotation of SynTagRus heavily relies on the syntactic component of the Meaning ⇔ Text theory by Igor Mel'čuk (see Mel'čuk 1974), which was later refined and extended by Juri Apresjan and his colleagues during the elaboration of a multipurpose linguistic processor ETAP (see Apresjan et al. 1992, 2010). For the reasons of space, I am skipping the details of this theory.

5 All compound prepositions are naturally considered to be microsyntactic units.

This unit, an adverbial of degree, consists of two permanent word elements, *v* and *silu,* and one variable element – an adjective modifying the noun *silu.* SynTagRus represents only one option of this unit – *v polnuju silu* 'in full swing' (plus two occurrences of the adverb *vpolsily* 'at half strength', which may be viewed as an option of the «v takuju-to silu» unit). In fact, Russian texts may contain other adjectives that occupy the variable position of the microsyntactic unit – *v nepolnuju silu* 'at reduced strength', *v polovinnuju silu* (a very close synonym of *vpolsily*), quantifier nouns (*v polovinu sily,* another equivalent of *vpolsily*) and even numerals like *tri sily* (something like 'using three strengths'), as in

(7) *Snova vzjalis' za sunduk, teper' uže v tri sily, i snova opustili – ne te sily* [Valentin Rasputin] 'They put their hands to the trunk, this time merging three strengths, but lowered them again – the strengths were wrong'.

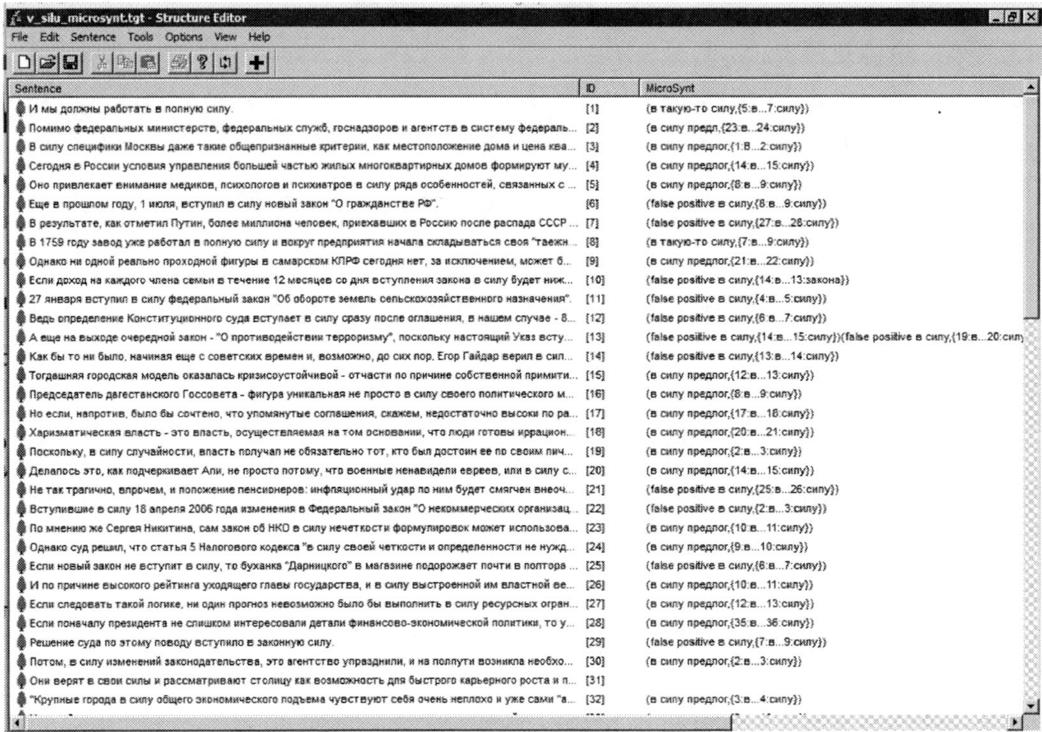

Fig. 2. Annotation of a SynTagRus fragment containing the binary subtree *v silu* with microsyntactic elements.

In 21 sentences of the samplng the subtree *v silu* occurred within expressions like *vstupat' v silu* 'come into effect', as in

(8) *Rešenie suda vstupilo v zakonnuju silu* 'The court's decision came into legal force'.

In my opinion, there is no syntactic idiom in (8); instead, we have to do with a specific meaning of the noun *sila* 'validity'. This meaning is specified in traditional dictionaries. What is important, however, is that the noun *sila* cannot be used freely in this meaning: it can only appear in combination with lexical finctions like IncepOper1 (*vstupat' v silu* 'come into force', FinOper1 (*utračivat' silu* 'be terminated') and with weakly idiomatic variants of Oper1 (*byt' v sile* 'be in force' and *ostavat'sja v sile* 'remain in force'.[6]

Since expressions like *vstupat' v silu* turn out to be very frequent, we believe that it is reasonable to leave them in the microsyntactic annotation of the corpus as false positives so that the respective contexts could be used in automatic disambigution of regular and microsyntactic units (e.g. with the help of machine learning techniques). We believe that such disambiguation will be possible in future.

---

6 Lexical functions present an important element of semantic and lexicographical components of the Meaning ⇔Text theory. The discussion of this issue, however, is far beyond the topic of my paper.

It is worth mentioning that in the whole sampling for *v silu* there is only one chance sentence which has nothing to do with any of the two syntactic idioms postulated above and at the same time contains no false positives: this is the sentence

(9) *Vošlo by v silu novoe pokolenie, osoznal by svoi interesy srednij klass* 'If the new generation gained strength, the middle class would become over of its interests'.

It should be emphasized that in this case SynTagRus provides a fairly satisfactory representation of syntactic idioms and freer collocations with *v silu*: two syntactic idioms and one lexical functional construction are amply covered. The author is aware of only one other syntactic idiom that contains the subtree *v silu* and is absent from SynTagRus: this is the adverbial meaning 'at a certain level', occurring in expressions like *igrat' v silu pervogo razrjada <pervorazrjadnika, grossmejstera>* etc. 'play at the level of the higher athletic rank, the first-rank sportsman, the grand master'

It cannot of course be excluded that there are other microsyntactic idioms based on this group of words: so far, however, we are aware of none.

4   A polysemous microsyntactic unit *kak by* and its context

Using the same strategy of the preliminary search of potential syntactic phrasemic units, we obtained a corpus sample of 116 sentences containing the *kak by* string, assuming that at least some of these sentences must contain phrasemic units. Fig. 3 below shows a fragment of this sample.

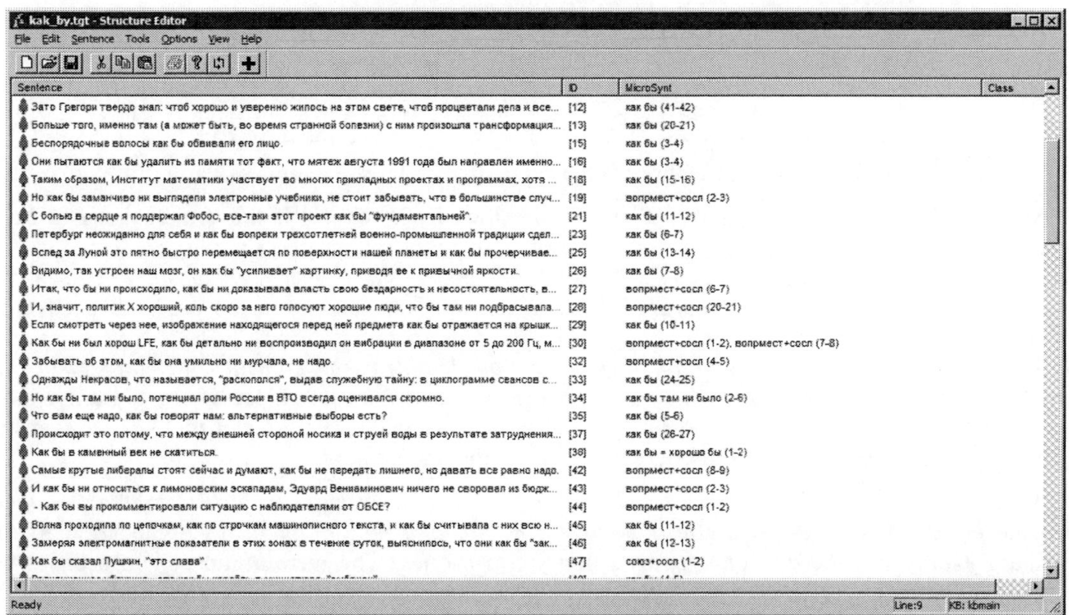

Sentence	ID	MicroSynt	Class
Зато Грегори твердо знал: чтоб хорошо и уверенно жилось на этом свете, чтоб процветали дела и все...	[12]	как бы (41-42)	
Больше того, именно там (а может быть, во время странной болезни) с ним произошла трансформация...	[13]	как бы (20-21)	
Беспорядочные волосы как бы обвивали его лицо.	[15]	как бы (3-4)	
Они пытаются как бы удалить из памяти тот факт, что мятеж августа 1991 года был направлен именно...	[16]	как бы (3-4)	
Таким образом, Институт математики участвует во многих прикладных проектах и программах, хотя ...	[18]	как бы (15-16)	
Но как бы заманчиво ни выглядели электронные учебники, не стоит забывать, что в большинстве случ...	[19]	вопрмест+сосл (2-3)	
С болью в сердце я поддержал Фобос, все-таки этот проект как бы "фундаментальней".	[21]	как бы (11-12)	
Петербург неожиданно для себя и как бы вопреки трехсотлетней военно-промышленной традиции сдел...	[23]	как бы (6-7)	
Вслед за Луной это пятно быстро перемещается по поверхности нашей планеты и как бы прочерчивае...	[25]	как бы (13-14)	
Видимо, так устроен наш мозг, он как бы "усиливает" картинку, приводя ее к привычной яркости.	[26]	как бы (7-8)	
Итак, что бы ни происходило, как бы ни доказывала власть свою бездарность и несостоятельность, в...	[27]	вопрмест+сосл (6-7)	
И, значит, политик Х хороший, коль скоро за него голосуют хорошие люди, что бы там ни подбрасывала...	[28]	вопрмест+сосл (20-21)	
Если смотреть через нее, изображение находящегося перед ней предмета как бы отражается на крышк...	[29]	как бы (10-11)	
Как бы ни был хорош LFE, как бы детально ни воспроизводил он вибрации в диапазоне от 5 до 200 Гц, м...	[30]	вопрмест+сосл (1-2), вопрмест+сосл (7-8)	
Забывать об этом, как бы она умильно ни мурчала, не надо.	[32]	вопрмест+сосл (4-5)	
Однажды Некрасов, что называется, "раскопался", выдав служебную тайну: в циклограмме сеансов с...	[33]	как бы (24-25)	
Но как бы там ни было, потенциал роли России в ВТО всегда оценивался скромно.	[34]	как бы там ни было (2-6)	
Что вам еще надо, как бы говорят нам: альтернативные выборы есть?	[35]	как бы (5-6)	
Происходит это потому, что между внешней стороной носика и струей воды в результате затруднения...	[37]	как бы (26-27)	
Как бы в каменный век не скатиться.	[38]	как бы = хорошо бы (1-2)	
Самые крутые либералы стоят сейчас и думают, как бы не передать лишнего, но давать все равно надо.	[42]	вопрмест+сосл (8-9)	
И как бы ни относиться к лимоновским эскападам, Эдуард Вениаминович ничего не своровал из бюдж...	[43]	вопрмест+сосл (2-3)	
- Как бы вы прокомментировали ситуацию с наблюдателями от ОБСЕ?	[44]	вопрмест+сосл (1-2)	
Волна проходила по цепочкам, как по строчкам машинописного текста, и как бы считывала с них всю н...	[45]	как бы (11-12)	
Замеряя электромагнитные показатели в этих зонах в течение суток, выяснилось, что они как бы "зак...	[46]	как бы (12-13)	
Как бы сказал Пушкин, "это слава".	[47]	союз+сосл (1-2)	

Fig. 3. Microsyntactic annotation of a corpus sample with sentences containing the *kak by* string.

A thorough study of these data shows a very interesting and complicated microsyntactic picture.

First of all, many of the sentences contain the phrasemic unit we shall call **kak by 1** that can be treated as a discourse particle with the semantics of comparison or uncertainty, as in (10) and (11):

(10) *Gazety, sledovatel'no, imejuščie dejstvitel'no obščestvennoe značenie, sut'* **kak by** *akushery obščestvennogo mnenija, pomogajuščie emu javit'sja na svet Božij* (N. Danilevskij) 'Therefore, the newspapers having a true public value are, **in a way**, obstetricians of the public opinion, helping it to be borne'.

Here the author compares newspapers to obstetricians and warns the reader that he exploits a metaphor, by using the *kak by* expression.

(11) *Tolpa sostojala iz ljuda prostogo, i čekistam bylo ne s ruki xvatat' **kak by** svoix – trudjaščixsja* (A. Tkačenko) 'The crowd were just common people, and the security agents did not think it fit to arrest those who were, **so to say**, of their own kind'.

Here the speaker considers the word *svoix* 'of their kind' not proper enough.

Intrinsically, **kak by 1** can almost be viewed as one word (which in internet discussions is even sometimes written without a space: *kakby*). In SynTagRus, the words *kak* and *by* are connected with the auxiliary syntactic relation reserved for syntactically integrated entities (*kak -> by*). The author is quite unclear whether *kak* here is a pronoun, a conjunction, or neither. In any case, it is the syntactic head of the unit, governed, in its turn, by the next word by a restrictive syntactic relation; see sentence (12) and its syntactic structure shown in Fig. 4:

 (12) *Besporjadočnye volosy kak by obvivali ego lico* ('The unruly hair as if twined itself around his face').

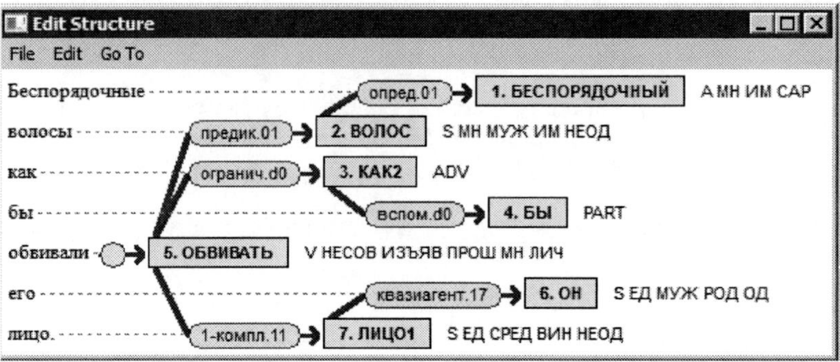

Fig. 4. Syntactic structure of (12) containg the phrasemic unit **kak by 1**.

Another syntactic phrasemic unit that can be identified in the corpus is the conjunction **kak by 2** which is only used as a strongly governed word with many predicates sharing the semantics of apprehension, such as the verbs *bojat'sja* 'to be afraid', *opasat'sja* 'to fear', *ispugat'sja* 'to be scared', *sledit'* 'to make sure', the nouns *bojazn', strax, opasenie* 'fear', and even the predicative adverbs *strashno, bojazno* 'fearful':

 (13) *V universitete Galilej poseščal takže lekcii po geometrii… i nastol'ko uvljoksja aetoj naukoj, čto otec stal opasat'sja, **kak by** aeto ne pomešalo izučeniju mediciny* (Wikipedia) 'In the university, Galileo also attended lectures in geometry… and became so enthusiastic about this science that his father started fearing lest it could interfere with his learning medicine'.

(14) *Vo Frajburge za nim [Gor'kim] po pjatam xodili špiki: nemeckie, — bojavšiesja, čto on sdelal revoljuciju, i sovetskie, — sledivšie, **kak by** on ne sdelal kontrrevoljuciju* (V. Khodasevich) 'In Freiburg, Gorky was closely followed by spies: German ones, who were afraid of him because he organized the revolution, and Soviet ones, who were making sure that he would not organize a counter-revolution'.

(15) *Smotri, **kak by** tebe ne požalet', čto smeješ'sja* (A. Herzen) 'Watch out you don't regret that you are laughing';

(16) *Vyvesti aeskadron iz stanicy bylo rešeno iz opasenija, **kak by** aeskadron ne vosstal, uznav ob areste Fomina* (M. Šoloxov) 'It was decided to draw out the squadron from the village, in fear that the squadron would rise if it learned about Fomin's arrest'.

(17) *Tolpa očutilas' neožidanno tak blizko k imperatoram, čto Rostovu, stojavšemu v perednix rjadax ejo, stalo strašno, **kak by** ego ne uznali* (L. Tolstoy) 'The crowd suddenly got so close to the emperors that Rostov, who was standing in its first rows, started to fear that he **could** be recognized'.

Sometimes the government pattern of this conjunction can be modified by the expletive pronoun *to*:

 (18) *S odnoj storony, neobxodimo bylo v celjax samooborony koe-čto pozaimstvovat', koe-čemu poučit'sja u Evropy; s drugoj storony, nado bylo opasat'sja togo, **kak by** pri aetom ne popast' v*

kul'turnuju, duxovnuju zavisimost' ot Evropy (N. Trubetskoj) 'On the one hand, it was necessary for self-defence to learn something from Europe; on the other hand, one had to **make sure not to** get into cultural and mental dependence on Europe'.

Semantic, syntactic and collocational properties of the syntactic idiom ***kak by 2*** are very interesting and need individual research. We can make only a few remarks here. First, the conjunction requires the presence of the negative particle *ne* as a direct dependent. Of the head verb of the subordinate close. Second, the verb has to be either a finite form in the past tense, or an infinitive (in the latter case, the implicit subject of the infinitive should coincide with the subject of the head predicate, cf. example 15 above and 19):

(19) *Ona snova pošla, opasajas', kak by ne natknut'sja gde-nibud' na policiju* [Vasil Bykov] 'She$_i$ went once again, fearing lest she$_i$ should run onto the police somewhere'.

As far as the embedment of *kak by 2* into the syntactic structure of the sentence is concerned, I believe that the most natural solution would be to view the first element of the idiom as a conjunction and subordinate it to the head predicate using a respective valency   relation; the verb of the subordinate clause should depend on *kak,* and *by* should be linked to this latter verb. Accordingly, the elements of the idioms turn out to be syntactically unlinked with each other, as in Fig. 5:

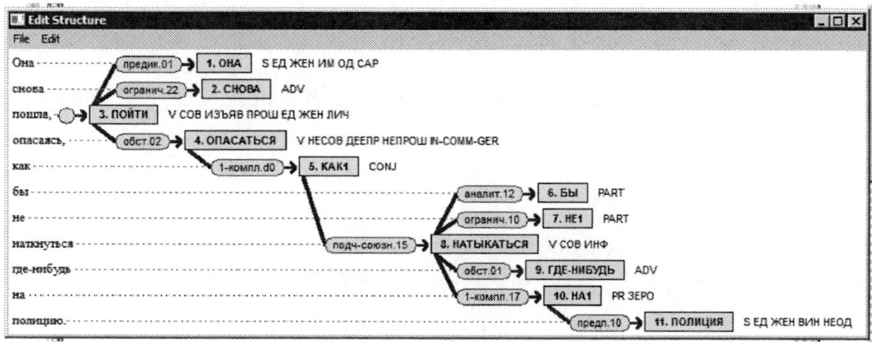

Fig. 5. The syntactic structure of the sentence with the embedded syntactic idiom *kak by 2*.

The next syntactic idiom composed of *kak* and *by* is a modal lexical unit that implicitly expresses the speaker's wish. Let us refer to this idiom as ***kak by 3***. It is represented in such corpus sentences as

(20) ***Kak by*** *v kamennyj vek ne skatit'sja* 'It would be good not to slide back into the stone age'

At first glance, this idiom is close to the microsyntactic unit *kak by 2* described above: in both cases, one has to do with the speaker's wish to avoid some unpleasant situation (and hence, with his fear that such a situation may happen. However the picture seems to me to be drastically different. Note that in (20) the verb *skatit'sja* 'slide back' belongs to the scope of the implicit predicate of the speaker's wish together **with the negation**; the speaker wishes no-slidng back to the stone age. In contrast, sentences with *kak by 2* contain the predicate of fear whose scope does not contain the negation. The approximate equivalence of (20) and

(21) *Bojus', kak by v kamennyj vek be skatit'sja* 'I fear lest we slide back into the stone age'

follows from the correlation of the semantics of wish and fear: *I fear X* is known to mean 'I expect X and I do not want X to happen'. In constructions with *kak by 3* the verbal negation is frequent but not at all obligatory, cf.

(22) *Kak by obojtis' bez etogo, ostaviv samuju sut'* [A.Bitov] 'I wish we could manage without it, leaving only the most crucial thing.

Another syntactic idiom appearing in the subcorpus is a discourse unit *kak by ne tak* ≈ 'contrary to expectations, the situation is different and much worse'. Normally, this unit forms a separate utterance or a separate clause:

(23) *Vy dumaete, teper' on po krajnej mere ujdet? Kak by ne tak!* [I.S.Turgenev] 'Do you think he will now at least leave?' Like hell he will'.

Finally, the subcorpus includes a very frequent parenthetic expression *kak by to ni bylo* 'be that as it may', with a variation *kak by tam ni bylo,* which can also be viewed as a microsyntactic unit:

(24) *Teper' vse eto bylo pozadi, no kak by tam ni bylo, videt' špiona Gardnera bylo emu neprijatno.* [Ju. Dombrovsky]. This was now all over but however that may be he did not like seeing the spy Gardner.

It is naturally rather easy to identify units like *kak by ne tak* or *kak by to ni* bylo due to their length and strict word order; yet, counterexamples are also possible, cf.

(25) *Vse kak by ne tak už ploxo* 'It seems that all is not so bad'

where the «shorter» idiom *kak by 1* can be detected

As in the first subcorpus containing units *v silu*, the present subcorpus has a number of sentences that do not involve microsyntactic units formed with *kak by.* In particular, some sentences contain construction with the emphatic particle *ni*:
(26) *Kak by nam ni xotelos' povysit' kačestvo školnogo obrazovanija, na eto potrebuetsja ešče mnogo let* 'However much we want to improve the quality of school education, this will require many years yet'.

Clearly neither *kak* nor *by* are constituent elements of this construction: *kak* may be replaced by any interrogative word, and *by* may be absent, as in
(27) *Čto on ni predprinimaet, ničego ne menjaetsja* 'Whatever he undertakes, nothing changes'.

Finally, some sentences represent a Wackernagel shift of the particle *by* forming the subjunctive mood into the position after *kak,* as in
(28) *Kak by ty otvetil* 'How would you answer'.

As in the first subcorpus, we leave «false positive» tags in all such cases.
To conclude, we need to note that in this case, too, the corpus is representative enough for the syntactic idioms postulated. Yet, we were able to find an interesting microsyntactic idiom formed with kak and by beyond the material of the corpus. It can be illustrated by a sentence present in the Russian National Corpus:
(29) — Kak by ne burja moskovskaja sobiraetsja, - pokrutil golovoj storož i povernul s pogosta von. [B.Evseev]. 'Isn't it the case that the Moscow tempest is approaching? – The watchman twisted his head and went away from the cemetery'
The first part of (29) means the following: There are signs that the Moscow tempest is approaching, which is undesirable. Importantly, in such cases a semantically void negation must be present – just like in the case with kak by 2. However it is not attached to the verb but immediately follows kak by, ths forming a new syntactic idiom which could be called kak by ne. This idiom has a rather close synonym – už ne (with an obligatory li particle). - 'Už bne burja li moskovskaja sobiraetsja?
It goes without saying that one cannot discuss all features of the newly developed resource – a corpus with microsyntactic annotation. It is to be hoped that I could demonstrate the fact that this resource is likely to be very helpful.

Acknowledgements

The author is grateful to the Russian Humanitarian Research Foundation for their support of this work (grant No. 15-04-00562).

References

Ju.D.Apresjan, I.M.Boguslavsky, L.L.Iomdin, A.V.Lazursky, L.G.Mitjushin, V.Z.Sannikov, L.L.Tsinman (1992). Lingvističeskij protessor dlja složnyx informatisonnyx sistem. [A linguistic processor for complex information systems.] Moscow, Nauka Publishers. 256 p. [In Russian.]

Ju.D.Apresjan, I.M.Boguslavsky, L.L.Iomdin, V.Z.Sannikov (2010). Teoretičeskie problemy russkogo sintaksisa: Vzaimodejstvie grammatiki i slovarja. [Theoretical Issues of Russian Syntax: Interaction of the Grammar and the Lexicon.] / Ju.D.Apresjan, ed. Moscow, Jazyki slavjanskix kul'tur. 408 p. [In Russian.]

Dayu Yuan, Ryan Doherty, Julian Richardson, Colin Evans, Eric Altendorf (2016). Word Sense Disambiguation with Neural Language Models. https://arxiv.org/pdf/1603.07012v1.pdf.

P.V.Dyachenko, L.L.Iomdin, A.V.Lazursky, L.G.Mityushin, O.Yu.Podlesskaya, V.G.Sizov, T.I.Frolova, L.L.Tsinman (2015). Sovremennoe sostojanie gluboko annotirovannogo korpusa tekstov russkogo jazyka (SynTagRus). [The current state of the deeply annotated corpus of Russian texts (SynTagRus)]. // Nacional'nyj korpus russkogo jazyka. 10 let proektu. Trudy Instituta russkogo jazyka im. V.V. Vinogradova. M. Issue 6, p. 272-299. [In Russian.]

Ch. Fillmore (1988). The Mechanisms of Construction Grammar. // Proceedings of the Fourteenth Annual Meeting of the Berkeley Linguistics Society. pp. 35-55.

A. Goldberg (1995). Constructions: A Construction Grammar Approach to Argument Structure. Chicago: University of Chicago Press.

B.L.Iomdin (2014). Mnogoznačnye slova v kontekste i vne konteksta. [Polysemous words in context and out of context.] Voprosy jazykoznaniya, No. 4. P. 87-103.

B.L.Iomdin, A.A.Lopukhina, K.A.Lopukhin, G.V.Nosyrev (2016). Word Sense Frequency of Similar Polysemous Words in Different Languages. // Computational Linguistics and Intellectual Technologies. Dialogue 2016, p. 214-225.

L.L.Iomdin (2013). Nekotorye mikrosintasičeskie konstruktsii v russkom jazyke s učastiem slova *što* v kačestve sostavnogo elementa. [Certain microsyntactic constructions in Russian which contain the word *što* as a constituent element.] Južnoslovenski filolog. Beograd, LXIX, 137-147. [In Russian.]

L.L.Iomdin (2014). Xorošo menja tam ne bylo: sintaksis i semantika odnogo klassa russkix razgovornyx konstruktsij. [Good thing I wasn't there: syntax and semantics of a class of Russian colloquial constructions]. // Grammaticalization and lexicalization in the Slavic languages. Proceedings from the 36th meeting of the commission on the grammatical structure of the Slavic languages of the International committee of Slavists. München-Berlin-Washington/D.C.: Verlag Otto Sagner. 436 p. (Die Welt der Slaven. Bd. 55), p. 423-436. [In Russian.]

L.L.Iomdin (2015). Konstruktsii mikrosintaksisa, obrazovannye russkoj leksemoj *raz.* [Constructions of microsyntax built by the Russian word *raz.*]. SLAVIA, časopis pro slovanskou filologii, ročník 84, sešit 3, s. 291-306. [In Russian.]

K.A.Lopukhin, A.A.Lopukhina (2016). Word Sense Disambiguation for Russian Verbs using Semantic Vectors and Dictionary Entries. // Computational Linguistics and Intellectual Technologies. Dialogue 2016, p. 393-405.

I.A.Mel'čuk (1974). Opyt teorii lingvističeskix modelej «Smysl ⇔ Tekst». [An experience of creating the theory of linguistic models of the Meaning ⇔ Text type.] Moscow, Nauka Publishers. [In Russian.]

R. Navigli (2009). Word sense disambiguation: A survey. ACM Comput. Survey,. 41(2):1–69.

A. Moro, A. Raganato, R. Navigli (2014). Entity Linking meets Word Sense Disambiguation: a Unified Approach. Transactions of the Association for Computational Linguistics (TACL), 2, pp. 231-244.

E.V.Rakhilina (ed.) (2010). Lingvistika konstruktsij. [The linguistics of constructions]. Moscow, Azbukovnik Publishers. 584 p. [In Russian.]

Alternations: From Lexicon to Grammar And Back Again

Markéta Lopatková
Charles University
Faculty of Mathematics and Physics
Prague, Czech Republic
lopatkova@ufal.mff.cuni.cz

Václava Kettnerová
Charles University
Faculty of Mathematics and Physics
Prague, Czech Republic
kettnerova@ufal.mff.cuni.cz

Abstract

An excellent example of a phenomenon bridging a lexicon and a grammar is provided by grammaticalized alternations (e.g., passivization, reflexivity, and reciprocity): these alternations represent productive grammatical processes which are, however, lexically determined. While grammaticalized alternations keep lexical meaning of verbs unchanged, they are usually characterized by various changes in their morphosyntactic structure.

In this contribution, we demonstrate on the example of reciprocity and its representation in the valency lexicon of Czech verbs, VALLEX how a linguistic description of complex (and still systemic) changes characteristic of grammaticalized alternations can benefit from an integration of grammatical rules into a valency lexicon. In contrast to other types of grammaticalized alternations, reciprocity in Czech has received relatively little attention although it closely interacts with various linguistic phenomena (e.g., with light verbs, diatheses, and reflexivity).

1 Introduction

Contemporary linguistic theories usually divide a language description into two components, a lexicon and a grammar. The grammar consists of general patterns rendered in the form of formal rules that are applicable to whole classes of language units. The lexicon, on the other hand, represents an inventory of language units with their specific properties. Nevertheless, the distribution of linguistic information between the grammar and the lexicon is not given by the language itself but it is purely an empirical issue. Thus linguistic frameworks can substantially differ from each other in the design of the grammar and the lexicon. In some theories a central role is performed by the grammar component, e.g., Chomskyan generative transformational grammar (Chomsky, 1965), while others put emphasis on the lexical component, e.g., the Lexical-Functional Grammar (Kaplan and Bresnan, 1982), the Head-Driven Phrase Structure Grammar (Pollard and Sag, 1994), and the Meaning-Text Theory (Mel'čuk, 1988).

There are several linguistic phenomena, e.g., agreement and semantics, which are consistently treated across various linguistic theories either in the grammar or lexical component, respectively. However, a language is typically abundant with borderline phenomena whose treatment either as grammatical or as lexical ones is strongly theory dependent. Moreover, some phenomena represent products of a close interaction between the grammar and the lexicon. An excellent example of linguistic phenomena bridging these components is provided by grammaticalized alternations, e.g., passive, reflexive and reciprocal alternations. These alternations represent fully (or almost fully) productive grammatical processes which are, however, lexically determined.

Grammaticalized alternations typically preserve lexical meaning and deep syntactic structure of verbs; however, they are characterized by various changes in surface syntactic structures. Morphologically rich languages provide an excellent opportunity to study grammaticalized alternations as the surface syntactic changes are manifested by changes in morphological expressions of the valency complementations affected by the alternations, as can be illustrated by examples with the Czech verb *potkat* 'meet' in (1). The deep syntactic structure of this verb is formed by two valency complementations 'Actor' (ACT) and

Proceedings of the Workshop on Grammar and Lexicon: Interactions and Interfaces,
pages 18–27, Osaka, Japan, December 11 2016.

'Patient' (PAT), which are expressed in the unmarked structure of grammaticalized alternations (active, unreciprocal and irreflexive) as subject in the nominative and direct object in the accusative, respectively (1b). This verb allows for the reciprocity of ACT and PAT, see (1c). Comparing with the unreciprocal structure in (1b), this structure is characterized by the following changes: (i) as subject, coordinated ACT in the nominative is expressed; this results in the change in verb agreement, and (ii) the direct object position corresponding to PAT is occupied by the clitic reflexive pronoun *se* expressed in the accusative; this reflexive pronoun corefers with the subject position.

Despite the changes in unreciprocal and reciprocal structures of the verb *potkat* 'meet', the meaning of the verb remains unchanged: in both structures, it denotes the same situation when two or more individuals accidentally or intentionally come together. Thus these changes cannot be explained as a consequence of polysemy of the given verb. The main difference between unreciprocal and reciprocal structures of this verb rather lies in the fact that the reciprocal structure (unlike the unreciprocal one) denotes complex event involving two propositions, which can be describe in the following way: *Peter met Claire in the theater and at the same time Claire met Peter in the theater.* This semantics is characteristic of reciprocal structures in general (Evans et al., 2007).

(1) a. *potkat* 'meet' ... ACT_{nom} PAT_{acc}
         reciprocity: ACT-PAT

     b. *Petr   potkal Kláru   v divadle.*
         $Peter_{ACT.nom.sg}$ $met_{pst.3sg}$ $Claire_{PAT.acc.sg}$ in the theater.
         'Peter met Claire in the theater.'

     c. *Petr   a   Klára   se   potkali v divadle.*
         $(Peter_{nom.sg}$ and_{conj} $Claire_{nom.sg.})_{ACT}$ $REFL_{PAT.acc}$ $met_{pst.3pl}$ in the theater
         'Peter and Claire met in the theater.'

While the surface syntactic formation of marked structures of grammaticalized alternations (passive, reflexive and reciprocal structures) is typically regular enough to be described by grammatical rules, a possibility to create these structures is lexically conditioned, i.e., this possibility is primarily given by the lexical meaning of verbs and thus it cannot be deduced from their deep and/or surface syntactic structures alone. For example, both the verbs *potkat* 'meet' and *absolvovat* 'undergo' are characterized by the same valency frames. However, only the former verb forms reciprocal structures, the latter one does not allow for reciprocity, see examples (1) and (2). The information on applicability of individual grammaticalized alternations thus must be stored in the lexicon.

(2) a. *absolvovat* 'undergo' ... ACT_{nom} PAT_{acc}
     b. *Petr   absolvoval   operaci.*
         $Peter_{ACT.nom.sg}$ $underwent_{pst.3sg}$ $operation_{PAT.acc.sg}$
         'Peter has undergone an operation.'

In this contribution, we demonstrate on the example of reciprocity and its representation in the valency lexicon of Czech verbs, VALLEX how the linguistic description of complex (and still systemic) changes characteristic of grammaticalized alternations can benefit from the integration of grammatical rules into a valency lexicon.

Let us stress that the representation of reciprocity proposed in this paper is restricted to reciprocity of verbs. However, reciprocity is characteristic of other parts-of-speech as well, esp. of nouns, e.g., *dohoda jedné válčící strany s druhou stranou* 'an agreement of one warring party with the other' vs. *dohoda mezi válčícími stranami* 'an agreement between warring parties'. Reciprocity of nouns has received little attention so far. Further, the interplay between reciprocity on the one hand and diatheses or reflexivity on the other is left aside here; this issue has not been sufficiently explored yet as well although their interactions brought about specific changes in surface syntactic structures. For example, in Czech, in contrast to the valency complementations involved in reciprocity in active light verb constructions, the valency complementations in reciprocity in passive light verb constructions have a strong tendency to be expressed as the valency complementations of nouns, e.g., *Dosud nebyla uzavřena dohoda válčících* *stran*$_{\text{reciprACT:nominal}}$. 'An agreement of warring party has not been made yet.' vs. *?Válčícími stranami*$_{\text{reciprACT:verbal}}$ *dosud nebyla uzavřena dohoda.* 'An agreement has not been made by warring party yet.'

2   Related Work

Grammaticalized alternations have been treated in the linguistic description of many languages as productive grammatical processes, the applicability of which can be fully predicted from syntactic structure of verbs. Thus their description entirely relies on the grammar alone, leaving the lexicon aside. As a result, an explicit representation of grammaticalized alternations of verbs is still missing in most contemporary lexical resources. Reciprocity, which serves here as an illustrative example of grammaticalized alternations, does not represent any exception. Although reciprocity is cross-linguistically attested as a widespread phenomenon, see esp. (Nedjalkov, 2007; König and Gast, 2008), from the important lexical resource, only FrameNet[1] introduces the information on reciprocity in the form of the non-lexical semantic frame 'Reciprocality'; this frame indicates that its daughter frames are endowed with frame elements that can be used symmetrically. However, FrameNet does not provide any systematic way for deriving reciprocal structures. Similarly, despite being based on Levin's classification of verbs within which reciprocity of English verbs is described in detail (Levin, 1993), VerbNet[2] does not explicitly distinguish between reciprocal structures and unreciprocal ones.

Reciprocity of Czech verbs has been theoretically elaborated within the Functional Generative Description in (Panevová, 1999; Panevová, 2007; Panevová and Mikulová, 2007). In these studies, the representation of reciprocity in a lexicon has been proposed as well. The theoretical results has been then applied in the Prague Dependency Treebank, and in the VALLEX lexicon, see Section 3. The systematic rule description of morphosyntactic changes brought about reciprocity has been introduced in (Skoumalová, 2001), (Urešová, 2011), and (Kettnerová et al., 2012b; Lopatková et al., 2016).

3   VALLEX and FGD

In this section, we describe main tenets of valency theory of the Functional Generative Description within which we formulate a representation of grammaticalized alternations. The proposed representation is then applied in the valency lexicon of Czech verbs, VALLEX[3] (Lopatková et al., 2016). The main output is a qualitatively and quantitatively enhanced version of this lexicon available for human users as well as for NLP applications which allows for obtaining all surface manifestations of Czech verbs.

The Functional Generative Description (FGD)[4] represents a stratificational dependency-oriented theoretical framework, see esp. (Sgall et al., 1986). Valency – as one of the core concepts – is related primarily to the tectogrammatical (deep syntactic) layer of the linguistic description, i.e., the layer of linguistically structured meaning, esp. (Panevová, 1994). Valency structure of verbs is captured in the form of valency frames. According to a main descriptive principle of the valency theory of FGD, differences in valency frames correlate with differences in lexical meaning; thus each meaning of a verb should be characterized by a single valency frame. As grammaticalized alternations bring about changes in valency frames of a verb while preserving its lexical meaning, they collide with this principle. We further demonstrate how this collision can be overcome when we carefully distribute the information on grammaticalized alternations between the lexicon and the grammar.

The valency theory of FGD has been applied in several valency lexicons, VALLEX, PDT-Vallex (Urešová, 2011),[5] and EngVallex (Urešová et al., 2016).[6] VALLEX, being the most elaborated one, forms a solid basis for the lexical component of FGD. For the purpose of representation of grammaticalized alternations, VALLEX is divided into a lexical part (i.e., the data component) and a grammatical part (i.e., the grammar component) (Kettnerová et al., 2012a).

---

[1] http://framenet2.icsi.berkeley.edu

[2] http://verbs.colorado.edu/verb-index/vn/reference.php

[3] http://ufal.mff.cuni.cz/vallex/3.0/

[4] FGD serves as the theoretical framework for the Prague Dependency Treebank (PDT), see http://ufal.mff.cuni.cz/pdt3.0/.

[5] http://lindat.mff.cuni.cz/services/PDT-Vallex/

[6] http://lindat.mff.cuni.cz/services/EngVallex/

Data component. The data component consists of an inventory of lexical units of verbs (corresponding to their individual meanings) with their respective valency frames underlying their deep syntactic structures. Each valency frame is modeled as a sequence of frame slots corresponding to valency complementations of a verb labeled by (rather coarse-grained) tectogrammatical roles such as 'Actor' (ACT), 'Patient' (PAT), 'Addressee' (ADDR), 'Effect' (EFF), 'Direction', 'Location', 'Manner', etc. Further, the information on obligatoriness and on possible morphological forms is specified for each valency complementation. The valency frames stored in the data component describe unmarked structures of grammaticalized alternations (i.e., active, unreciprocal, irreflexive). In addition to information on various other syntactic properties, each lexical unit of a verb bears information on the possibility to create marked syntactic structures of grammaticalized alternations (i.e., passive, reciprocal and reflexive).

The data component of VALLEX stores valency information on 2 722 verb lexemes (associating lexical units and verb forms of a verb). These verb lexemes are represented by 4 586 verb lemmas and describe 6 711 lexical units (VALLEX thus covers more than 96% of verb occurrences in the sub-corpus of the Czech National Corpus SYN2000).[7]

Grammar component. The grammar component represents a part of the overall grammar of Czech. It stores formal rules directly related to valency structure of verbs. These rules allow users to derive marked structures of grammaticalized alternations (i.e., passive, reciprocal or reflexive).[8] Let us stress that grammaticalized alternations typically preserve deep syntactic structures of lexical units of verbs, i.e., the number and type of their valency complementations remain unchanged; it is their morphosyntactic structure that changes. These changes are manifested by changes in morphological forms of the valency complementations affected by grammaticalized alternations. The rules contained in the grammar component thus describe the systemic changes in morphological forms of the given valency complementations. Further, these rules can determine changes in lexical expressions of valency complementations involved in grammaticalized alternations.

In the current stage of the project, the grammar component of VALLEX stores rules for the following grammaticalized alternations:

- *Diatheses.* Diatheses represent a core type of grammaticalized alternations. In Czech linguistics, five types of diatheses are distinguished (Panevová et al., 2014): passive, deagentive, resultative, dispositional and recipient passive diatheses; they are covered by 17 formal rules, detailed description can be found in (Lopatková et al., 2016).

- *Reflexivity.* Reflexivity represents a peripheral type of grammaticalized alternations in Czech (Kettnerová et al., 2014). Reflexive structures denote the actions which ACT performs on himself; thus two valency complementations – one of which being expressed as subject – share the same reference, e.g., *Petr*$_{ACT}$ *se viděl v zrcadle.* ≈ *Petr*$_{ACT}$ *viděl sám sebe*$_{PAT}$ *(= Petra* $_{PAT}$*) v zrcadle.* 'Peter$_{ACT}$ saw himself$_{PAT}$ in the mirror.' In VALLEX, reflexivity is covered by 4 formal rules.

- *Reciprocity.* Reciprocity (similarly as reflexivity) represents a peripheral type of grammaticalized alternations; on reciprocity we further illustrate the representation of grammaticalized alternations in VALLEX, see the following Section 4.

4 Reciprocity

The description of reciprocity (as well as other types of grammaticalized alternations) may benefit from the distinction between a *situational meaning* and a *structural meaning*. The situational meaning portrays a situation described by a lexical unit of a verb which is characterized by a set of situational participants

---

[7]http://ucnk.ff.cuni.cz/

[8]In this contribution, we leave aside lexicalized alternations. These alternations associate pairs of lexical units of verbs characterized by systemic shifts in their lexical meaning which are exhibited across groups of semantically similar verbs. Changes in surface syntactic structures of these lexical units result from changes in their deep structures. For example, two lexical units of the verb *znít* 'sound' (e.g., *Sálem zní chorál.* 'A choral singing sounds in the hall.' – *Sál zní chorálem.* 'The hall sounds with choral singing.') manifest similar changes in their deep and surface syntactic structures as lexical units of the verbs *hučet* 'roar', *chrastit* 'rattle', *bzučet* 'buzz', *blýskat se* 'shine', *vonět* 'smell', etc. For representation of lexicalized alternations in VALLEX see esp. (Kettnerová et al., 2012a).

related by particular relations (Mel'čuk, 2004; Apresjan, 1992).[9] This type of the verbal meaning can be characterized by semantic roles, by lexical conceptual structures, by semantic graphs, etc. For the purpose of simplification, we further describe the situational meaning by a set of semantic roles assigned to situational participants; we explicitly call attention to relations among participants only where it is relevant. As for the structural meaning, it represents a structural part of the meaning of a lexical unit of a verb – in FGD, it corresponds to the valency frame and its members are represented by individual valency complementations.

Grammaticalized alternations differ from each other in systemic changes in the correspondence between situational participants and valency complementations and their mapping onto surface syntactic positions. Reciprocity is characterized by a symmetrical relation into which two situational participants enter;[10] as a result of this symmetry, each valency complementation onto which these two situational participants are mapped in unreciprocal structure corresponds to both situational participants at the same time. Despite the complex correspondence between situational participants and valency complementations, the mapping of valency complementations onto surface syntactic positions is maintained, see Figure 1.

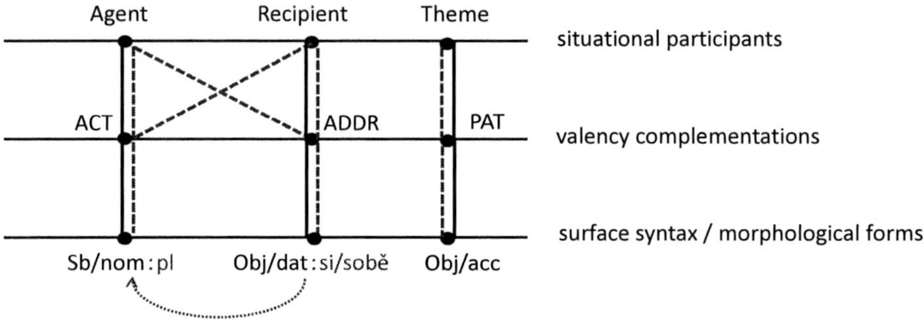

Figure 1: Correspondence among situational participants, valency complementations and their morphological forms for example (3); the solid lines mark the correspondence in the unreciprocal structure, the dashed lines mark the correspondence in the reciprocal structure.

The symmetrical relation between two situational participants expressed in reciprocal structures has specific morphological and lexical markers. First, the surface position that is more prominent – prototypically subject (if subject is not involved, it is direct object) – has a plural meaning. This meaning can be expressed syntactically as coordination, morphologically as plural, or lexically as a collective noun. Second, the less prominent surface syntactic position is lexically expressed by the reflexive pronoun coreferring with the more prominent surface position.Reciprocity in Czech has thus the same marking as reflexivity; however, additional grammatical and/or lexical markers usually disambiguate between reciprocity and reflexivity, see also the comment on reciprocity and reflexivity at the end of this Section.

Let us exemplify the above described changes in morphosyntactic structure of reciprocal constructions on the verb *svěřovat* 'to entrust', example (3). The situational meaning of this verb is characterized by three situational participants: 'Agent', 'Recipient' and 'Theme'; its structural meaning is described by the valency frame consisting of three valency complementations: ACT, ADDR, and PAT (3a). In unreciprocal constructions, each situational participant corresponds to a single valency complementation ('Agent' to ACT, 'Recipient' to ADDR, and 'Theme' to PAT), see Figure 1 and example (3b). In reciprocal constructions, 'Agent' and 'Recipient' enter into symmetry; as a result, ACT and ADDR with which 'Agent' and 'Recipient' are linked in unreciprocal structure, respectively, correspond to both these

---

[9]Such part of the verbal meaning is not syntactically structured, see esp. (Mel'čuk, 2004). Following the FGD principles, we do not formalize the concept of situational meaning here; instead, we use just intuitive and informal labels for situational participants.

[10]Rarely triplets of situational participants are in symmetry, e.g., *Petr, Jan a Pavel se sobě navzájem představili.* 'Peter, John and Paul introduced themselves to each other.'. We leave these more complex cases of reciprocity aside here.

participants at the same time. Nevertheless, the mapping of ACT and ADDR onto surface syntactic position remains unchanged: ACT is still expressed as subject and ADDR as indirect object (3c) and (3d). In these reciprocal structures, the reciprocal relation between situational participants and their complex mapping onto valency complementations are grammatically marked (i) by the plural meaning of the subject position encoded by coordination (paratactic in (3c) or hypotactic in (3d)), and (ii) by the reflexive pronoun expressed in the indirect position, which corefers with subject.

(3)   a. *svěřovat* 'entrust' ... ACT_{nom} $ADDR_{dat}$ PAT_{acc}
        reciprocity: ACT-ADDR

       b. *Jana   svěřuje   děti   sestře Marii.*
          $Jane_{ACT.nom.sg}$ $entrusts_{pres.3sg}$ $children_{PAT.acc}$ $sister\ Mary_{ADDR.dat.sg}$
          'Jane entrusts her children to her sister Mary.'

       c. *Jana   a   Marie   si   (vzájemně)   svěřují   děti.*
          $(Jane_{nom.sg}$ and_{conj} $Mary_{nom.sg})_{ACT}$ $REFL_{ADDR.dat}$ (to each other) $entrust_{pres.3pl}$ $children_{PAT.acc}$
          'Jane entrusts her children to Mary and at the same time Mary entrusts her children to Jane.'

       d. *Jana   s   Marií   si   (vzájemně)   svěřují   děti.*
          $(Jane_{nom.sg}$ $with_{prep}$ $Mary_{instr.sg})_{ACT}$ $REFL_{ADDR.dat}$ (to each other) $entrust_{pst.3pl}$ $children_{PAT.acc}$
          'Jane entrusts her children to Mary and at the same time Mary entrusts her children to Jane.'

However, the reflexive pronoun, as one of the grammatical markers of reciprocity, is not prototypically expressed with the verbs that bear the feature of reciprocity in their lexical meanings, see (4c) and (5c).

(4)   a. *diskutovat* 'discuss' ... ACT_{nom} $ADDR_{s+instr}$ $PAT_{acc,nad+instr,o+loc}$
        reciprocity: ACT-ADDR

       b. *Přednášející   diskutoval   s   kolegou   hebrejsky.*
          $lecturers_{ACT.nom.sg}$ $discussed_{pst.3sg}$ $with\ colleague_{ADDR.s+instr}$ Hebrew
          'The lecturer discussed with his colleague in Hebrew.'

       c. *Přednášející   spolu   diskutovali   hebrejsky.*
          $lecturers_{ACT.nom.pl}$ $together\ discussed_{pst.3pl}$ Hebrew
          'The lecturers discussed with each other in Hebrew.'

Example (5) illustrates the above described changes in morphosyntactic structure of reciprocal constructions when subject is not involved. The reciprocity is grammatically marked by the plural meaning of the direct object position expressing PAT; in this case, the indirect position of EFF is not expressed on the surface (and the reciprocal interpretation is thus often stressed by lexical expressions like *spolu* 'together' or *vzájemně* 'each other').

(5)   a. *porovnat* 'compare' ... ACT_{nom} PAT_{acc} $EFF_{s+instr}$
        reciprocity: PAT-EFF

       b. *Článek   porovnává   prognózu   se skutečností   ...*
          $paper_{ACT.nom.sg}$ $compares_{pres.3sg}$ $prognosis_{PAT.acc.sg}$ $with\ reality_{EFF.s+instr.sg}$ ...
          'The paper compares the prognosis with the reality...'

       c. *Článek   spolu / vzájemně   porovnává   prognózu   a   skutečnost   ...*
          $paper_{ACT.nom}$ $together\ /\ each\ other\ compares_{pres.3sg}$ $(prognosis_{acc.sg}$ and_{conj} $reality_{acc.sg})_{PAT}$ ...
          'This paper compares the prognosis and the reality...'

In the data component of the VALLEX lexicon, the information on the possibility of a lexical unit of a verb to create reciprocal constructions is recorded in the attribute 'reciprocity' assigned to the given lexical unit; the value of this attribute is the pair (or triplet in exceptional cases) of the valency complementations involved in reciprocity (e.g., ACT-PAT for *potkat* 'meet' (1a), ACT-ADDR for *svěřovat* 'entrust' (3a) and *diskutovat* 'discuss' (4a), and PAT-EFF for *porovnat* 'compare' (5a)).

In VALLEX, reciprocity is indicated with more than 30% of lexical units of verbs, see Table 1; the vast majority belongs to the reciprocity affecting subject as the more prominent position. Let us stress that a single lexical unit may create reciprocal constructions involving different pairs of valency complementations, as is exemplified by (6).

LUs in total	6 711
LUs with indicated reciprocity	2 039
reciprocity involving subject	2 074
reciprocity not involving subject	93

Table 1: Basic statistics of reciprocity in VALLEX.

(6)   a.   *lhát* 'lie' ... ACT_{nom} ADDR_{dat} $\text{PAT}_{o+\text{loc},dcc}$
reciprocity: ACT-ADDR
reciprocity: ACT-PAT

b.   *Jan   manželce   lhal   o   svých výdajích.*
$\text{John}_{\text{ACT.nom.sg}}$ $\text{wife}_{\text{ADDR.dat.sg}}$ $\text{lied}_{\text{pst.3sg}}$ about his $\text{expenses}_{\text{PAT}.o+\text{loc}}$

'John lied to her wife about his expenses.'

c.   *John   a   jeho manžleka   si   lhali   o   svých výdajích.*
$(\text{John}_{\text{nom.sg}}$ and_{conj} his $\text{wife}_{\text{nom.sg}})_{\text{ACT}}$ $\text{REFL}_{\text{ADDR.dat}}$ $\text{lied}_{\text{pst.3pl}}$ about their $\text{expenses}_{\text{PAT}.o+\text{loc}}$

'John and his wife lied to each other about their expenses.'

d.   *John   a   jeho manžleka o   sobě   soudci   lhali.*
$(\text{John}_{\text{nom.sg}}$ and_{conj} his $\text{wife}_{\text{nom.sg}})_{\text{ACT}}$ about $\text{REFL}_{\text{PAT}.o+\text{loc}}$ $\text{judge}_{\text{ADDR.dat.sg}}$ $\text{lied}_{\text{pst.3pl}}$

'John and his wife lied to the judge about each other.'

Comment on reciprocity and reflexivity: With verbs allowing for reciprocity alongside with syntactic reflexivity, the lexical expressions bearing reciprocal meaning disambiguate between reciprocal and reflexive structures. For example, the Czech sentence in (6d) can be interpreted either as reciprocal ('John and his wife lied to the judge about each other'), or as reflexive ('John and his wife lied to the judge about themselves'); its homonymy can be eliminated by the presence of the lexical marker (e.g., *vzájemně* 'each other'). The formal overlap between markers of reciprocity and reflexivity is not limited to Czech but it is attested as a pervasive cross-linguistic phenomenon, see (Maslova, 2008).

5   System of Rules for Reciprocity in VALLEX

Reciprocity, as one of productive grammatical processes, can be described by grammatical rules. Let us demonstrate the system of rules characterizing changes in reciprocal surface syntactic structures of lexical units of verbs, as they are captured in the grammar component of VALLEX. We illustrate this system on one of the core types of reciprocity, on reciprocity involving ACT and ADDR (e.g., (3c), (3d) and (4c)); this type of reciprocity is indicated in the data component of the lexicon with 614 lexical units of verbs. The proposed rules – applied to the valency frames stored in the data component of the lexicon – allow for the derivation of grammatical patterns describing reciprocal structures. In case of reciprocity involving ACT and ADDR, two rules are successively applied to the relevant valency frames: the basic rule and one of the set of supplementary rules.

- *The basic rule.* The basic rule describes changes common for all lexical units of verbs allowing for the given type of reciprocity, namely a plural meaning of ACT and the resulting change in subject-verb agreement, see Figure 2.

- *The supplementary rules.* There are six supplementary rules formulated for reciprocity involving ACT and ADDR; their choice depends on the morphological form of ADDR; the overview of supplementary rules is given in Figure 3. These rules determine the morphological form of the reflexive pronoun expressing ADDR. Further, lexical expressions stressing reciprocal meaning are specified as their choice is conditioned by the form of ADDR.

Let us demonstrate one of the supplementary rules in more detail, see Figure 4 and example (7). This rule is applied to lexical units of verbs under the following conditions: they have the value ACT-ADDR in the attribute reciprocity (recipr: ACT-ADDR), their ADDR is in the dative (ADDR(dative)), and they are

24

Reciprocity ACT-ADDR		
Basic rule: change of verb form, agreement		
conditions:	recipr: ACT-ADDR ACT(nominative) & ADDR	
actions:	agreement: form of ACT:	number+gender+person, ACT * → nom : plural

Figure 2: The basic rule for the ACT-ADDR reciprocity (the asterisk indicates that all forms of ACT, the nominative as well as other possible morphological forms, are subject to the given change).

functor	original form		reciprocal form(s)	comment on the form of the reflexive pronoun	lexical expressions
ADDR	dat	→	si / sobě	dative clitic or strong form (with irreflexive verbs)	*navzájem, vzájemně* and/or *mezi sebou* `each other, one another'
	dat	→	sobě / ∅	dative strong form (with reflexive verbs)	* *navzájem, vzájemně* and/or *mezi sebou* `each other, one another'
	acc	→	se / sobě	accusative clitic or strong form	*navzájem, vzájemně* and/or *mezi sebou* `each other, one another'
	gen	→	sebe / ∅	genitive strong form	* *navzájem, vzájemně* and/or *mezi sebou* `each other, one another'
	s+instr `with'	→	∅	not expressed (verbs with reciprocity feature in their lexical meanings)	*spolu* `together' and/or *navzájem, vzájemně* and/or *mezi sebou* `each other, one another'
	k+dat `to'	→	k sobě		
	mezi+4 `between'	→	mezi sebe		
	na+4 `to'	→	na sebe	strong form in the respective case	*vzájemně, navzájem* `each other, one another'
	na+6 `to'	→	na sobě		
	proti+3 `against'	→	proti sobě		
	před+4 `before'	→	před sebe		
	před+7 `before'	→	před sebou		

* emphasizing lexical expression must be present if the reflexive pronoun is not expressed on the surface

Figure 3: Reciprocity ACT-ADDR: change of forms of ADDR (overview).

represented by the reflexive lemmas (SE|SI).[11] The rule determines that in reciprocal structures, ADDR is expressed either in the strong form of the reflexive pronoun, or it is not expressed at all (*sobě* / ∅) (the asterisk indicates that all forms of ADDR, the dative as well as all other possible morphological forms, are subject to the given change). Further, the rule stipulates that in reciprocal structures, ADDR in the prescribed form is obligatorily present in the deep structure. In case that ADDR has the null lexical form, either of the listed lexical expressions must be expressed, see example (7c). The absence of the reflexive pronoun in reciprocal structures of reflexive verbs results from the haplology of the clitic form of the reflexive pronoun and the reflexive morpheme of verb lemmas, see (Rosen, 2014). As the haplology occurs, one of the main grammatical markers of reciprocal meaning is missing and its role is taken over by the lexical expressions (in reciprocal structures of irreflexive verbs, these lexical expressions emphasize the reciprocal meaning but they are not the main markers of reciprocity, see e.g. (3c)).

(7) a. *svěřovat se* 'confide', reflexive variant … ACT_{nom} $ADDR_{dat}$ $PAT_{s+instr}$
reciprocity: ACT-ADDR

---

[11]With these verbs, the particles *se* and *si* are classified as word-forming morphemes representing a part of their verb lemmas: *Reflexive tantum verbs* are verbs without corresponding irreflexive counterparts, e.g., *bát se* 'fear' (**bát*), *setkávat se* 'meet' (**setkávat*), *dít se* 'happen' (though the verb *dít* 'say' exists, it has completely different lexical meaning so these two verbs are classified as homographs). With *derived reflexive verbs*, the reflexive variants are systematically semantically related to their irreflexive variants, e.g., they express unintentional activities (e.g., *šířit* 'disseminate' – *šířit se* 'spread') or they signal reciprocity (*potkat* 'meet' – *potkat se* 'meet (together)', *svěřovat* 'entrust' – *svěřovat se* 'confide'), see also (Kettnerová and Lopatková, 2014).

<table>
<tr><td colspan="3">Reciprocity ACT-ADDR
Supplementary rule: ACT(nominative)-ADDR(dative), reflexive verbs</td></tr>
<tr><td>conditions:</td><td colspan="2">recipr: ACT-ADDR
ADDR(dative) & SE|SI</td></tr>
<tr><td rowspan="2">actions:</td><td>form of ADDR:
obligatoriness:</td><td>* → sobě / ∅
ADDR
if ADDR is not expressed, emphasizing lexical expression
must be present on the surface</td></tr>
<tr><td>lexical expressions:</td><td>navzájem, vzájemně and/or mezi sebou
`each other, one another'</td></tr>
</table>

Figure 4: The supplementary rule for the ACT_{nom}-$ADDR_{dat}$ reciprocity with reflexive verbs.

b. *Jana   se svěřuje   Marii   (se svými problémy).*
   Jane$_{ACT.nom.sg}$ confides$_{pres.3sg}$ to Mary$_{ADDR.dat.sg}$ (with her troubles)$_{PAT.s+instr}$
   'Jane confides (her troubles) to Mary.'

c. *Jana   a   Marie   se vzájemně   svěřují.*
   (Jane$_{nom.sg}$ and$_{conj}$ Mary$_{nom.sg}$)$_{ACT}$ to each other confide$_{pres.3pl}$
   'Jane and Mary confide to each other.'

d. *Sobě   se Jana   a   Marie   svěřují,   rodičům ale nikdy.*
   REFL$_{ADDR.dat}$ (Jane$_{nom.sg}$ and Mary$_{nom.sg}$)$_{ACT}$ confine$_{pres.3pl}$ but never to their parents
   'Jane and Mary confide to each other but never to their parents.'

In (7c) and (7d), the reciprocity of ACT and ADDR is expressed by (i) the coordinated ACT corresponding to subject (the basic rule, Figure 2) and (ii) either by the dative strong form of the reflexive pronoun *sobě* (7d), or in case that the reflexive pronoun is not present, by the lexical expression *vzájemně* 'each other' (7c) (the supplementary rule, Figure 4).

Conclusion

In this contribution, we have shown how the linguistic description of complex (but still systemic) changes characteristic of grammaticalized alternations can benefit from the integration of grammatical rules into a valency lexicon. As a case study, we have presented reciprocity in Czech: although a possibility to create reciprocal structures is lexically conditioned, their morphosyntactic structures can be derived by a set of formal rules. Based on detailed empirical observations, we have presented a model aiming at an economic and theoretically well-founded description of valency behavior of verbs as it has been developed for VALLEX, the Valency Lexicon of Czech Verbs.

Acknowledgements

The work on this project was partially supported by the grant GA 15-09979S of the Grant Agency of the Czech Republic. This work has been using language resources developed, stored, and distributed by the LINDAT/CLARIN project of the Ministry of Education, Youth and Sports of the Czech Republic (project LM2015071).

References

Yuri D. Apresjan. 1992. *Lexical Semantics: User's Guide to Contemporary Russian Vocabulary*. Karoma Publishers, Ann Arbor, MI.

Noam Chomsky. 1965. *Aspects of the Theory of Syntax*. MIT Press, Cambridge, MA.

Nicholas Evans, Alice Gaby, and Rachel Nordlinger. 2007. Valency mismatches and the coding of reciprocity in Australian languages. *Linguistic Typology*, 11:541–597.

Ronald M. Kaplan and Joan Bresnan. 1982. Lexical-Functional Grammar: A Formal System for Grammatical Representation. In J. Bresnan, editor, *The Mental Representation of Grammatical Relations*, pages 173–281. MIT Press, Cambridge.

Václava Kettnerová and Markéta Lopatková. 2014. Reflexive Verbs in a Valency Lexicon: The Case of Czech Reflexive Morphemes. In A. Abel, C. Vettori, and N. Ralli, editors, *Proceedings of the XVI EURALEX International Congress: The User in Focus*, pages 1007–1023, Italy, Bolzano/Bozen. EURAC research.

Václava Kettnerová, Markéta Lopatková, and Eduard Bejček. 2012a. The Syntax-Semantics Interface of Czech Verbs in the Valency Lexicon. In R. V. Fjeld and J. M. Torjusen, editors, *Proceedings of the XV EURALEX International Congress*, pages 434–443, Oslo, Norway. University of Oslo.

Václava Kettnerová, Markéta Lopatková, and Zdeňka Urešová. 2012b. The Rule-Based Approach to Czech Grammaticalized Alternations. In Sojka P., A. Horák, I. Kopeček, and K. Pala, editors, *Proceedings of TSD 2012*, number 7499 in LNAI, pages 158–165, Berlin / Heidelberg. Springer Verlag.

Václava Kettnerová, Markéta Lopatková, and Jarmila Panevová. 2014. An Interplay between Valency Information and Reflexivity. *The Prague Bulletin of Mathematical Linguistics*, (102):105–126.

Ekkerhard König and Volker Gast. 2008. *Reciprocals and Reflexives. Theoretical and Typological Explorations*. Mouton de Gruyter, Berlin – New York.

Beth C. Levin. 1993. *English Verb Classes and Alternations: A Preliminary Investigation*. The University of Chicago Press, Chicago and London.

Markéta Lopatková, Václava Kettnerová, Eduard Bejček, Anna Vernerová, and Zdeněk Žabokrtský. 2016. *Valenční slovník českých sloves*. Karolinum Press, Prague. (in press).

Elena Maslova. 2008. Reflexive Encoding of Reciprocity: Cross-Linguistic and Language-Internal Variation. In E. König and V. Gast, editors, *Reciprocals and Reflexives. Theoretical and Typological Explorations*, pages 225–258. Mouton de Gruyter, Berlin and New York.

Igor A. Mel'čuk. 1988. *Dependency Syntax: Theory and Practice*. State University of New York Press, Albany.

Igor A. Mel'čuk. 2004. Actants in Semantics and Syntax I. *Linguistics*, 42(1):1–66.

Vladimir P. Nedjalkov. 2007. *Typology of Reciprocal Constructions*. John Benjamins Publishing Company, Amsterdam – Philadelphia.

Jarmila Panevová and Marie Mikulová. 2007. On Reciprocity. *The Prague Bulletin of Mathematical Linguistics*, 87:27–40.

Jarmila Panevová, Eva Hajičová, Václava Kettnerová, Markéta Lopatková, Marie Mikulová, and Magda Ševčíková. 2014. *Mluvnice současné češtiny 2, Syntax na základě anotovaného korpusu*. Karolinum, Praha.

Jarmila Panevová. 1994. Valency Frames and the Meaning of the Sentence. In P. A. Luelsdorff, editor, *The Prague School of Structural and Functional Linguistics*, pages 223–243. John Benjamins Publishing Company, Amsterdam – Philadelphia.

Jarmila Panevová. 1999. Česká reciproční zájmena a slovesná valence. *Slovo a slovesnost*, 60(4):269–275.

Jarmila Panevová. 2007. Znovu o reciprocitě. *Slovo a slovesnost*, 68(2):91–100.

Carl Pollard and Ivan A. Sag. 1994. *Head-Driven Phrase Structure Grammar*. University of Chicago Press, Chicago – London.

Alexandr Rosen. 2014. Haplology of Reflexive Clitics in Czech. In E. Kaczmarska and M. Nomachi, editors, *Slavic and German in Contact: Studies from Areal and Contrastive Linguistics*, volume 26 of *Slavic Eurasian Studies*, pages 97–116. Slavic Research Center, Sapporo.

Petr Sgall, Eva Hajičová, and Jarmila Panevová. 1986. *The Meaning of the Sentence in Its Semantic and Pragmatic Aspects*. Reidel, Dordrecht.

Hana Skoumalová. 2001. *Czech Syntactic Lexicon*. Ph.D. thesis, Charles University in Prague, Prague.

Zdeňka Urešová, Eva Fučíková, and Jana Šindlerová. 2016. CzEngVallex: a bilingual Czech-English valency lexicon. *The Prague Bulletin of Mathematical Linguistics*, 105:17–50.

Zdeňka Urešová. 2011. *Valence sloves v Pražském závislostním korpusu*. Ústav formální a aplikované lingvistiky, Praha.

Extra-Specific Multiword Expressions for
Language-Endowed Intelligent Agents

Marjorie McShane and Sergei Nirenburg
Cognitive Science Department
Rensselaer Polytechnic Institute
Troy, NY 12180 USA
{margemc34,zavedomo}@gmail.com

Abstract

Language-endowed intelligent agents benefit from leveraging lexical knowledge falling at different points along a spectrum of compositionality. This means that robust computational lexicons should include not only the compositional expectations of argument-taking words, but also non-compositional collocations (idioms), semi-compositional collocations that might be difficult for an agent to interpret (e.g., standard metaphors), and even collocations that could be compositionally analyzed but are so frequently encountered that recording their meaning increases the efficiency of interpretation. In this paper we argue that yet another type of string-to-meaning mapping can also be useful to intelligent agents: remembered semantic analyses of actual text inputs. These can be viewed as super-specific multi-word expressions whose recorded interpretations mimic a person's memories of knowledge previously learned from language input. These differ from typical annotated corpora in two ways. First, they provide a full, context-sensitive semantic interpretation rather than select features. Second, they are are formulated in the ontologically-grounded metalanguage used in a particular agent environment, meaning that the interpretations contribute to the dynamically evolving cognitive capabilites of agents configured in that environment.

1   Introduction

Language-endowed intelligent agents benefit from access to knowledge of many types of string-to-meaning pairings. The most obvious ones are recorded in the lexicon, which must include not only argument-taking words (along with the lexical, syntactic, and semantic constraints on their arguments) but also a large inventory of multiword expressions (MWEs). MWE is an umbrella term covering many types of entities, a short list of which includes:

- Competely fixed idioms: *It's do or die*
- Idioms with variable slots: [someone] *kicked the bucket*
- Common metaphorical usages that are not semantically opaque: [someone] *is in deep water*
- Frequent phrases that are semantically compositional but for which any other word choice would sound unnatural: *What's for dinner? How can I help you?* (Recording these can speed up analysis as well as ensure the correct paraphrase during generation.)

But what if we were to expand an agent's repository of string-to-meaning pairings even beyond traditional MWEs to full utterances, no matter their linguistic status? What if the agent had access to the correct semantic analyses of a large corpus of inputs such as, "That kid just kicked me in the shins!", "Because I said so!", "If you don't do this within the next five minutes the tank will explode.", and "Scalpel!!"? We hypothesize that memories of successful past language analyses could bootstrap the analysis of new inputs in the ways described in Section 4. We hypothesize further that modeling agents with such a repository is psychologically plausible and, therefore, should be implemented in human-inspired computational cognitive systems.

Proceedings of the Workshop on Grammar and Lexicon: Interactions and Interfaces,
pages 28–37, Osaka, Japan, December 11 2016.

In our earlier writings (e.g., Nirenburg and Raskin 2004; McShane et al. 2005a, 2015) we have described our Ontological Semantics (OS) approach to the lexicon overall, and to MWEs in particular. Some of that material will be summarized here by way of background. But the novel aspect of this contribution involves expanding the notion of useful string-to-meaning pairings to include the agent's repository of previously analyzed inputs. Computing and combining many types of heuristic evidence toward the larger goal of achieving deep semantic analysis contrasts sharply with most current work in NLP, which tends to treat individual phenomena in isolation (MWEs *or* word-sense disambiguation *or* reference resolution) and tends to avoid pursuing the full analysis of text meaning.

The paper is organized as follows. We begin with brief overviews of OS language analysis (Section 2) and the OS lexicon (Section 3). We then consider the text-meaning representations of actual inputs as super-specific MWEs, which can contribute to a knowledge base that supports the analysis of subsequent inputs (Section 4). We conclude with thoughts about how a repository of sentence-to-meaning pairings could serve the wider community as a more fully specified alternative to traditional corpus annotation methods (Section 5). We conclude by commenting on the issues posited to guide the formulation of submissions for this workshop (Section 6).

2　Language Analysis with Ontological Semantics (OS)

The goal of OS text analysis is to automatically generate fully specified, disambiguated, ontologically-grounded text meaning representations (TMRs) of language input. For example, the TMR for the input *John is addressing the situation* is:

```
CONSIDER-1
      AGENT         HUMAN-1
      THEME         STATE-OF-AFFAIRS-1
      TIME          find-anchor-time
      textpointer   addressing
      from-sense    address-v2
HUMAN-1
      HAS-NAME      John
      GENDER        male
      textpointer   John
      from-sense    *proper-name*
STATE-OF-AFFAIRS-1
      textpointer   situation
      from-sense    situation-n1
```

This TMR is headed by a numbered instance of the concept CONSIDER, which is the contextual interpretation of "address". The AGENT of this action is an instance of HUMAN, which is further specified in its own frame as being named John and being male. The THEME of CONSIDER is an instance of the concept STATE-OF-AFFAIRS. The TIME is the time of speech, whose filler is a call to a procedural-semantic routine that attempts to determine when, in absolute terms, the sentence was uttered. If the agent cannot determine that time, then the call to the meaning procedure remains in the TMR, providing an indication of relative time with respect to the other propositions in the text. This is just one example of how OS treats underspecification – an essential aspect of meaning representation. The italicized features are just a couple of the types of metadata stored along with TMRs: the string that gave rise to the frame (textpointer), and the lexical sense used for the analysis (from-sense).

The concepts referred to in TMRs are not merely symbols in an upper-case semantics. They are grounded in a 9,000-concept, property-rich ontology developed to support semantically-oriented NLP, script-based simulation, and overall agent reasoning (McShane and Nirenburg 2012). The information stored about concepts in the ontology is always available to support agent reasoning should that information be needed; however, it is not copied into every TMR. For example, the TMR for the sentence *A dog is barking* will include an instance of DOG (e.g., DOG-1) but it will not include all of the ontological information about typical dogs, such as [HAS-OBJECT-AS-PART: SNOUT, TAIL, FUR], [AGENT-OF GROWL, PLAY-FETCH] , etc. There are three reasons for not copying all of this ontological information into the TMR: first, it is not in the text, and the TMR captures text meaning; second, it is available in the ontology already, should it be needed, making copying redundant; and third, this generic information about dogs might not even apply to this particular dog, which might have no tail, might have never growled a single time in its entire life, and might have no idea why people throw balls into the distance all the time.

A prerequisite for automatically generating TMRs is OS's highly specified lexicon, which we now briefly describe.

3   The OS Lexicon

The OS English lexicon currently contains nearly 30,000 senses. Each sense description contains: metadata for acquirers (definition, example, comments); syntactic and semantic zones (syn-struc and sem-struc) linked by coreferential variables; and, optionally, a meaning-procedures zone that includes calls to procedural semantic routines (for words like *yesterday* and *respectively*).

Consider, for example, the first two verbal senses for *address*, shown in Table 1 using a simplified formalism. Syntactically, both senses expect a subject and a direct object in the active voice, filled by $var1 and $var2, respectively.[1] However, in address-v1, the meaning of the direct object (^$var2) is constrained to a HUMAN (or, less commonly, any ANIMAL), whereas in address-v2 the meaning of the direct object is constrained to an ABSTRACT-OBJECT. The constraints appear in italics because they are virtually available, being accessed from the ontology by the analyzer at runtime. This difference in constraint values permits the analyzer to disambiguate: if the direct object is abstract, as in *He addressed the problem*, then *address* will be analyzed as CONSIDER; by contrast, if the direct object is human, as in *He addressed the audience*, then *address* will be analyzed as SPEECH-ACT.

Table 1. Two verbal senses for the word *address*. The symbol ^ indicates "the meaning of".

address-v1			address-v2		
anno			anno		
definition "to talk to"			definition "to consider, think about"		
example "He addressed the crowd."			example "He addressed the problem."		
syn-struc			syn-struc		
subject	$var1		subject	$var1	
v	$var0		v	$var0	
directobject	$var2		directobject	$var2	
sem-struc			sem-struc		
SPEECH-ACT			CONSIDER		
AGENT	^$var1 *(sem HUMAN)*		AGENT	^$var1 *(sem HUMAN)*	
BENEFICIARY	^$var2 *(sem HUMAN) (relax.-to ANIMAL)*		THEME	^$var2 *(sem ABSTRACT-OBJECT)*	

These examples highlight several aspects of the OS lexicon. First, it supports the combined syntactic and semantic analysis of text. Second, the metalanguage for describing its sem-strucs is the same one used in the ontology. And third, the sem-strucs—and, often, the associated syn-strucs—from the lexicon for one language can be ported into the lexicon of another language with minimal modification (McShane et al. 2005a), which greatly enhances the multilingual applicability of the OS suite of resources.

The simplest method of representing lexical meaning in an ontological semantic environment is to map a lexeme directly onto an ontological concept: e.g., dog → DOG. In the case of argument-taking lexemes, the syntactic arguments and semantic roles need to be appropriately associated using variables, as shown our *address* senses above. However, not every word meaning is necessarily represented by a single ontological concept. In some cases, property-based specifications of concepts are provided in the lexicon (for a discussion of what makes it into the ontology, see McShane et al. 2005a). For example, *asphalt* (v.) is described as a COVER event whose THEME must be a ROADWAY-ARTIFACT and whose INSTRUMENT is ASPHALT.

---

[1] Variables are written, by convention, as $var followed by a distinguishing number. Variables permit us to map textual content from the input to elements of the syn-struc, then link each syn-struc element with its semantic realization in the sem-struc.

asphalt-v1
  anno
    definition "to cover a roadway in asphalt"
    example   "The workers asphalted the country road."
  syn-struc
    subject $var1
    v $var0
    directobject $var2
  sem-struc
    COVER
      AGENT   ^$var1 *(sem HUMAN)*
      THEME   ^$var2 (sem ROAD-SYSTEM-ARTIFACT)
      INSTRUMENT ASPHALT

Using this lexical sense, among others, to process the input *He asphalted the driveway yesterday* generates the following TMR, presented without metadata:

COVER-1
    AGENT   HUMAN-1
    THEME   DRIVEWAY-1
    INSTRUMENT ASPHALT
    TIME   combine-time (find-anchor-time -1 DAY) ; *find the time of speech and subtract a day*
HUMAN-1
    GENDER   male

As we see, generating TMRs essentially involves: a) copying the content of sem-strucs into TMR frames; 2) converting bare concept names (COVER) into instances (COVER-1); and 3) replacing variables by their associated concept instances (^$var1 → HUMAN-1).

The lexicon includes a large inventory of MWEs, such as *someone takes someone by surprise.*

take-v4
  anno
    definition "MWE: s.o. takes s.o. by surprise = s.o. surprises s.o. else"[2]
    example   "The clowns took us by surprise."
    comments "Non-agentive subjects are covered by a conversion recorded as a meaning-procedure"
  syn-struc
    subject $var1
    v $var0
    directobject $var2
    pp
      prep $var3 (root by)
      obj $var4 (root surprise)
  sem-struc
    SURPRISE
      AGENT   ^$var1 *(sem ANIMAL) (RELAXABLE-TO ORGANIZATION)*
      THEME   ^$var2 *(sem ANIMAL) (RELAXABLE-TO ORGANIZATION)*
    ^$var3 null-sem+
    ^$var4 null-sem+
  meaning-procedure
    change-agent-to-caused-by (value ^$var1)

As should be clear by now, the combination of syntactic expectations and semantic constraints renders every argument-taking lexical sense *construction-like*. So, although non-idiomatic argument-taking word senses do not require particular lexemes to be used as their arguments, they do semantically constrain the set of meanings that can be used to fill case-role slots, resulting in what might be thought of as broadly specified constructions. This is not a peculiar side-effect of the theory of OS; instead, we hypothesize that this is how people think about language, and how intelligent agents con-

---

[2] If the meaning of the subject is non-agentive, the procedural semantic routine *change-agent-to-caused-by* will be triggered. E.g., *His arrival took me by surprise* will be analyzed as SURPRISE (CAUSED-BY COME (AGENT HUMAN) (GENDER male)). An alternative approach would be to simply record another lexical sense that expects a non-agentive subject.

figured to act like people need to learn to think about it. In short, a sufficiently fine-grained lexical specification of argument-taking words – supported by ontological knowledge about the concepts they invoke – is a long way toward being a construction, and constructions are a superclass of what are typically considered multi-word expressions.

Now we turn to the new contribution of this paper: exploring how we can use a repository of stored TMRs as super-specific MWEs that can serve as an additional knowledge base for agent reasoning about language.

4   TMRs as Super-Specific MWEs

When intelligent agents configured within the OntoAgent cognitive architecture carry out natural language understanding, they store the resulting string-to-meaning correlations in a TMR repository. Let us consider the content of the TMR repository alongside the agent's other core knowledge bases, the ontology and the fact repository. The **ontology** describes types of objects and events using the ontological metalanguage; it has no connection to natural language whatsoever. The **TMR repository** contains pairings of text strings with their semantic interpretations, the latter recorded as ontologically-grounded TMRs. Each TMR is supplied with confidence scores along many parameters. These scores permit the agent to reason about whether its level of understanding of the input is sufficient (a) to merit storing the information to memory, and (b) to support subsequent reasoning about action (McShane and Nirenburg 2015). The **fact repository**, for its part, models the agent's memory of concept instances. Like the ontology, it is recorded exclusively using the ontological metalanguage – there are no links to natural language. This is quite natural because agent memories do not derive exclusively from language understanding: e.g., when an agent supplied with a physiological simulation (such as a virtual patient) experiences symptoms, it remembers them as meaning representations with no associated text strings; similarly, when an agent reasons about its task or its interlocutor, it remembers its conclusions and their rationale in the form of meaning representations. In principle, though we are still working out the details, the fact repository should also reflect (a) decision-making about what is worth remembering (i.e., the information should be sufficiently relevant and of sufficiently high quality), (b) the merging of individual memories into generalizations (365 instances of taking a given medication every evening should be merged into the memory of taking the medication every evening for a year), and (c) possibly even forgetting the kinds of things that a regular person would forget – depending on how lifelike one wants the agent to be. In short, the TMR repository is one source of input to the fact repository, and it is the fact repository – along with the ontology – that supports agent reasoning.

It is very difficult for intelligent agents to compute full, completely disambiguated and contextually correct interpretations of natural language utterances – which is presumably the reason why mainstream NLP has sidelined this goal in favor of pursuits with nearer-term payoffs. We will work through just a sampling of the many challenges of full language interpretation that we think will be better handled by agents that are configured to use a TMR repository as a source of evidence.

Challenge 1: Polysemy. Most words are polysemous, with the challenges of disambiguation exploding exponentially with increasing sentence length. But many words are used in frequent combinations. The remembered interpretations of such combinations help human readers save effort in language analysis, and they should serve as the agent's default interpretation as well. For example, when reading *He gave the dog a bone*, any human and human-emulating agent should immediately think "furry canine companion" not "contemptible person" – though the latter interpretation is not excluded based on ontological constraints (one can, in fact, hand a bone to a person).

Stored analyses can be particularly helpful for disambiguation when the input words are used *outside of* a highly predictive dependency structure. For example, disambiguating *horse* in *The horse was eating hay* is straightforward using OS methods since only animate entities can eat things, and the alternative meanings of *horse* (a sawhorse or pommel horse) are inanimate. However, disambiguation is not as easy for *She put some hay down beside the horse*, because "beside the horse" is a free adjunct, and the ontology can be expected to contain only the weakest semantic constraints on where something can be put down. The disambiguation heuristic that people use in such contexts is frequency of co-occurrence.[3] That is, in any context with *hay* – understood as mown, dried grass (not 'bed', as used

---

[3] This is being explored by distributional semantics; however, since that paradigm works on uninterpreted text strings, it provides no direct support for our agent's goal of ontologically-grounded disambiguation.

in various idiomatic expressions) any *horse* that is mentioned is likely to be an animal. Our agent can use the TMR repository as a search space, seeking combinations of two or more *words of input* along with their corresponding *concepts in TMR*. The closer the alignment between the incoming and stored input strings – and/or the closer the alignment between candidate interpretations of the incoming string and the interpretation of the stored string – the more confident the result of this method of disambiguation. Formalizing similarity metrics is, of course, key to optimizing this process.

Challenge 2: Non-canonical syntax. The OS lexicon records syntactic expectations for argument-taking words such as verbs. For example, one sense of *manage* expects an infinitival complement (xcomp) and is used to analyze inputs like *He managed to close the door.* But what if an input says *He managed close the door,* which lacks infinitival 'to'? As people, we know that this might reflect a typo, a mistake by a non-native-speaker, or a transcription error by an automatic speech recognizer; moreover, we might think it trivial to even think twice about this example. But for a machine, it is anything but trivial to determine whether *almost* matching lexically recorded expectations is good enough. For example, whereas *kick the bucket* can mean 'to die', *kick the buckets* (plural) cannot. So we do not want our agents to assume that all recorded constraints are relaxable – they have to be smarter about making related judgments.

Returning to the non-canonical "managed close the door", let us assume that the agent already processed the canonical input *Charlie managed to close the door* and stored the results in the TMR repository. Let's assume further that the new input is *The fire chief managed close the door,* for which the external parser we use, from the CoreNLP toolset (Manning et al. 2014), does not recognize that *close the door* is intended to be an xcomp. So our agent cannot directly align the parser output with the xcomp expected in the lexical sense for *manage*. As before, the agent can use the TMR repository as a search space and look for approximate string-level matches of "*managed close the door*". If it finds "managed to close the door," it can judge the similarity between the stored and new text strings and, if close enough, use the stored analysis to guide the new analysis. The natural extension is to relax the notion of similarity beyond surface string matching. The first level of relaxation might be to replace 'close' by any verb and 'the door' by an NP referring to any PHYSICAL-OBJECT, generating the following search query: **manage + V$_{BARE}$ + NP$_{PHYSICAL-OBJECT}$.** This would match stored inputs like *She managed to drink the espresso in 5 seconds flat,* whose associated stored TMR would provide the needed clue for how to combine the meanings of *manage* and *close* in our syntactically corrupted input. However, if this first level of relaxation fails to match a stored input, an even more relaxed pattern would remove the semantic constraint from the direct object, resulting in **manage + V$_{BARE}$ + NP,** which would match inputs like *The tallest guy managed to win the race* ('race' is semantically an event, not an object), and would serve equally as a point of analogy for our *manage close the door* example.

Challenge 3. Literal vs. metaphorical meanings. Many expressions can be used in a literal or a metaphorical meaning, with the overall context being the only clue for disambiguation. For example, outside of contexts involving war, gangs or mafias, *I'm going to kill him!* typically indicates anger or, at most, the intention to punish someone for having done something undesirable. Similarly common are the metaphorical uses of *I hit him hard* and *I'm totally drowning!* We believe that the best way to prepare intelligent agents to analyze conventional metaphors (and most metaphorical usages are, indeed, conventional) is to record them in the lexicon. But runtime disambiguation, then, remains an issue. A good heuristic will be to simply check the TMR repository and see whether there is a frequency difference between the metaphorical and non-metaphorical usages, which should be the case, e.g., for *I'm going to kill him!*

Challenge 4. Exaggerations. People exaggerate all the time. (Get it?!) *Grandma drinks 20 cups of tea a day. If you go ½ mile-an-hour over the speed limit on that street they'll give you a ticket. Being a musician is tough, you earn like $1,000 a year.* Intelligent agents need to recognize exaggerations, which can be hyperboles or litotes, and convert them into their respective abstract representations which, in English, can be conveyed as *drinking a whole lot of tea, going slightly over the speed limit,* and *earning very little money.* The most direct way for an agent to detect an exaggeration is to compare the stated value with expectations stored in the ontology. For example, if the ontology says that people are generally not more than 7 feet tall, then saying that someone is 20 feet tall is surely an exaggeration. However, an ontology can be expected to cover typical heights of people, it very well might not cover things like "normal daily beverage consumption," "minimal speed infraction for getting a ticket" or "normal income range per year" – especially since the latter can differ greatly across different cultures and social groups. For these cases, the TMR repository can be of help.

The TMR repository should contain *interpretations,* not literal renderings, of inputs, for which many kinds of reasoning can be needed. For example, the agent must reason about non-literal language ("You're a pig" does not introduce an instance of the animal PIG into the context), about indirect speech acts ("Can you pass the pepper?" is a request not a question), as well as about exaggerations ("Grandma drinks 20 cups of tea a day" means she drinks a whole lot of tea). Focusing on exaggerations, the correct, interpreted TMR that is stored in an agent's TMR repository should reflect the conversion of an exaggerated scalar value into the highest – or, for litotes, lowest – value on the abstract scale. Compare the basic and reasoning-enhanced TMRs for our tea example, shown in Table 1.

Table 1. The basic and reasoning-enhanced TMRs for "Grandma drinks 20 cups of tea a day". The reasoning-enhanced TMR converts the exaggerated value into an abstract one.

Basic TMR		Reasoning-enhanced TMR	
DRINK-1		DRINK-1	
AGENT	GRANDMOTHER-1	AGENT	GRANDMOTHER-1
THEME	TEA-BEVERAGE-1	THEME	TEA-BEVERAGE-1
CONSUMPTION-RATE	**20 (MEASURED-IN CUP-PER-DAY)**	**CONSUMPTION-RATE**	**1**
TIME	find-anchor-time	TIME	find-anchor-time
TEA-BEVERAGE		TEA-BEVERAGE-1	
QUANTITY	**20 (MEASURED-IN CUP)**	**QUANTITY**	**1**

The reasoning-enhanced TMR asserts that drinking 20 cups a day is an exaggeration by aligning a tex-string value of "20 cups" with the "QUANTITY 1," the maximum value on an abstract scale from zero to 1. (If the ontology does not contain any relevant clues to guide this reasoning, it will need to be provided manually by the knowledge acquirer who is validating the results of the automatically-generated TMRs; see the discussion in the next section.) Once the agent detects this mismatch, it can use it to automatically enhance its ontology with a corresponding generalization: normal tea consumption is considerably less than 20 cups per day. Of course, we don't know how much less since the speaker of the exaggeration could have said anything from 20 to 1000 to a million cups a day. But, even though not maximally specific, this information can still be useful for reasoning about future inputs that include tea consumption. For example, if the agent subsequently receives the input "Joe drank 50 cups of tea yesterday", it can automatically – i.e., with no human intervention this time – hypothesize, with high confidence, that this is an exaggeration and automatically carry out the conversion from a specific scalar value to an abstract value.

Challenge 5. Elliptical and fragmentary utterances. Natural language text is full of elliptical and fragmentary utterances, some of which are stereotypical: *More cream, please* is a request for more cream; *Scalpel!* is a demand to be handed a scalpel; and *Anything else?* asks whether the speaker can give, or help the interlocutor with, anything else. One of the ways an agent can analyze these is by referring to ontological scripts – a method that is similar to the ontology-checking method of determining the normal range of heights for humans discussed above. So, if a robotic agent is configured to hand a surgeon implements during surgery, it will have the expectation that the physician's mention of a tool is a request to be handed the implement. (We are, of course, simplifying the actual complexity of the knowledge structures and the reasoning involved for reasons of space.) However, if the agent does not have recorded ontological scripts for a given domain it can still use the TMR repository to hypothesize what elliptical utterances might mean. For example, if the reasoning-enhanced TMR for "Scalpel!" is

```
REQUEST-ACTION-1
     AGENT          HUMAN-1     ; the speaker
     BENEFICIARY    HUMAN-2     ; the interlocutor
     THEME          TRANSFER-POSSESSION-1
TRANSFER-POSSESSION-1
     AGENT          HUMAN-2
```

    BENEFICIARY   HUMAN-1
    THEME   SCALPEL-1

then the agent can use this as a template for analyzing such inputs as "Coffee!" and "Another pickle, please!" Moreover, if the agent leverages this reasoning rule successfully – as determined by the fact that the TMR for "Coffee!" that it automatically generates is judged by a person to be correct – it can posit a generalization such as: When a sentence contains a mention of a PHYSICAL-OBJECT in isolation, or with the addition of select adverbs (e.g., please, now, here), this is a request to be given the object, as formally represented in a TMR structure like the one shown above. This generalization cannot be stored in the ontology like our generalization about quantities of tea because it relates not just to concepts but also to linguistic realizations of utterances, which are not within the purview of ontology.

5   Creating and Using a High-Quality TMR Repository

Because of all of the challenges listed above – as well as many more that we did not mention – it is difficult within the current state of the art for agents to generate perfect, reasoning-enhanced TMRs fully automatically. The most obvious way of creating the kind of high-quality TMR repository we have been talking about is for people to manually vet and, if necessary, correct TMRs automatically generated by the agent in the course of its normal operation. To return to an earlier example, if the agent has no information at all about normal tea-drinking practices, it has no way to know that 20 cups a day is an exaggeration: a person would have to correct the basic TMR that refers to the 20 cups, editing it to refer to the abstract value (QUANTITY 1). Only then can the agent detect future exaggerations in this realm.

Our past experience has shown that, given the appropriate tools, the process of semi-automatically creating gold-standard TMRs is not prohibitively difficult or time-consuming, and it is much faster than creating TMRs from scratch by hand. Although a gold-standard TMR repository has clear uses for intelligent agents configured within the OntoAgent architecture, it could also be viewed as a semantically deep alternative or supplement to traditional corpus annotation efforts, as we have discussed previously (McShane et al. 2005b).

6   Conclusion

We conclude by directly commenting on the issues posited to guide the crafting of submissions for this workshop.

Novelty: To the best of our knowledge, the proposed approach to using stored semantic interpretations of real texts to support the runtime analysis of new inputs is novel. However, it builds upon several existing theories and technologies: the theory of Ontological Semantics and its implementation in the OntoSem2 language processing system; the lexical and ontological knowledge bases used in that system; the OntoAgent cognitive architecture; and past work on compositionality, multiword expressions, and reasoning by analogy, among others.

Status of the Implementation: The theory of Ontological Semantics has recently been given a new implementation, called OntoSem2. It differs from its predecessor, OntoSem (McShane et al. 2016), in that it analyzes inputs incrementally and uses an architecture that is not a strict pipeline: e.g., reference resolution can be carried out before semantic analysis when applicable. OntoSem2 can already generate TMRs in fully automatic mode, though not yet for as broad a range of contexts as its predecessor. We are currently implementing the TMR repository that we have been discussing. The reasoning processes for dynamically leveraging the TMR repository have not yet been implemented. Although they will require more detailed specifications than have been provided here, formulating those specifications is a workaday task, as we understand the problem space well.

Benefits. Deep-semantic analysis will permit intelligent agents to effectively and naturally communicate with people during task-oriented collaboration. Agents must understand their task, their world, and how their interlocutors' utterances fit into their mental model in order to function with human-like proficiency.

Limitations. The limitations of this approach to language analysis are that, at least at present, it is best suited to agent applications that focus on specific domains, rather than applications that cover all possible domains. For example, it makes sense for an agent to learn ontological facts about tea consumption only if it operates in a domain where that is important – e.g., as a medical assistant or an addiction counselor; and we can expect that human time in correcting TMRs will be best spent only if correcting TMRs in a specific domain of interest. The results of such human intervention can then inform language processing and reasoning in that same domain.

Benefit/Limitation Analysis. If we want intelligent agents to use language with human-like proficiency, we need to provide them with the same types of knowledge and resources as humans seem to use. Most of the NLP community has judged that achieving human-level proficiency is not sufficiently important to merit the requisite development time. We disagree, believing that people will not be satisfied with what knowledge-lean NLP can offer for very much longer.

Competing Approaches. The competing approaches are knowledge-lean NLP, along with its useful near-term applications that do not, however, support human-level reasoning by intelligent agents.

Next Steps. The next steps in making OS text processing useful are: a) continuing to develop the analysis engine; b) operationalizing notions like "sufficiently-close matching" (of new inputs to stored analyses) and reasoning by analogy; c) creating a large TMR repository; and d) testing all of these capabilities in demonstration systems with virtual agents and robots – all of which is in progress.

Outside Interest and Competing Approaches. Few groups are working on automating deep-semantic natural language understanding. Much of computational semantics is currently devoted to corpus annotation and the supervised machine learning that it supports; but the depth of those annotations is, in most cases, significantly less than what we describe here.

New Information About Language Functioning. We hypothesize that people have, and use, the equivalent of a TMR repository during language understanding. For example, if you hear just "The cat ran out…" what do you predict comes next? Perhaps *the door, of the room, of the yard, into the street*? It is likely that *something* comes to mind, and that something derives from ontological knowledge about the world as well as past experience with individuals in it. This paper has described how we have tried to lasso that knowledge into a form that is usable by intelligent agents.

Finally, given our collective decades-long experience working on these issues, we do not underestimate the number of devils in the details of operationalizing analogy detection, approximate matching, and so on. However, we have treated countless such devils before and have come to believe that they are, almost always, quite benign – they just require close attention and dedicated conceptual and descriptive work.

Acknowledgments

This research was supported in part by Grant N00014-16-1-2118 from the U.S. Office of Naval Research. Any opinions or findings expressed in this material are those of the authors and do not necessarily reflect the views of the Office of Naval Research. Our thanks to Igor Boguslavsky for his insightful commentary on a draft of this paper.

References

Manning, C. D., Surdeanu, M., Bauer, J., Finkel, J., Bethard, S. J., & McClosky, D. 2014. The Stanford CoreNLP Natural Language Processing Toolkit. *Proceedings of the 52nd Annual Meeting of the Association for Computational Linguistics: System Demonstrations,* pp. 55–60. Stroudsburg, PA: The Association for Computational Linguistics.

McShane, M., Nirenburg, S. and Beale, S. 2005a. An NLP lexicon as a largely language independent resource. *Machine Translation,* 19(2): 139-173.

McShane, M., Nirenburg, S., Beale, S. and O'Hara, T. 2005b. Semantically rich human-aided machine annotation. *Proceedings the Workshop on Frontiers in Corpus Annotation II: Pie in the Sky,* pp. 68-75, at the 43rd Annual Meeting of the Association for Computational Linguistics (ACL-05). Stroudsburg, PA: Association for Computational Linguistics.

McShane, M. and Nirenburg, S. 2012. A knowledge representation language for natural language processing, simulation and reasoning. *International Journal of Semantic Computing,* 6(1): 3-23.

McShane, M. and Nirenburg, S. 2015. Decision-making during language understanding by intelligent agents. *Artificial General Intelligence,* Volume 9205 of the series Lecture Notes in Computer Science, pp. 310-319.

McShane, M., Nirenburg, S. and Beale, S. 2015. The Ontological Semantic treatment of multiword expressions. *Lingvisticæ Investigationes*, 38(1): 73-110. John Benjamins Publishing Company.

McShane, M., Nirenburg, S. and Beale, S. 2016. Language understanding with Ontological Semantics. *Advances in Cognitive Systems* 4:35-55.

Nirenburg, S. and Raskin, V. 2004. *Ontological Semantics*. Cambridge, Mass.: The MIT Press.

Universal Dependencies: A Cross-Linguistic
Perspective on Grammar and Lexicon

Joakim Nivre
Department of Linguistics and Philology
Uppsala University

`joakim.nivre@lingfil.uu.se`

Abstract

Universal Dependencies is an initiative to develop cross-linguistically consistent grammatical annotation for many languages, with the goal of facilitating multilingual parser development, cross-lingual learning and parsing research from a language typology perspective. It assumes a dependency-based approach to syntax and a lexicalist approach to morphology, which together entail that the fundamental units of grammatical annotation are words. Words have properties captured by morphological annotation and enter into relations captured by syntactic annotation. Moreover, priority is given to relations between lexical content words, as opposed to grammatical function words. In this position paper, I discuss how this approach allows us to capture similarities and differences across typologically diverse languages.

1 Introduction

Multilingual research on syntax and parsing has for a long time been hampered by the fact that annotation schemes vary enormously across languages, which has made it very hard to perform sound comparative evaluations and cross-lingual learning experiments. The basic problem is illustrated in Figure 1, which shows three parallel sentences in Swedish, Danish and English, annotated according to the guidelines of the Swedish Treebank (Nivre and Megyesi, 2007), the Danish Dependency Treebank (Kromann, 2003), and Stanford Typed Dependencies (de Marneffe et al., 2006), respectively. The syntactic structure is identical in the three languages, but because of divergent annotation guidelines the structures have very few dependencies in common (in fact, none at all across all three languages). As a result, a parser trained on one type of annotation and evaluated on another type will be found to have a high error rate even when it functions perfectly.

Universal Dependencies (UD) seeks to tackle this problem by developing an annotation scheme that makes sense in a cross-linguistic perspective and can capture similarities as well as idiosyncrasies among typologically different languages. However, the aim is not only to support comparative evaluation and cross-lingual learning but also to facilitate multilingual natural language processing and enable comparative linguistic studies. To serve all these purposes, the framework needs to have a solid linguistic foundation and at the same time be transparent and accessible to non-specialists. In this paper, I discuss the basic principles underlying the UD annotation scheme with respect to grammar and lexicon. A more general introduction to UD can be found in Nivre et al. (2016) and on the project website.[1]

2 Grammatical Relations and Content Words

The UD annotation scheme is based on *dependency*, which means that it focuses on grammatical relations between linguistic units, rather than on the internal constituent structure of these units. In this respect, it adheres to the language typology tradition, where concepts like *subject* and *object*, although far from controversial as language universals, have proven more useful than notions of constituency in cross-linguistic investigations.[2]

---

[1] See http://universaldependencies.org.

[2] See, for example, the World Atlas of Language Structures (WALS) at http://wals.info.

Proceedings of the Workshop on Grammar and Lexicon: Interactions and Interfaces,
pages 38–40, Osaka, Japan, December 11 2016.

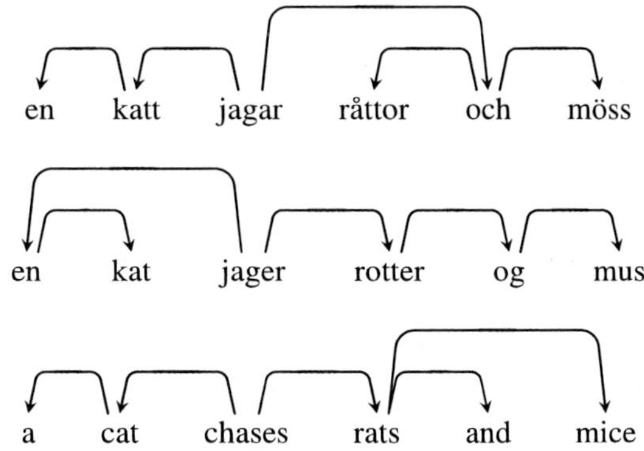

Figure 1: Divergent annotation of Swedish (top), Danish (middle) and English (bottom).

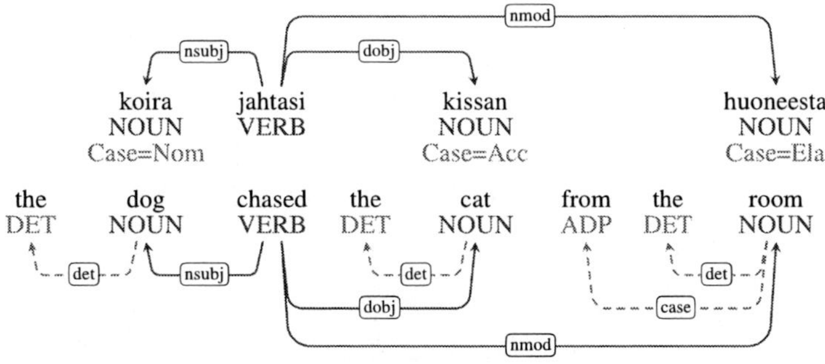

Figure 2: Simplified UD annotation for equivalent sentences in Finnish (top) and English (bottom).

The UD annotation scheme also subscribes to a version of *lexicalism*, which means that the units that enter into grammatical relations are words, more precisely lexical words (or content words), which can be assumed to be more constant across languages. By contrast, function words and bound morphemes are treated as part of the grammatical structure. The former are attached to the lexical word they modify with special functional relations. The latter are captured by morphological features associated with words in a holistic fashion.

The UD annotation scheme is illustrated in Figure 2 with two parallel sentences from Finnish (top) and English (bottom). In both languages, the sentence consists of a single verb and three nouns that act as nominal subject (*nsubj*), direct object (*dobj*) and nominal modifier (*nmod*) of the verb, respectively. What differs is primarily the grammatical encoding of nominals in the two languages. In English, all nouns have a definite article acting as determiner (*det*); *room* in addition is accompanied by the preposition *from*, which is analyzed as a case marker (*case*) indicating that it is not a core argument. In Finnish, no noun is specified by a function word, but all nouns have a morphological case inflection, which shows up as a morphological feature on the noun.[3]

3   Conclusion

The UD project tries to provide cross-linguistically consistent grammatical annotation for typologically diverse languages. To capture similarities and differences across languages, UD uses a representation consisting of three components: (i) dependency relations between lexical words; (ii) function words modifying lexical words; and (iii) morphological features associated with words. This system has so far been applied successfully to over 50 languages.

---

[3]In both languages, nouns and verbs have additional features that have been suppressed here to highlight the contrast between the two languages.

References

Marie-Catherine de Marneffe, Bill MacCartney, and Christopher D. Manning. 2006. Generating typed dependency parses from phrase structure parses. In *Proceedings of the 5th International Conference on Language Resources and Evaluation (LREC)*.

Matthias Trautner Kromann. 2003. The Danish Dependency Treebank and the DTAG treebank tool. In *Proceedings of the 2nd Workshop on Treebanks and Linguistic Theories (TLT)*, pages 217–220.

Joakim Nivre and Beáta Megyesi. 2007. Bootstrapping a Swedish treeebank using cross-corpus harmonization and annotation projection. In *Proceedings of the 6th Workshop on Treebanks and Linguistic Theories (TLT)*, pages 97–102.

Joakim Nivre, Marie-Catherine de Marneffe, Filip Ginter, Yoav Goldberg, Jan Hajič, Christopher D. Manning, Ryan McDonald, Slav Petrov, Sampo Pyysalo, Natalia Silveira, Reut Tsarfaty, and Dan Zeman. 2016. Universal Dependencies v1: A multilingual treebank collection. In *Proceedings of the 10th International Conference on Language Resources and Evaluation (LREC)*.

The Development of Multimodal Lexical Resources

James Pustejovsky, Nikhil Krishnaswamy, Tuan Do, Gitit Kehat
Department of Computer Science
Brandeis University
Waltham, MA 02453 USA
{jamesp,nkrishna,tuandn,gititkeh}@brandeis.edu

Abstract

Human communication is a multimodal activity, involving not only speech and written expressions, but intonation, images, gestures, visual clues, and the interpretation of actions through perception. In this paper, we describe the design of a multimodal lexicon that is able to accommodate the diverse modalities that present themselves in NLP applications. We have been developing a multimodal semantic representation, VoxML, that integrates the encoding of semantic, visual, gestural, and action-based features associated with linguistic expressions.

1 Motivation and Introduction

The primary focus of lexical resource development in computational linguistics has traditionally been on the syntactic and semantic encoding of word forms for monolingual and multilingual language applications. Recently, however, several factors have motivated researchers to look more closely at the relationship between both spoken and written language and the expression of meaning through other modalities. Specifically, there are at least three areas of CL research that have emerged as requiring significant cross-modal or multimodal lexical resource support. These are:

- **Language visualization and simulation generation**: Creating images from linguistic input; generating dynamic narratives in simulation environments from action-oriented expressions;(Chang et al., 2015; Coyne and Sproat, 2001; Siskind, 2001; Pustejovsky and Krishnaswamy, 2016; Krishnaswamy and Pustejovsky, 2016)

- **Visual Question-Answering and image content interpretation**: QA and querying over image datasets, based on the vectors associated with the image, but trained on caption-image pairings in the data; (Antol et al., 2015; Chao et al., 2015a; Chao et al., 2015b)

- **Gesture interpretation**: Understanding integrated spoken language with human or avatar-generated gestures; generating gesture in dialogue to supplement linguistic expressions;(Rautaray and Agrawal, 2015; Jacko, 2012; Turk, 2014; Bunt et al., 1998)

To meet the demands for a lexical resource that can help drive such diverse applications, we have been pursuing a new approach to modeling the semantics of natural language, *Multimodal Semantic Simulations (MSS)*. This framework assumes both a richer formal model of events and their participants, as well as a modeling language for constructing 3D visualizations of objects and events denoted by natural language expressions. The Dynamic Event Model (DEM) encodes events as programs in a dynamic logic with an operational semantics, while the language VoxML, Visual Object Concept Modeling Language, is being used as the platform for multimodal semantic simulations in the context of human-computer communication, as well as for image- and video-related content-based querying.

Prior work in visualization from natural language has largely focused on object placement and orientation in static scenes (Coyne and Sproat, 2001; Siskind, 2001; Chang et al., 2015). In previous work (Pustejovsky and Krishnaswamy, 2014; Pustejovsky, 2013a), we introduced a method for modeling natural language expressions within a 3D simulation environment, Unity. The goal of that work was to

Proceedings of the Workshop on Grammar and Lexicon: Interactions and Interfaces,
pages 41–47, Osaka, Japan, December 11 2016.

evaluate, through explicit visualizations of linguistic input, the semantic presuppositions inherent in the different lexical choices of an utterance. This work led to two additional lines of research: an explicit encoding for how an object is itself situated relative to its environment; and an operational characterization of how an object changes its location or how an agent acts on an object over time. The former has developed into a semantic notion of situational context, called a *habitat* (Pustejovsky, 2013a; McDonald and Pustejovsky, 2014), while the latter is addressed by dynamic interpretations of event structure (Pustejovsky and Moszkowicz, 2011b; Pustejovsky, 2013b; Mani and Pustejovsky, 2012; Pustejovsky, 2013a). The requirements on a "multimodal simulation semantics" include, but are not limited to, the following components:

- A minimal embedding space (MES) for the simulation must be determined. This is the 3D region within which the state is configured or the event unfolds;

- Object-based attributes for participants in a situation or event need to be specified; e.g., orientation, relative size, default position or pose, etc.;

- An epistemic condition on the object and event rendering, imposing an implicit point of view (POV);

- Agent-dependent embodiment; this determines the relative scaling of an agent and its event participants and their surroundings, as it engages in the environment.

In the sections that follow, we outline briefly the components of a multimodal lexical entry to address the needs stated above by the CL community for the first two areas. Integration of gesture interpretation and modeling is presently ongoing work in our lab.

2   VoxML: a Language for Concept Visualization

While both experience and world knowledge about objects and events can influence our behavior, as well as the interpretation and consequences of events, such factors are seldom involved in representing the predicative force of a particular lexeme in a language. Some representations, such as Qualia Structure (Pustejovsky, 1995) do provide additional information that can be used to map a linguistic expression to a minimal model of the event, and then from there to a visual output modality such as one that may be produced by a computer system, and so requires a computational framework to model it. Still, such languages are not in themselves rich enough to create useful minimal models.

To remedy this deficit, we have developed modeling language VoxML (Visual Object Concept Markup Language) for constructing 3D visualizations of natural language expressions (Pustejovsky and Krishnaswamy, 2016). VoxML forms the scaffold used to link lexemes to their visual instantiations, termed the "visual object concept" or *voxeme*. In parallel to a lexicon, a collection of voxemes is termed a *voxicon*. There is no requirement on a voxicon to have a one-to-one correspondence between its voxemes and the lexemes in the associated lexicon, which often results in a many-to-many correspondence. That is, the lexeme *plate* may be visualized as a [[SQUARE PLATE]], a [[ROUND PLATE]][1], or other voxemes, and those voxemes in turn may be linked to other lexemes such as *dish* or *saucer*.

Each voxeme is linked to an object geometry (if a noun—OBJECT in VoxML), a DITL program (if a verb or VoxML PROGRAM), an attribute set (VoxML ATTRIBUTEs), or a transformation algorithm (VoxML RELATIONs or FUNCTIONs). VoxML is used to specify the "episemantic" information beyond that which can be directly inferred from the geometry, DITL (Pustejovsky and Moszkowicz, 2011a), or attribute properties.

In order to demonstrate the composition of the linguistic expression plus the VoxML encoded information into a fully-realized visual output, we have developed, **VoxSim** (Krishnaswamy and Pustejovsky, 2016), a visual semantic simulator built on top of the Unity game engine (Goldstone, 2009).[2]

---

[1]Note on notation: discussion of voxemes in prose will be denoted in the style [[VOXEME]] and should be taken to refer to a visualization of the bracketed concept.

[2]The VoxSim Unity project and source may be found at https://github.com/nkrishnaswamy/voxicon.

VoxSim does not rely on manually-specified categories of objects with identifying language, and instead procedurally composes the properties of voxemes in parallel with the lexemes to which they are linked. Input is a simple natural language sentence, which is part-of-speech tagged, dependency-parsed, and transformed into a simple predicate-logic format.

From tagged and parsed input text, all NPs are indexed to objects in the scene. A reference to *a/the ball* causes the simulator to attempt to locate a voxeme instance in the scene whose lexical predicate is "ball," while an occurrence of *a/the block* prompts an attempt to locate a voxeme with the lexical predicate "block". Attributive adjectives impose a sortal scale on their heads, so *small block* and *big block* single out two separate blocks if they exist in the scene, and the VoxML-encoded semantics of "small" and "big" discriminates the blocks based on their relative size. *red block* vs. *green block* results in a distinction based on color, a nominal attribute, while *big red block* and *small red block* introduce scalar attribution, and can be used to disambiguate two distinct red blocks by iteratively evaluating each interior term of a formula such as *big(red(block))* until the reference can be resolved into a single object instance in the scene that has all the signaled attributes[3]. The system may ask for clarification (e.g., *"Which block?"*) if the object reference is still ambiguous.

An OBJECT voxeme's semantic structure provides *habitats*, situational contexts or environments which condition the object's *affordances*, which may be either "Gibsonian" and "telic" *affordances* (Gibson et al., 1982; Pustejovsky, 1995; Pustejovsky, 2013a). Affordances are used as attached behaviors, which the object either facilitates by its geometry (Gibsonian) (Gibson et al., 1982), or purposes for which it is intended to be used (telic) (Pustejovsky, 1995). For example, a Gibsonian affordance for [[CUP]] is "grasp," while a telic affordance is "drink from." Following from the convention that agents of a VoxML PROGRAM must be explicitly singled out in the associated implementation by belonging to certain entity classes (e.g., humans), affordances describe what *can be done to* the object, and not what actions it *itself* can perform. Thus an affordance is notated as HABITAT $\rightarrow$ [EVENT]RESULT, and an instance such as $H_{[2]} \rightarrow [put(x, on([1]))]support([1], x)$ can be paraphrased as "In habitat-2, an object x can be put on component-1, which results in component-1 supporting x." This procedural reasoning from habitats and affordances, executed in real time, allows VoxSim to infer the complete set of spatial relations between objects at each state and track changes in the shared context between human and computer. Thus, simulation becomes a way of tracing the consequences of linguistic spatial cues through a narrative.

A VoxML entity's interpretation at runtime depends on the other entities it is composed with. A cup on a surface, with its opening upward, may afford containing another object, so to place an object $in(cup)$, the system must first determine if the intended containing object (i.e., the cup) affords containment by default by examining its affordance structure.

If so, the object must be currently situated in a *habitat* which allows objects to be placed partially or completely inside it (represented by RCC relations PO, TPP, or NTPP). In VoxML, [[CUP]] is encoded as a concave object with rotational symmetry around the Y-axis and reflectional symmetry across the XY and YZ planes, meaning that it opens along the Y-axis. Its HABITAT further situates the opening along its positive Y-axis, meaning that if the cup's opening along its +Y is currently unobstructed, it affords containment. Previously established habitats, i.e., "The cup is flipped over," may activate or deactivate these and other affordances.

The spatial relations operating within the context of a verbal program, such as "put the spoon in the cup," enforce constraints that requires a test against the current situational context before a value assignment can be made. Given *put*, if the "placed object" is of a size that is too large to fit inside the mentioned object, VoxSim conducts a series of calculations to see if the object, when reoriented along any of its three orthogonal axes, will be situated in a configuration that allows it to fit inside the region bounded by the ground object's containing area. The containing area is situated relative to one of the ground object's orthogonal axes, and which axis and orientation this is is encoded in the ground object's VoxML type semantics. For example, the symmetrical and concave properties of [[CUP]] compose to situate the cup's opening along its *positive* Y-axis. So, to place a [[SPOON]] in a [[CUP]], assuming

---

[3]See (Pustejovsky and Krishnaswamy, forthcoming) for details on discriminating and referencing objects through sortal and scalar descriptions.

objects of typical size, [[SPOON]] must be reoriented so that its world-space bounding box aligning with the [[CUP]]'s Y-axis is smaller than the bounds of the [[CUP]]'s opening in that same configuration.

3   Video Event Recognition

Now let us turn the language-to-visualization strategy on its head. The same modeling language, VoxML, can be used to help detect and recognize events and actions in video. This task has received increasing attention in the scientific community, due to its relevance to a wide variety of applications (Ballan et al., 2011) and there have been calls for annotation infrastructure that includes video (Ide, 2013).

Our lab has begun bootstrapping a dataset of videos annotated with event-subevent relations using ECAT, an internally-developed video annotation tool (Do et al., 2016). This annotation tool allows us to annotate videos of labeled events with object participants and subevents, and to induce what the common subevent structures are for the labeled superevent. Using the Microsoft Kinect®, we are currently recording videos of a test set of human actions interacting with simple objects, such as blocks, cylinders, and balls. Both human bodies (rigs) and these objects can be tracked and annotated as participants in a recorded motion event; this labeled data can then be used to build a corpus of *multimodal semantic simulations* of these events that can model object-object, object-agent, and agent-agent interactions through the durations of said events. This library of simulated motion events can serve as a novel resource of direct linkages from natural language to event visualization, indexed through the multimodal lexical representation for the event, its voxeme.

We are also interested in leveraging VoxML PROGRAMs to facilitate machine learning algorithms in activity recognition. Our motivation is that modeling actions as a rigorous dynamic structures allows us to represent action as labelled state transition systems. Therefore, we can model their similarity and difference using classical graph similarity approaches. For example, we aim to reveal in the data the intuition that there is a similarity between "I toss a ball" and "I jump in the air", i.e. a *figure* object moving in the same manner in relative to *ground* object. This is different from other activity recognition approaches, such as (Shahroudy et al., 2016), in which the authors directly used supervision learning on different classes of activities.

We have begun creating lexical resources using movie databases, such as MPII Movie Description Dataset (Rohrbach et al., 2015), which has parallel movie snippets and descriptions. These descriptions are transcribed from audio descriptions for the visually impaired. Therefore, they are highly event-centric, describing the most salient events in each movie snippet. By annotating them using the same annotation framework as mentioned above for the 3D motion capture, we aim to create a rich word sense resource. In turn, we hope that we can use these modes of representation to discover the difference between *canonical* and *non-canonical* uses of activity verbs.

4   Image Grounding for the Lexicon

Finally, another aspect of multimodal lexicalized meaning that we are investigating, and which has become increasingly popular among both the computer vision and NLP communities, is the creation and usage of vision-language datasets. These datasets typically contain still images along with a set of textual annotations, such as nouns, attributes and verbs, or full descriptive sentences or Q&A pairs, for each image in the dataset. They are mostly used in the training and evaluation of tasks sitting at the intersection of vision and language, such as image description generation, visual question answering and image retrieval, but they are also used in tasks such as action and affordance recognition, to support and expand previous "vision-only" techniques with linguistic information.

As the field is growing, more time and effort are being spent on the creation of large-scale vision-language datasets (Krishna et al., 2016; Lin et al., 2014), as well as smaller task-oriented ones for tasks like the ones mentioned above (Chao et al., 2015a; Chao et al., 2015b). However, we found that many of the existing datasets suffer from problems making them difficult to use in a consistent way (Kehat and Pustejovsky, 2016). Some of the main difficulties are: vocabulary issues (both limited or sparse);

lack of validation or averaging process that leads to information loss; a heavy bias originated in both the authors pre-assumptions and annotators attentio; and underdefined visual actions/concepts. The last problem, which is perhaps the most challenging of all, is related to the fact that in the majority of datasets, verbs and actions are considered the same. However, in reality, one verb can describe multiple different visually defined actions, and the same visual action can be matched to more than one verb. While most of the existed datasets do not distinguish between the two, there are new attempts to solve this inherent ambiguity, as well as to define what a visually defined action is (Gella et al., 2016; Ronchi and Perona, 2015; Yatskar et al., 2016).

5   Conclusion and Future Directions

We have described our initial steps towards the design and development of a multimodal lexical resource, based on a modeling language that admits of multiple representations from different modalities. These are not just linked lists of modal expressions but are semantically integrated and interpreted representations from one modality to another. The language VoxML and the resource Voxicon are presently being used to drive simulations using multiple modalities within the DARPA Communicating with Computers program.

Acknowledgements

This work is supported by a contract with the US Defense Advanced Research Projects Agency (DARPA), Contract W911NF-15-C-0238. Approved for Public Release, Distribution Unlimited. The views expressed are those of the authors and do not reflect the official policy or position of the Department of Defense or the U.S. Government. We would like to thank Scott Friedman, David McDonald, Marc Verhagen, and Mark Burstein for their discussion and input on this topic. All errors and mistakes are, of course, the responsibilities of the authors.

References

Stanislaw Antol, Aishwarya Agrawal, Jiasen Lu, Margaret Mitchell, Dhruv Batra, C Lawrence Zitnick, and Devi Parikh. 2015. Vqa: Visual question answering. In *Proceedings of the IEEE International Conference on Computer Vision*, pages 2425–2433.

Lamberto Ballan, Marco Bertini, Alberto Del Bimbo, Lorenzo Seidenari, and Giuseppe Serra. 2011. Event detection and recognition for semantic annotation of video. *Multimedia Tools and Applications*, 51(1):279–302.

Harry Bunt, Robbert-Jan Beun, and Tijn Borghuis. 1998. *Multimodal human-computer communication: systems, techniques, and experiments*, volume 1374. Springer Science & Business Media.

Angel Chang, Will Monroe, Manolis Savva, Christopher Potts, and Christopher D. Manning. 2015. Text to 3d scene generation with rich lexical grounding. *arXiv preprint arXiv:1505.06289*.

Yu-Wei Chao, Zhan Wang, Yugeng He, Jiaxuan Wang, and Jia Deng. 2015a. Hico: A benchmark for recognizing human-object interactions in images. In *Proceedings of the IEEE International Conference on Computer Vision*, pages 1017–1025.

Yu-Wei Chao, Zhan Wang, Rada Mihalcea, and Jia Deng. 2015b. Mining semantic affordances of visual object categories. In *Proceedings of the IEEE Conference on Computer Vision and Pattern Recognition*, pages 4259–4267.

Bob Coyne and Richard Sproat. 2001. Wordseye: an automatic text-to-scene conversion system. In *Proceedings of the 28th annual conference on Computer graphics and interactive techniques*, pages 487–496. ACM.

Tuan Do, Nikhil Krishnaswamy, and James Pustejovsky. 2016. Ecat: Event capture annotation tool. *Proceedings of ISA-12: International Workshop on Semantic Annotation*.

Spandana Gella, Mirella Lapata, and Frank Keller. 2016. Unsupervised visual sense disambiguation for verbs using multimodal embeddings. *In Proceedings of the Human Language Technology Conference of the North American Chapter of the Association for Computational Linguistics, 182-192. San Diego.*

James Jerome Gibson, Edward S Reed, and Rebecca Jones. 1982. *Reasons for realism: Selected essays of James J. Gibson.* Lawrence Erlbaum Associates.

Will Goldstone. 2009. *Unity Game Development Essentials.* Packt Publishing Ltd.

Nancy Ide. 2013. An open linguistic infrastructure for annotated corpora. In *The People's Web Meets NLP*, pages 265–285. Springer.

Julie A Jacko. 2012. *Human computer interaction handbook: Fundamentals, evolving technologies, and emerging applications.* CRC press.

Gitit Kehat and James Pustejovsky. 2016. Annotation methodologies for vision and language dataset creation. *IEEE CVPR Scene Understanding Workshop (SUNw), Las Vegas.*

Ranjay Krishna, Yuke Zhu, Oliver Groth, Justin Johnson, Kenji Hata, Joshua Kravitz, Stephanie Chen, Yannis Kalantidis, Li-Jia Li, David A Shamma, Michael Bernstein, and Li Fei-Fei. 2016. Visual genome: Connecting language and vision using crowdsourced dense image annotations.

Nikhil Krishnaswamy and James Pustejovsky. 2016. Multimodal semantic simulations of linguistically under-specified motion events. *Proceedings of Spatial Cognition.*

Tsung-Yi Lin, Michael Maire, Serge Belongie, James Hays, Pietro Perona, Deva Ramanan, Piotr Dollár, and C Lawrence Zitnick. 2014. Microsoft coco: Common objects in context. In *European Conference on Computer Vision*, pages 740–755. Springer.

Inderjeet Mani and James Pustejovsky. 2012. *Interpreting Motion: Grounded Representations for Spatial Language.* Oxford University Press.

David McDonald and James Pustejovsky. 2014. On the representation of inferences and their lexicalization. In *Advances in Cognitive Systems*, volume 3.

James Pustejovsky and Nikhil Krishnaswamy. 2014. Generating simulations of motion events from verbal descriptions. *Lexical and Computational Semantics (* SEM 2014)*, page 99.

James Pustejovsky and Nikhil Krishnaswamy. 2016. VoxML: A visualization modeling language. In Nicoletta Calzolari (Conference Chair), Khalid Choukri, Thierry Declerck, Sara Goggi, Marko Grobelnik, Bente Maegaard, Joseph Mariani, Helene Mazo, Asuncion Moreno, Jan Odijk, and Stelios Piperidis, editors, *Proceedings of the Tenth International Conference on Language Resources and Evaluation (LREC 2016)*, Paris, France, May. European Language Resources Association (ELRA).

James Pustejovsky and Nikhil Krishnaswamy. forthcoming. Envisioning language: The semantics of multimodal simulations.

James Pustejovsky and Jessica Moszkowicz. 2011a. The qualitative spatial dynamics of motion. *The Journal of Spatial Cognition and Computation.*

James Pustejovsky and Jessica L Moszkowicz. 2011b. The qualitative spatial dynamics of motion in language. *Spatial Cognition & Computation*, 11(1):15–44.

James Pustejovsky. 1995. *The Generative Lexicon.* MIT Press, Cambridge, MA.

James Pustejovsky. 2013a. Dynamic event structure and habitat theory. In *Proceedings of the 6th International Conference on Generative Approaches to the Lexicon (GL2013)*, pages 1–10. ACL.

James Pustejovsky. 2013b. Where things happen: On the semantics of event localization. In *Proceedings of ISA-9: International Workshop on Semantic Annotation.*

Siddharth S Rautaray and Anupam Agrawal. 2015. Vision based hand gesture recognition for human computer interaction: a survey. *Artificial Intelligence Review*, 43(1):1–54.

Anna Rohrbach, Marcus Rohrbach, Niket Tandon, and Bernt Schiele. 2015. A dataset for movie description.

Matteo Ruggero Ronchi and Pietro Perona. 2015. Describing common human visual actions in images. *arXiv preprint arXiv:1506.02203.*

Amir Shahroudy, Jun Liu, Tian-Tsong Ng, and Gang Wang. 2016. Ntu rgb+ d: A large scale dataset for 3d human activity analysis. *arXiv preprint arXiv:1604.02808*.

Jeffrey Mark Siskind. 2001. Grounding the lexical semantics of verbs in visual perception using force dynamics and event logic. *J. Artif. Intell. Res.(JAIR)*, 15:31–90.

Matthew Turk. 2014. Multimodal interaction: A review. *Pattern Recognition Letters*, 36:189–195.

Mark Yatskar, Luke Zettlemoyer, and Ali Farhadi. 2016. Situation recognition: Visual semantic role labeling for image understanding. *In Proceedings of the Conference of Computer Vision and Pattern Recognition (CVPR)*.

Part II:

Regular Papers

On the Non-canonical Valency Filling

Igor Boguslavsky

A.A.Kharkevich Institute for Information Transmission Problems,
Russian Academy of Sciences, Russia /
Universidad Politécnica de Madrid, Spain
Bolshoy Karetny per. 19, build.1, Moscow 127051 Russia /
Campus de Montegancedo,
28660 Boadilla del Monte (Madrid) España.

`bogus@iitp.ru`

Abstract

Valency slot filling is a semantic glue, which brings together the meanings of words. As regards the position of an argument in the dependency structure with respect to its predicate, there exist three types of valency filling: active (canonical), passive, and discontinuous. Of these, the first type is studied much better than the other two. As a rule, canonical actants are unambiguously marked in the syntactic structure, and each actant corresponds to a unique syntactic position. Linguistic information on which syntactic function an actant might have (subject, direct or indirect object), what its morphological form should be and which prepositions or conjunctions it requires, can be given in the lexicon in the form of government patterns, subcategorization frames, or similar data structures. We concentrate on non-canonical cases of valency filling in Russian, which are characteristic of non-verbal parts of speech, such as adverbs, adjectives, and particles, in the first place. They are more difficult to handle than canonical ones, because the position of the actant in the tree is governed by more complicated rules. A valency may be filled by expressions occupying different syntactic positions, and a syntactic position may accept expressions filling different valencies of the same word. We show how these phenomena can be processed in a semantic analyzer.

1 Introduction

Discovering the predicate-argument structure of the sentence is an important step in constructing its semantic structure. Identifying arguments of predicates (or, in a different terminology, valency slot filling) is a semantic glue that combines the meanings of words together. It is in fact the main mechanism of meaning amalgamation.

What information is needed to discover the predicate-argument structure of the sentence? First of all, one needs a dictionary that contains the following information for each argument-bearing word:

(a) analytical definition of the meaning of the word should be given; among other things, it should represent all valency slots (by means of variables);

(b) each valency slot should be assigned the information on how it can be filled; this information includes primarily the data on the syntactic position of the actant in the syntactic structure (subject, direct or indirect object), what prepositions or conjunctions are needed to introduce it and what lexico-grammatical form it can have. This information is provided by subcategorization frames, government patterns and similar data structures.

Besides the dictionary, for identifying the actants in the text, the syntactic structure of the sentence should be available, because different actants have different syntactic positions with respect to the predicate.

This aspect – different syntactic positions of actants with respect to the predicate – did not receive sufficient attention in the literature, neither in linguistics nor in computational linguistics. To a large extent, only verbs and nouns are considered as argument-bearing words and subcategorization frames seem a sufficient tool to identify arguments in the sentence. However, other parts of speech, such as adjectives, adverbs, particles, conjunctions, and prepositions are equally entitled to be classed as

Proceedings of the Workshop on Grammar and Lexicon: Interactions and Interfaces,
pages 51–60, Osaka, Japan, December 11 2016.

argument-bearing words. Moreover, being non-prototypical predicates, they substantially enlarge our knowledge of the ways predicates use to instantiate their valencies.

The paper is structured as follows. First, we will discuss different ways of valency filling paying special attention to the patterns that cannot be described by means of subcategorization frames (Section 2). Then we will present our case study – syntactic properties and non-canonical valency instantiation of the words *edinstvennyj* and *tol'ko* in Russian (Section 3). This is the main contribution of the paper. However, we would also like to show that this approach is implementable in a semantic analyser. With this aim in view, we will briefly introduce semantic analyser SemETAP (Section 4) and show how it treats these phenomena (Section 5). We will conclude in Section 6.

2 Valency Slot Filling

First of all, we have to draw the readers' attention to the fact that we understand the concepts of *valency* and *actant* somewhat broader than it is often done. Here we follow the tradition of the Moscow Semantic School (MSS), which in its turn, shares these notions with the Meaning – Text theory (Apresjan 1974, Mel'čuk 1974). For MSS, the starting point in defining the concept of valency is the semantic analysis of the situation denoted by the given word. Analytical semantic definition of a word, constructed according to certain requirements (Apresjan 1999), should explicitly present all obligatory participants of the situation denoted by this words. For a word L to have a certain valency slot it is necessary, though insufficient, that a situation denoted by L should contain a corresponding participant in the intuitively obvious way. Another condition is that this participant should be expressible in a sentence along with L in a systematic way (Mel'čuk 2004a, 2004b). A word or a phrase that denotes such a participant is said to fill (or, instantiate) the valency slot and is called an actant (or, argument).

In this respect, all types of words that denote situations with obligatory participants (which we call predicates) – verbs, (some) nouns, adjectives, adverbs, prepositions, particles etc. – are on equal footing and obey the same principles of description.

Deciding on the set of valency slots is not the whole story. Besides that, one needs to exhaustively describe all the ways these slots can be filled and **not only canonical** ones. We lay special emphasis on describing the whole spectrum of possible syntactic realization of arguments, because non-canonical valency filling significantly complicates the task of detecting arguments of the predicates.

The MSS framework represents the sentence at various levels of representation. In particular, each sentence has a syntactic structure and a semantic structure. In the semantic structure of the sentence, predicates and their actants are always connected by predicate-argument relations directed from the predicate to the argument. For example, (1a) is represented as (1b):

(1a) *John bought a house.*

(1b) hasAgent(Buy, John), hasObject(Buy, House)

In the syntactic structure it is not always that simple. The syntactic position of the actant with respect to its predicate may be more diverse, if we take into account all kinds of actant-bearing words and all possible syntactic realizations of the actants. From this point of view, we distinguish three types of valency slot filling: ACTIVE, PASSIVE, and DISCONTINOUS ones (Boguslavsky 2003). If a predicate **subordinates** its actant in the syntactic structure by means of an immediate dependency relation, we will say that such a valency filling is ACTIVE. This is the most typical (canonical) case. If a predicate **is subordinated** to its actant, we will say that the filling is PASSIVE. If there is **no direct syntactic link** between the predicate and the actant, the valency filling is DISCONTINOUS.

Let us give some examples. In (2) the verb *to precede* subordinates both its actants A1 and A2 (the subject and the object), and therefore the valency filling is active.

(2) *The workshop* [A1] *precedes* [L] *the main conference* [A2].

Preposition *before* denotes the same situation as the verb *to precede* and therefore has the same valencies. However, in the syntactic structure, these valencies are filled in a different way. In (3), A1 is filled passively, and A2 – actively:

(3) *The workshop* [A1] *before* [L] *the conference* [A2].

Passive valency filling is characteristic for prepositions, conjunctions, adjectives, adverbs and particles.

One of the valencies of the quantifiers, such as *all, some, most,* etc. is filled by the noun they are connected to and another one – by the verb, with which they do not have any direct syntactic link. Therefore, it is a case of a discontinuous valency filling:

(4) *Most* [L] *delegates* [A1] *supported* [A2] *the resolution.*

A regular source of the discontinuous valency filling are subject- and object-oriented adverbials. To give an example, let us compare sentences (5a) and (5b):

(5a) *John has a habit of getting up early.*

(5b) *By habit, John got up early.*

Habit has two valencies – person Q ('John') and situation P ('get up early') – and both of them are instantiated both in (5a) and in (5b). However, in neither case is *habit* syntactically connected to *John.*

As for (5a), actant Q of *habit* is detached from *habit* and connected to *has* because *has* is the value of Lexical Function Oper1 (in Melčukian sense). The functions of the Oper-Func family have a property of syntactically attracting some actants of their arguments. In (5b), actant Q of *habit* can only be the subject of the main verb (*get up*), and therefore *habit* instantiates valency Q in the discontinuous way. Cf. sentences (6a)-(6b) that show that *by habit* is subject-oriented and takes the subject of the main verb as its actant. In (6a) it is John's habit that is referred to, and in (6b) it is Mary's habit.

(6a) *By habit, John borrowed $100 from Mary.*

(6b) *By habit, Mary lent $100 to John.*

Active valency filling is mostly typical for verbs and nouns and is particularly well fit for slot instantiation. First of all, actants are directly connected to the predicate. Besides, each valency slot has its own set of surface realizations. If a word has several valency slots, their means of realization, are, as a rule, clearly contrasting. Different actants are marked by different means – cases, prepositions, conjunctions. Different actants of the same word cannot intersect: no word can normally participate in the filling of different valencies of the same predicate at the same time. As a rule, there is a one-to-one correspondence between the actants and their syntactic positions. However, it may so happen that this correspondence does not hold, and a valency may be filled by expressions that occupy different syntactic positions. This is called diathesis alternation, or modification (Mel'čuk, Xolodovič 1970, Padučeva 2003, Partee 2005):

(7a) The farmers loaded the truck with (the) hay.

(7b) The farmers loaded (the/some) hay on the truck.

However, these are relatively rare situations that do not undermine the general rule. It is in the nature of things that the actants are marked in the syntactic structure in an unambiguous way, and each actant corresponds, as a rule, to a unique syntactic position. An attempt to extend this observation to passive and discontinuous valency slots reveals interesting surprises (Boguslavsky 2009). The data presented below show that this one-to-one correspondence can be violated in a number of ways. We will see that a valency may be filled by expressions occupying different syntactic positions, and a syntactic position may accept expressions filling different valencies. Moreover, the same word can belong to more than one actant of the same predicate.

Below, we will examine in detail two such words – the Russian adjective *edinstvennyj* and the particle *tol'ko*, both meaning 'only'. These words are of considerable interest from the point of view of the valency filling typology.

3 Case study: *edinstvennyj – tol'ko* 'only'

From the point of view of the argument structure, it is very instructive to contrast two Russian words – particle *tol'ko* and adjective *edinstvennyj,* both of which basically mean 'only'. In different contexts, a few other English words may be appropriate translations (*only – single – sole – unique – alone*), but for simplicity's sake we will only use the basic equivalent 'only' in the glosses of the examples below. These words give us a rare opportunity to observe dramatic differences in terms of valency filling when the words are practically synonymous. Indeed, both words claim that a certain object is – in some aspect – unique (a more precise definition will be given below). Valency instantiation differences have the result that the sentences that have a similar structure behave differently, while sentences of different composition manifest identical valency filling patterns.

For example, in (8a) and (8b) the words *edinstvennyj* and *tol'ko* are interchangeable (up to the syntactically determined word order). In (9a) and (9b) replacing one word for the other drastically modifies the meaning of the sentence, and in (10a)-(10c) the relationship between *edinstvennyj* and *tol'ko* is even queerer: if one substitutes *tol'ko* for *edinstvennyj* in the same noun phrase, the sentence will become anomalous, but if one introduces *tol'ko* in a different noun phrase, the resulting sentence will be synonymous to the original one:

(8a) *Ivan edinstvennyj menja ponimaet.*
    lit. Ivan only me undertstands
    'Only Ivan undertsands me'

(8b) *Menja ponimaet tol'ko Ivan.*
    lit. me understands only Ivan
    'only Ivan understands me'

(9a) *V uglu stojal edinstvennyj stul.*
    lit. in corner stood only chair
    'There was only one chair in the corner'

(9b) *V ugly stojal tol'ko stul.*
    lit. in corner stood only chair
    'There was only a chair in the corner'

(10a) *Edinstvennym drugom Ivana byl Petr.*
    lit. only friend of-Ivan was Peter
    'Peter was the only Ivan's friend'

(10b) **Tol'ko drugom Ivana byl Petr.*
    lit. only friend of-Ivan was Peter

(10c) *Drugom Ivana byl tol'ko Petr.*
    lit. friend of-Ivan was only Peter
    'Peter was the only Ivan's friend'

Another mystery of *edinstvennyj* which is also connected to the argument structure is related to the correspondence between *edinstvennyj NP* and *edinstvennyj iz NP* 'only of NP'. In (11a) *edinstvennyj NP* can be replaced by *edinstvennyj iz NP* without any semantic shift (cf. (11b)). In (12a) such a substitution results in an anomaly (cf. (12b)).

(11a) *Panteon – edinstvennoe antičnoe sooruženie, došedšee do našix dnej s nepovreždennym kupolom.*
    lit. Pantheon – only ancient building having-come to our days with intact cupola
    'Pantheon is the only ancient building that has survived until now with the cupola intact'

(11b) *Panteon – edinstvennoe iz antičnyx sooruženij, došedšee do našix dnej s nepovreždennym kupolom.*
    lit. Pantheon – only of ancient buildings having-come to our days with intact cupola
    'Pantheon is the only one of ancient buildings that has survived until now with the cupola intact'

(12a) *Ivan vybral edinstvennyj nadežnyj put'.*
    'Ivan chose the only reliable way'

(12b) **Ivan vybral edinstvennyj iz nadežnyx putej.*
    '*Ivan chose the only one of the reliable ways

To explain these facts, one should first give analytical definition of both words, that fixes their valencies, and then describe how they can be filled.

3.1 Meaning and valency slots of *edinstvennyj*.

A detailed analysis of valency instantiation of *edinstvennyj* and *tol'ko* can be found in (Boguslavsky 1996). Here we will only give a brief review with some refinements.

Edinstvennyj is used in several syntactic contexts, and in each of them the valencies are filled in a different way. It is the copulative construction that is the most transparent from this point of view. Here all the valencies are filled by clearly distinguishable phrases:

(13) *Petr – edinstvennyj čelovek, kotoromu Ivan doverjaet.*

'Peter is the only person whom Ivan trusts'

Therefore this construction can be used as an input of the semantic definition:

(14) *Q jest' edinstvennyj R, kotoryj P* 'Q is the only R which P' = '(Q is R which P); among all Rs there is no one except (this) Q, which would have property P'

Here, the parentheses enclose the part of the sentence meaning which serves as the context for *edinstvennyj*. In sentence (13), the subject 'Peter' fills valency Q, 'person' – valency R, and the clause 'whom Ivan trusts' – valency P. Applying the definition (14) to (13), given these variable instantiations, will yield the following meaning: 'Peter is a person whom Ivan trusts; among all the (relevant) people, there is no other (= different from Peter) person whom Ivan trusts'.

Valency P is obligatory in all contexts, R and Q are optional.

As a rule, **valency Q**, is expressed by means of the copulative construction (cf. (13)) or another one which presupposes the copulative construction at a deeper level. Two characteristic constructions of this type are the appositive construction (cf. (15)) and the co-predicative one (cf. (16)):

(15) *Petr [Q], edinstvennyj čelovek, kotoromu Ivan doverjaet, znaet o nem vse.*

'Peter [Q], the only person whom Ivan trusts, knows everything about him'

(16) *Petr [Q] edinstvennyj pol'zuetsja doveriem Ivana.*

lit. Peter [Q] only enjoys trust of-Ivan

'Peter is the only one who enjoys Ivan's trust'

In spite of the fact that *edinstvennyj* agrees with *Petr* in case, number and gender, as is proper for adjective + noun phrases in Russian, it is not its regular modifier, being syntactically linked to the verb rather than to the noun. This is what happens in general in co-predicative constructions, as opposed to the modificative ones. In co-predicative and modificative constructions, *edinstvennyj* fills its valencies quite differently. This becomes obvious if we compare the co-predicative phrase (17a) and the modificative one (17b):

(17a) *Angličanin edinstvennyj prišel vovremja.*

lit. Englishman only came on-time

'the Englishman was the only one to come on time'

(17b) *Edinstvennyj angličanin prišel vovremja.*

lit. only Englishman came on-time

'the only Englishman came on time'

In both cases the Englishman is set off to other people according to some property, but these properties are quite different in (17a) and (17b). In (17a) no one else came on time, and in (17b) no one else was an Englishman.

One should also take into account that there are two types of co-predicative constructions in Russian, which affects the valency instantiation of *edinstvennyj*: in the subject-copredicative construction (as in (17a)) the adjective refers to the subject of the sentence, while in the object-copredicative construction (as in (18)) it refers to the object:

(18) *Ja ljublju ee edinstvennyju.*

lit. I love her only

'I love only her'

The thing that is interesting about the modificative construction (Adjective + Noun) is that the modified noun fills two valencies of *edinstvennyj* at a time – Q and P. If we come back to sentence (17b), we will see that in its semantic structure 'Englishman' occurs twice: 'besides (this) Englishman, there is no one who is an Englishman'. It is to be noted that these two occurrences of 'Englishman' differ in their referential status: in the position of Q the status is referential ('this Englishman'), while in the position of P it is predicative ('be an Englishman').

The copulative construction manifests a similar case, if *edinstvennyj* is not a noun modifier. The subject also plays two roles with respect to *edinstvennyj* – Q and P. This becomes obvious if we compare (19a) and (19b):

(19a) *Holiday Inn – edinstvennaja gostinitsa na ostrove.*

'Holiday Inn is the only hotel on the island'

(19b) *Eta gostinitsa – edinstvennaja na ostrove.*

lit. this hotel (is) only on island

'This hotel is the only one on the island'.

In (19a), the actants of *edinstvennyj* are as follows: Holiday Inn = Q, hotel = P; island = R. All the valencies filled in (19a) are also filled in (19b). Both sentences say that a certain hotel is the only one on the island. Hence, the valencies P and Q that are filled in (19a) by different phrases in (19b) correspond to the single occurrence of *hotel*.

Valency P is filled as follows:

- if *edinstvennyj* is a co-predicate (cf. (17a) and (18)), valency P is filled by the predicate of the sentence;

- if *edinstvennyj* is a modifier (cf. (20a) and (20b)) or a head of the elective construction (cf. (20c)) of a noun which has a restrictive attribute, valency P is filled by this attribute.

(20a) *edinstvennoe gosudarstvo* [R], *soxranivšee* [P] *svoju konstitutsiju*

    lit. only state [R] that-preserved [P] its constitution

    'the only state to preserve its constitution' = 'among the states [R] there is no other that preserved [P] its constitution'

(20b) *edinstvennoe kardinal'noe* [P] *sredstvo* [R] *ot golovnoj boli*

    'the only radical [P] remedy [R] for headache' = 'among remedies [R] there is no other that is radical [P]'

(20c) *edinstvennyj iz moix druzej* [R], *kto živet* [P] *za gorodom*

    lit. only of my friends [R] who lives [P] out of town

    'the only one of my friends who lives out of town' = 'among my friends [R] there is no other who lives [P] out of town'

Valency R is filled either by a locative phrase (cf. *edinstvennyj passažir v kupe* 'the only passenger in the compartment'), or the elective prepositions *iz* 'of' and *sredi* 'among' (cf. *edinstvennyj jurist sredi nas* 'the only lawyer among us'), or by a modified noun, if it has a restrictive attribute (cf. (13), (20a), (20b)).

One more actant configuration that arises due to the phrasal stress on *edinstvennyj* is noteworthy. Let us compare sentence (21a), in which *edinstvennyj* is pronounced with a neutral intonation, and (21b), where this word is stressed:

(21a) *My upustili edinstvennuju vozmožnost' perelomit' situatsiju.*

    lit. 'we missed only opportunity to reverse the situation'

    'we missed the unique opportunity to reverse the situation'

(21b) *Eto neprijatno soznavat', no, poxože, my vospol'zovalis'* ↓*edinstvennym blagom svobody.*

    'It is frustrating to realize, but it seems we made use of only one asset of freedom'.

In both cases, *edinstvennyj* is a noun phrase modifier without any restrictive attributes, which makes both sentences similar from the point of view of the valency instantiation rules presented above. However, sentence (21a) is interpreted as predicted: 'we missed an opportunity to reverse the situation; there was no other opportunity'. This interpretation is obtained with Q = opportunity, P = be an opportunity, and R not instantiated. In (21b), on the contrary, the modified noun phrase ('asset of freedom') fills valency R, P is instantiated by the predicate of the sentence ('make use'), and Q is not instantiated at all: 'we made use of an asset of freedom; of all the assets of freedom, there is no other one we made use of'. This dramatic shift in valency instantiation has been provoked by the phrasal stress that falls on *edinstvennyj*.

3.2 Meaning and valency slots of *tol'ko*

As mentioned above, particle *tol'ko* is synonymous with *edinstvennyj* (in one of its senses), but differs in its syntactic potential and valency instantiation patterns. First of all, *tol'ko* is a particle, while *edinstvennyj* is an adjective. Therefore their syntactic behaviours are quite different. *Tol'ko* cannot occur in many syntactic contexts characteristic of *edinstvennyj* (cf., e.g. *Eta gostinitsa edinstvennaja - *Eta gostinitsa tol'ko*). On the other hand, *tol'ko* may be connected to a word of any part of speech and cannot have its own dependents (cf. *edinstvennyj iz nas - *tol'ko iz nas*).

In most (but not all) contexts the following rule holds true: (a) valency Q is filled by the phrase to which *tol'ko* is subordinated syntactically and which it immediately precedes; (b) valency P is filled by a verb which is the head of the clause to which *tol'ko* belongs; (c) valency R is filled by phrases headed by prepositions *iz* 'of' and *sredi* 'among'.

(22) *Iz* [R] *vsego spiska literatury on soslalsja* [P] *tol'ko na knigu* [Q] 1974 *goda.*

lit of the whole list of references he referred only to the book of 1974 year
'of [R] the whole reference list he only referred [P] to the 1974 book [Q]'
Now, we can come back to sentences (8)-(12) and explain the differences observed.

3.3 *Tol'ko* vs. *edinstvennyj*: valency filling.

In the light of what we learned of the argument properties of *edinstvennyj* and *tol'ko*, we can now explain the facts presented in (8)-(12) above.

In sentences (8a) and (8b) *edinstvennyj* and *tol'ko* have different syntactic links: *tol'ko* depends on *Ivan*, and *edinstvennyj* is a co-predicate and depends on the predicate *ponimaet* 'understands'. Nevertheless, the sentences are synonymous, since *edinstvennyj* and *tol'ko* fill their valencies in the same way. Co-predicative constructions are the only[1] context in which *edinstvennyj* fills valency P by the main VP, just as *tol'ko* does.

In sentences (9a)-(9b), the situation is inverse: both words depend on the same noun (*stul* 'chair'), but valency P is filled in different ways. Therefore, the sentences are not synonymous.

Sentences (10a)-(10c) contain a copulative construction. *Edinstvennyj* belongs to the predicative NP, and fills Q by the subject of the copula. Since *tol'ko* should be placed before actant Q, it is natural that, to preserve the synonymy, *tol'ko* should be moved to the subject NP.

As opposed to *edinstvennyj*, *tol'ko* is a rhematizer and cannot be placed in the thematic position. Therefore, (10b) not only is non-synonymous with (10a), but is also ungrammatical. If we change the communicative perspective, sentence (10b) will become grammatical (*Petr byl tol'ko drugom Ivana* 'Peter was only Ivan's friend (but not a brother)') but will remain non-synonymous with (10a).

Let us now turn to sentences (11a) and (12a). In both cases, NP to which *edinstvennyj* is connected ('ancient building' vs. 'way') has a restrictive attribute ('having come' vs. 'reliable'). According to the rules above, in both cases the NP fills valency R, and the attribute – valency P. An alternative way to fill R is use the *iz* 'of' + N group ('of ancient buildings' vs. 'of the ways'). However, in (11b) the introduction of this construction leads to success, while in (12b) it doesn't.

The fact is that the *iz*-group fills valency R as a whole. It cannot include extraneous elements. This is what happened in (12b). The group 'of reliable ways' contains the word 'reliable', which in fact fills valency P and not R: *edinstvennyj nadežnyj put'* 'the only reliable way' means that there is no other way that is reliable. If we take this word out of the *iz*-group, the sentence will become quite correct:

(23) *Ivan vybral edinstvennyj iz putej, kotoryj byl nadežnym.*

'Ivan chose the only of the ways that was reliable'

As for sentence (11a), this problem does not arise, since the participle *došedšee* 'having-come' does not belong to the *iz*-group, but is connected directly to *edinstvennyj*. This follows from the fact that *došedšee* (nom, sg) does not agree in case and number with *sooruženij* 'buildings' (gen, pl) but with *edinstvennoe* (nom, sg). Otherwise, the sentence would be as ungrammatical as (12b):

(24) **Panteon – edinstvennoe* (nom, sg) *iz antičnyx sooruženij* (gen, pl) *, došedšix* (gen, pl) *do našix dnej s nepovreždennym kupolom.*

lit. Pantheon – only (nom, sg) ancient building (gen, pl) having-come (gen, pl) to our days with intact cupola.

4. SemETAP semantic analyzer.

The semantic analyzer SemETAP, under development in the Computational Linguistics lab of the Kharkevich Institute for Information Transmission Problems of the Russian Academy of Sciences, is aiming at performing semantic analysis based on both linguistic and extra-linguistic knowledge. This analyzer includes a wide-coverage linguistic processor capable of building coherent semantic structures for Russian, a knowledge-extensive lexicon, which contains a variety of types of lexical information, an ontology, which describes objects in the domain and their properties, a repository of ground-level facts, a set of common-sense axioms, and an inference engine (Boguslavsky 2011, Boguslavsky et al. 2013). The text is processed in three steps: 1) building of dependency syntactic structure (SyntS), 2) building of basic semantic structure (BSemS), and 3) building of extended

---

[1] except for the cases of diathesis modification under phrasal stress – cf. above.

semantic structure (ExtSemS). Most of the predicate-argument links are established in SyntS. Here belong all cases of the active (see above, Section 2) valency filling, which correspond to immediate dependency links between the predicate and the argument. Passive and discontinuous valency filling is performed at the level of BSemS. It is there that the actants discussed in the previous section are presented. ExtSemS is obtained by means of various semantic procedures based on common sense axioms, context data, ground-level facts, etc. A similar distribution of knowledge between the levels is adopted in the Onto-Sem approach (Nirenburg, Raskin 2004).

5. Non-prototypical valency filling in SemETAP

Let us go back to our case study. For convenience, we will repeat below the sentences under discussion.

(8a) *Ivan edinstvennyj menja ponimaet.*
    lit. Ivan only me undertstands
    'Only Ivan undertsands me'

(8b) *Menja ponimaet tol'ko Ivan.*
    lit. me understands only Ivan
    'only Ivan understands me'

(9a) *V uglu stojal edinstvennyj stul.*
    lit. in corner stood only chair
    'There was only one chair in the corner'

(9b) *V ugly stojal tol'ko stul.*
    lit. in corner stood only chair
    'There was only a chair in the corner'

SyntSs of these sentences do not contain explicit information on the actants of *edinstvennyj* and *tol'ko*. SyntSs of (8a) and (8b) obtained by the ETAP parser are shown in Fig. 1 and 2. In (8a) *edinstvennyj* (word 2) is connected to the verb *ponimaet* 'understands' (word 4) by the subject-copredicative dependency relation. In (8b) *tol'ko* (word 3) is linked to *Ivan* (word 4) by the restrictive dependency relation.

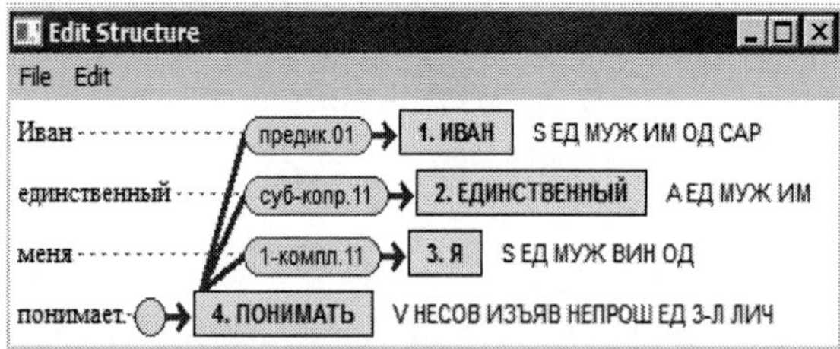

Fig. 1. SyntS of (8a) *Ivan edinstvennyj menja ponimaet*

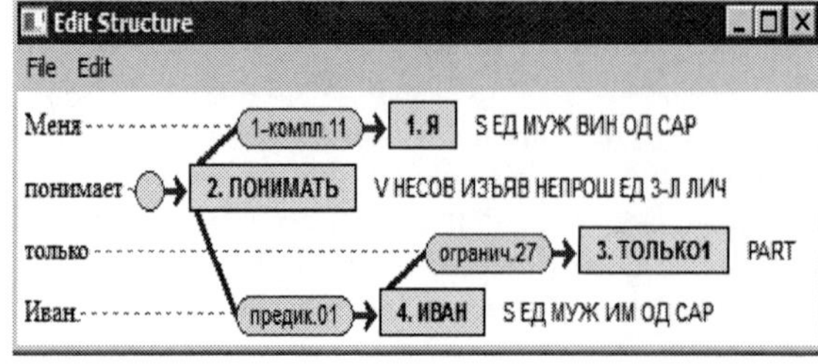

Fig. 2 SyntS of (8b) *Menja ponimaet tol'ko Ivan*

In spite of completely different SyntSs, synonymous sentences (8a) and (8b) get an identical BSemS shown in Fig. 3. In this BSemS, both *edinstvennyj* and *tol'ko* have the same equivalent – Only. Its actants Q, R and P, described in section 3, are connected to this concept by means of relations hasObject (for valency Q), hasSource (for valency R) and hasAttribute (for valency P).

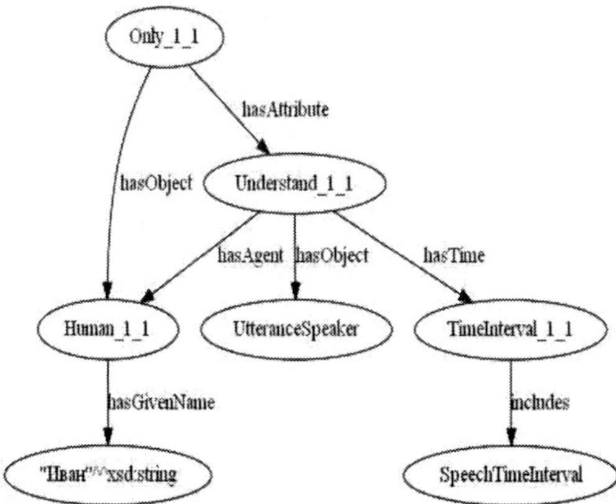

Fig. 3 BSemS of both (8a) and (8b)

SyntSs of sentences (9a) and (9b) are very similar. In both cases, *edinstvennyj/tol'ko* is connected to the same noun *stul* 'chair'. However, as can be seen in Fig. 4 and 5, the BSemSs of these sentences are noticeably different. They differ in how valency P of these words is instantiated. In (9b) it is filled by the main verb: 'there is nothing except the chair [Q] that is standing [P] in the corner'. In (9a), both Q and P are filled by the same concept – chair (leaving aside the difference in the referential status): 'there is nothing except the chair [Q] standing in the corner that is a chair [P]'.

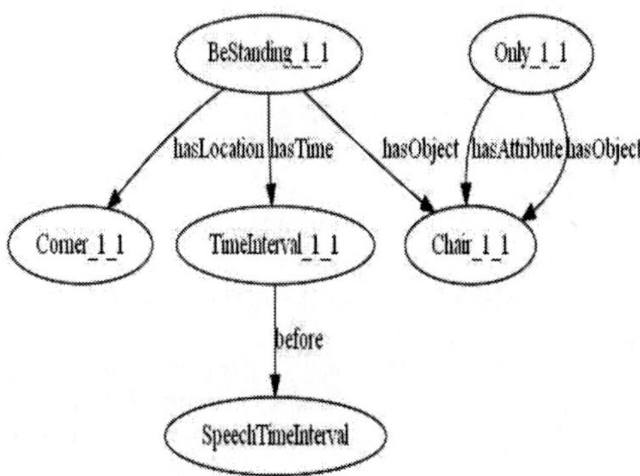

Fig. 4 BSemS of (9a) *V uglu stojal edinstvennyj stul*

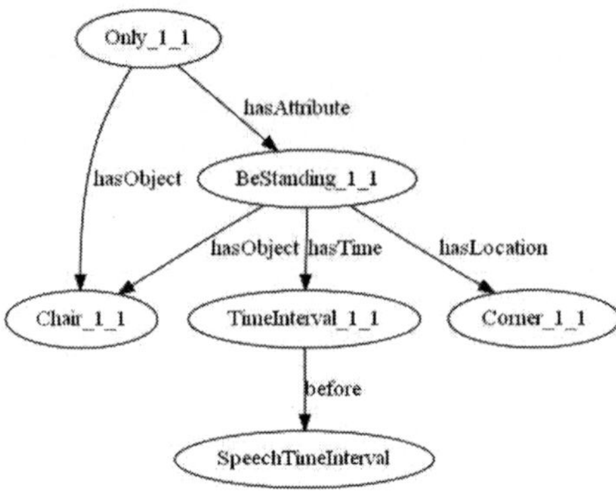

Fig. 5 BSemS of (9b) *V uglu stojal tol'ko stul*

6 Conclusion

Non-canonical valency filling received less attention, both in linguistics and in computational linguistics, than well-studied cases of active valency filling, when actants are directly subordinated to predicates in a dependency structure and different actants are always represented by non-intersecting phrases. We show that the inventory of valency filling is not restricted to that. Actants can be connected to predicates in different ways. They can subordinate their predicate and even have no direct connection with it. It is also possible that the same word participates in the filling of different valencies of the same predicate. We have shown how these phenomena can be handled in a semantic analyser.

Acknowledgements

This work was supported by the RSF grant 16-18-10422, which is gratefully acknowledged.

References.

Apresjan Ju.D. 1974. Leksicheskaja semantika. Nauka, Moscow.

Apresjan Ju.D. 1999. Otechestvennaja teoreticheskaja semantika v konce XX stoletija. Izv. AN, serija lit. i jazyka, № 4.

Boguslavsky I. 1996. Sfera dejstvija leksicheskix edinic. Shkola Jazyki russkoj kul'tury, Moscow.

Boguslavsky I. 2003. On the Passive and Discontinuous Valency Slots. In: Proceedings of the 1st International Conference on Meaning-Text Theory, pp. 129-138. Ecole Normale Supérieure, Paris, June 16–18.

Boguslavsky I. 2005. Valentnosti kvantornyx slov. In: Kvantifikativnyj aspekt jazyka. Moskva, p. 139-165.

Boguslavsky I. 2009. Enlarging the Diversity of Valency Instantiation Patterns and Its Implications // Lecture Notes In Artificial Intelligence. Logic, Language, and Computation: 7th International Tbilisi Symposium on Logic, Language, and Computation (TbiLLC'2007). Tbilisi, Georgia, October 1-5, 2007. Berlin; Heidelberg: Springer-Verlag. P. 206-220.

Boguslavsky I.M. 2011. "Semantic Analysis Based on Linguistic and Ontological Resources"; Proceedings of the 5th International Conference on the Meaning - Text Theory. Barcelona. Igor Boguslavsky and Leo Wanner (Eds.). P. 25-36, 2011.

Boguslavsky I.M., V.G.Dikonov, L.L.Iomdin, S.P. Timoshenko. 2013. "Semantic representation for NL understanding"; Computational Linguistics and Intellectual Technologies. Papers from the Annual International Conference "Dialogue". Issue 12(19), Moscow, RGGU Publishers. P. 132-144.

Mel'čuk I. 2004a. Actants in semantics and syntax I: actants in semantics, Linguistics, 42(1), 1-66.

Mel'čuk I. 2004b. Actants in semantics and syntax II: actants in syntax, Linguistics, 42(2), 247-291.

Mel'čuk I.A. and Xolodovič A.A. 1970. Zalog (Opredelenie. Ischislenie). Narody Azii I Afriki, n° 4, 111-124.

Nirenburg, Raskin. 2004. Ontological Semantics. The MIT Press. Cambridge, Massachusetts. London, England.

Padučeva E. 2003. Diathesis: some extended applications of the term. In: Proceedings of the 1st International Conference on Meaning-Text Theory. Paris, École Normale Supérieure, June 16–18.

Partee B. 2005. Diathesis Alternations and NP Semantics. // East West Encounter: Second International Conference on Meaning – Text Theory. Jazyki slavjanskoj kultury. Moskva.

Improvement of VerbNet-like resources by frame typing

Laurence Danlos
Université Paris Diderot
ALPAGE INRIA
Laurence.Danlos@inria.fr

Mathieu Constant
Université de Lorraine
ATILF CNRS

Lucie Barque
Université Paris 13
ALPAGE INRIA
Barque@univ-paris13.fr

Mathieu.Constant@univ-lorraine.fr

Abstract

Verbǝnet is a French lexicon developed by "translation" of its English counterpart — VerbNet (Kipper-Schuler, 2005) — and treatment of the specificities of French syntax (Pradet et al., 2014; Danlos et al., 2016). One difficulty encountered in its development springs from the fact that the list of (potentially numerous) frames has no internal organization. This paper proposes a type system for frames that shows whether two frames are variants of a given alternation. Frame typing facilitates coherence checking of the resource in a "virtuous circle". We present the principles underlying a program we developed and used to automatically type frames in Verbǝnet. We also show that our system is portable to other languages.

1   Introduction

VerbNet is a broad-coverage resource for English verbs in which verbs are grouped according to shared syntactic behaviors, namely surface realizations of their argument structure and syntactic alternations they are involved in (Kipper-Schuler, 2005; Kipper et al., 2006). Based on the hypothesis that verbs with similar semantics share similar syntactic properties (Levin, 1993), VerbNet extends Levin's classification up to 270 hierarchically organized verb classes. VerbNet has proven useful for NLP thanks to its high coverage (more than five thousand distinct verbs), useful verb separation and systematic coding of thematic roles. In particular, VerbNet is widely used in Semantic Role Labelling (SRL), a task that has grown steadily in importance: it serves as an aid to information extraction (Surdeanu et al., 2003), question-answering (Shen and Lapata, 2007), event extraction (Exner and Nugues, 2011), plagiarism detection (Osman et al., 2012), machine translation (Bazrafshan and Gildea, 2013), or stock market prediction (Xie et al., 2013).

Given the success of VerbNet, equivalent ressources for other languages have been developed, including Italian (Busso and Lenci, 2016), Portuguese (Scarton et al., 2014) and others. For French, a French Verbǝnet was first automatically derived from English VerbNet (Pradet et al., 2014); next the focus turned to accounting for the syntactic specificities of French – for example the existence of pronominal forms (noted as *se V*) which are illustrated in (1) for the middle alternation (Danlos et al., 2016).

(1) a. Le boucher a coupé le rumsteak = `Agent V Patient` *(The butcher cut the rump steak)*

  b. Le rumsteak se coupe facilement = `Patient se V<+middle> ADV` *(The rump steak cuts easily)*

During the development of French Verbǝnet, problems were encountered owing to the lack of structure in the list of frames for a given class in the original English resource. The aim of this paper is to propose a solution to these problems. We first explain why the current organization of the information is detrimental to the resource quality (Section 2). Then, after highlighting differences between English VerbNet and its French counterpart in terms of optionality and order of complements (Section 3), we explain how frames are automatically typed for French and how this typing helps to enhance the resource (Section 4). Finally, Section 5 discusses the portability of the typing program to other languages.

Proceedings of the Workshop on Grammar and Lexicon: Interactions and Interfaces,
pages 61–70, Osaka, Japan, December 11 2016.

2   Problems with frame structuring in VerbNet

In VerbNet, verb classes are organized in a hierarchy in which sub-classes inherit properties of parent classes. The components of a class are 1) **Members**, a list of verbs – considered in one of their senses, if polysemous – belonging to the class; 2) **Roles**, a list of thematic roles shared by the members, with each thematic role optionally further characterized by certain selectional restrictions;[1] and 3) **Frames** which is a list of frames characterizing the syntactico-semantic behavior of the members. Each frame consists of a **syntactic surface construction**, an EXAMPLE sentence, a SYNTAX field in which thematic roles are mapped to syntactic complements, and a SEMANTICS field that indicates how the participants are involved in the event. As an illustration, Figure 1 shows the list of the seven frames that describe the get-13.5.1 class.[2] This class includes verbs that denote an action consisting of obtaining something (e.g *buy, catch, order, reach*). This kind of action generally implies the following thematic roles: Agent, Theme, Source, Beneficiary and Asset.

FRAMES	
NP V NP	
EXAMPLE	"Carmen bought a dress."
SYNTAX	AGENT V THEME
SEMANTICS	HAS_POSSESSION(START(E), ?SOURCE, THEME) TRANSFER(DURING(E), THEME) HAS_POSSESSION(END(E), AGENT, THEME) CAUSE(AGENT, E)
NP V NP PP.SOURCE	
EXAMPLE	"Carmen bought a dress from Diana."
SYNTAX	AGENT V THEME {FROM} SOURCE
SEMANTICS	HAS_POSSESSION(START(E), SOURCE, THEME) TRANSFER(DURING(E), THEME) HAS_POSSESSION(END(E), AGENT, THEME) CAUSE(AGENT, E)
NP V NP PP.BENEFICIARY	
EXAMPLE	"Carmen bought a dress for Mary."
SYNTAX	AGENT V THEME {FOR} BENEFICIARY
SEMANTICS	HAS_POSSESSION(START(E), ?SOURCE, THEME) TRANSFER(DURING(E), THEME) HAS_POSSESSION(END(E), AGENT, THEME) CAUSE(AGENT, E) BE
NP V NP.BENEFICIARY NP	
EXAMPLE	"Carmen bought Mary a dress."
SYNTAX	AGENT V BENEFICIARY THEME
SEMANTICS	HAS_POSSESSION(START(E), ?SOURCE, THEME) TRANSFER(DURING(E), THEME) HAS_POSSESSION(END(E), AGENT, THEME) CAUSE(AGENT, E) BE
NP V NP PP.ASSET	
EXAMPLE	"Carmen bought a dress for $50."
SYNTAX	AGENT V THEME {FOR} ASSET
SEMANTICS	HAS_POSSESSION(START(E), ?SOURCE, THEME) TRANSFER(DURING(E), THEME) HAS_POSSESSION(END(E), AGENT, THEME) CAUSE(AGENT, E) CO
NP.ASSET V NP	
EXAMPLE	"$50 won't even buy a dress."
SYNTAX	ASSET V THEME
SEMANTICS	HAS_POSSESSION(START(E), ?SOURCE, THEME) TRANSFER(DURING(E), THEME) HAS_POSSESSION(END(E), ?AGENT, THEME) CAUSE(?AGENT, E)
NP V NP PP.SOURCE NP.ASSET	
EXAMPLE	"FMC has bought 565,000 shares from Nortek Inc. at $23.50 a share."
SYNTAX	AGENT V THEME {FROM} SOURCE {AT FOR} ASSET
SEMANTICS	HAS_POSSESSION(START(E), SOURCE, THEME) HAS_POSSESSION(END(E), AGENT, THEME) TRANSFER(DURING(E), THEME) COST(E, ASSET)

Figure 1: List of frames for the get-13.5.1 class.

One can see in Figure 1 that frames differ in the number of complements (e.g. one complement in the 1st and 6th frames, two complements in the 2nd and 3rd frame, etc.), in their syntactic nature (e.g. Beneficiary is realized as a prepositional complement in the 3rd frame, as a direct complement in the 4th frame), in their syntactic function (e.g. Asset is realized as an oblique complement in the 5th frame, as the subject in the 6th frame), etc. In addition to these cases, it must be noted that if a given argument can be realized in different ways (nominal, infinitival, sentential, etc.), then there is one frame by type of realization. This is illustrated in Figure 2 showing the list of frames for the urge-58-1 class with two frames according to the realization of Topic. The non-nominal syntactic realizations of a thematic role are specified in syntactic restrictions, which are written between (angle) brackets.

In summary, there can be quite a number of frames in English VerbNet for a given class. The problem we want to highlight is the absence of organization and typing in the list of frames. First, alternation variants are not explicitly related, which is a loss of information for any NLP system using VerbNet.

---

[1] The terms thematic and semantic roles refer to the very same notion.

[2] Because of lack of room, the SEMANTICS field is cut.

FRAMES

NP V NP

EXAMPLE "I advised him."

SYNTAX AGENT V RECIPIENT

SEMANTICS URGE(DURING(E), AGENT, RECIPIENT, ?TOPIC)

NP V NP S_ING

EXAMPLE "I advised him to come."

SYNTAX AGENT V RECIPIENT TOPIC <+OC_TO_INF>

SEMANTICS URGE(DURING(E), AGENT, RECIPIENT, TOPIC)

NP V NP THAT S

EXAMPLE "I advised him that he should come."

SYNTAX AGENT V RECIPIENT TOPIC <+THAT_COMP>

SEMANTICS URGE(DURING(E), AGENT, RECIPIENT, TOPIC)

Figure 2: List of frames for the urge-58-1 class.

For instance, the 3rd and 4th frames in Figure 1 are not explicitly related as variants in the "Benefactive Alternation" (Levin, 1993, pp 48-49). The information that they describe exactly the same situation is thereby lost. By the same way, the alternations that induce a change of meaning — e.g. the "locative alternation" (Levin, 1993, pp 49-55) — are not identified and so the change in meaning is lost. Next, it is difficult to know whether a combination of complements is either impossible or possible but not coded. For example, the sentence *Carmen bought a dress from Diana for Mary* seems to be correct but no frame explicitly encodes this configuration. Similarly, the sentence in the 4th frame *Carmen bought Mary a dress* can be extended with a `Source` complement (*Carmen bought Mary a dress from Diana*) or an `Asset` complement (*Carmen bought Mary a dress for $50*) but there is no frame for such extensions.

Our point is not to criticize the coding of the get-13.5.1 class or any class but to emphasize that the absence of organization and/or typing in the list of frames for a given class can lead to errors, incoherencies and oversights, because the linguist is not guided in her work when creating the list of frames. In Section 4, we propose a solution to overcome this problem. We first underscore the differences in frame coding between the English and French resources.

3 Optionality and order of complements in French Verbənet

As stated previously, the French Verbənet was initially created by adapting the English resource to French, which means that the structure of this French resource is nearly identical to that of the English one (Pradet et al., 2014). It was developed using a web interface available at `https://verbenet.inria.fr` and illustrated in Figure 3 for the Settle-89 class.

However, there are two points where the French Verbənet differs from the English VerbNet.[3] The first one is that sub-structures, i.e. structures in which an optional complement is unexpressed, are never coded for French while they are sometimes coded for English. The second one is that the order of complements is not coded in French Verbənet. A prime example of the different coding choices between English VerbNet and French Verbənet is given in the class send-11.1. It has five frames in English given in Figure 4, while it has only one frame in French, which corresponds to the fourth one in Figure 4 (*Nora a envoyé le livre de Paris à Londres / Nora sent the book from Paris to London*). We will see that these different coding choices have implications for the automatic frame typing program (Section 5).

The choice not to encode sub-structures in French Verbənet is due to the fact that an unexpressed complement may lead to different interpretations. Considering only optional objects, (Levin, 1993, pp 33-40) identified eight unexpressed object alternations such as "Unspecified object Alternation" (*Mike ate the cake* → *Mike ate*) or "Characteristic property of Agent Alternation" (*That dog bites people* → *That dog bites*). In conclusion, it's not informative to simply encode a sub-structure as acceptable without stating to which situation it corresponds. For example, the frame for *That dog bites* should be typed as a variant in the "Characteristic property of Agent Alternation". For French Verbənet, such a work has not

[3]We remind the reader (Section 1) that the differences between French and English VerbNet due to the discrepancies between the two languages are discussed in (Danlos et al., 2016) and left aside here.

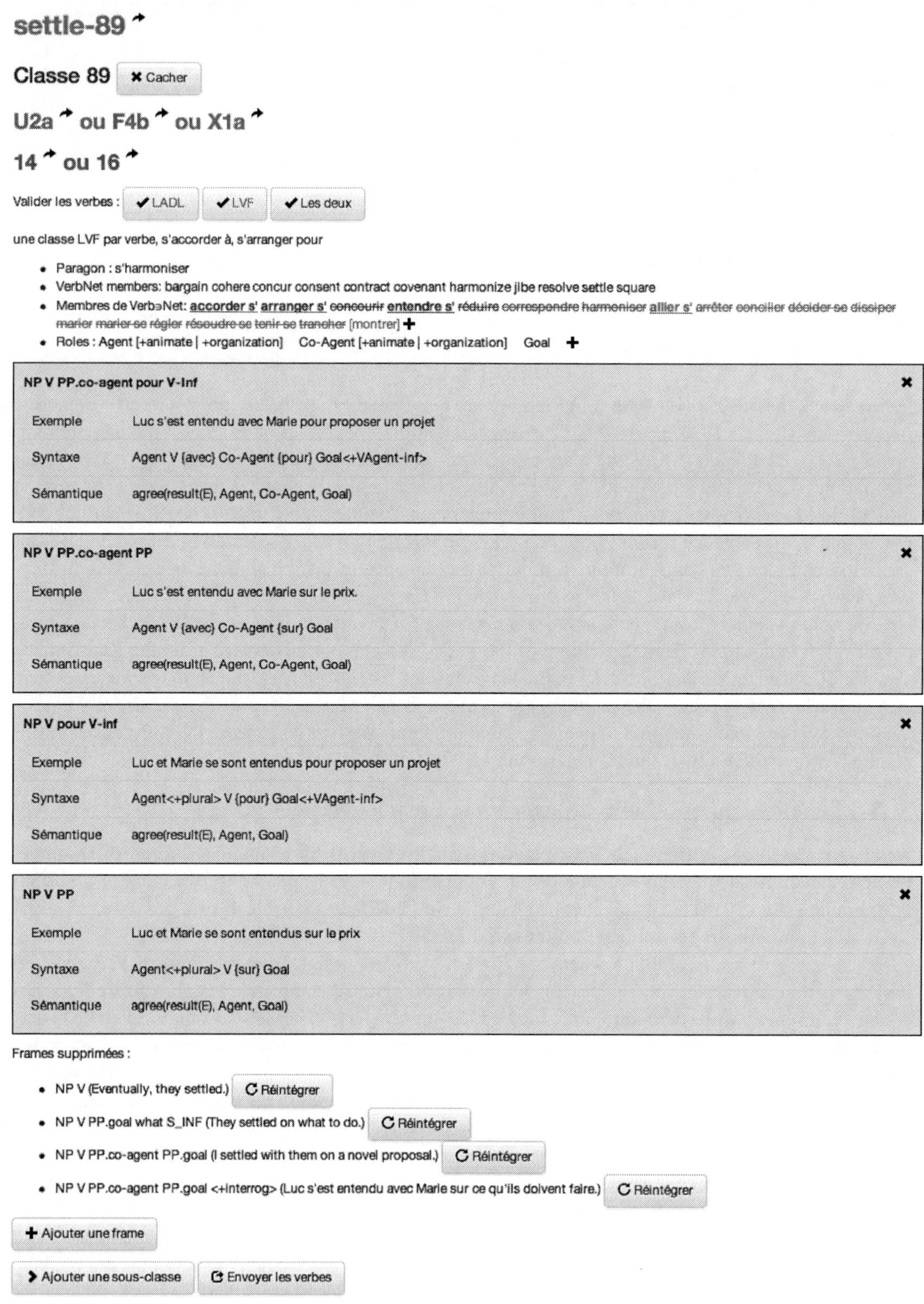

Figure 3: Web interface for editing and viewing Verbǝnet.

FRAMES	
NP V NP	
EXAMPLE	"Nora sent the book."
SYNTAX	AGENT V THEME
SEMANTICS	MOTION(DURING(E), THEME) CAUSE(AGENT, E)
NP V NP PP.INITIAL_LOCATION	
EXAMPLE	"Nora sent the book from Paris."
SYNTAX	AGENT V THEME {{+SRC}} INITIAL_LOCATION
SEMANTICS	MOTION(DURING(E), THEME) LOCATION(START(E), THEME, INITIAL_LOCATION) CAUSE(AGENT, E)
NP V NP PP.DESTINATION	
EXAMPLE	"Nora sent the book to London."
SYNTAX	AGENT V THEME {TO} DESTINATION
SEMANTICS	MOTION(DURING(E), THEME) LOCATION(END(E), THEME, DESTINATION) CAUSE(AGENT, E)
NP V NP PP.INITIAL_LOCATION PP.DESTINATION	
EXAMPLE	"Nora sent the book from Paris to London."
SYNTAX	AGENT V THEME {{+SRC}} INITIAL_LOCATION {TO} DESTINATION
SEMANTICS	MOTION(DURING(E), THEME) LOCATION(START(E), THEME, INITIAL_LOCATION) LOCATION(END(E), THEME, DESTINATION)
NP V NP PP.DESTINATION PP.INITIAL_LOCATION	
EXAMPLE	"TransCanada is shifting its HQ to Calgary from Toronto."
SYNTAX	AGENT V THEME {TO} DESTINATION {{+SRC}} INITIAL_LOCATION
SEMANTICS	MOTION(DURING(E), THEME) LOCATION(START(E), THEME, INITIAL_LOCATION) LOCATION(END(E), THEME, DESTINATION)

Figure 4: List of frames for the send-11.1 class.

yet been done, and so no sub-structure is coded.[4]

The choice not to encode the order of complements is due to the fact that the order of the complements of a verb in French does not depend on the verb itself but on the "weight" of the complements, the weight being computed according to the number of words (Gross, 1975) or other factors described in (Thuilier, 2012). [5] In English VerbNet, it happens that two frames in a class differ only by the order of the complements. This is the case in the class send-11.1, where the last two frames in Figure 4 differ only by the order of `Initial-Location` and `Destination` complements.

4 French Verbənet: version with typed frames

The typed version of Verbənet from the English-like version has been created automatically [6]. In this typed version, any frame is typed so as to show explicitly whether it is "canonical" or obtained by an alternation. Before going into detail, let us provide an illustrative example. The settle-89 class, which was shown in Figure 3 in the English-like version, is shown in the typed version in Figure 5. The type of the first frame is **Canonique** (canonical). The type of the second one is **Canonique avec Goal[+V-inf]** which states that the `Goal` complement is realized as an infinitival phrase, while it is understood that is is realized as a noun phrase — the default value — in the canonical frame. The type of the third frame is **Alt. Symetrique** which states that this frame is obtained from the canonical one by the alternation named "Simple reciprocal Alternation (intransitive)" in (Levin, 1993, pp 62-63). The type of the last frame is **Alt. Symetrique avec Goal[+V-inf]** which states that the `Goal` complement is realized as an infinitival phrase in the symmetrical (reciprocal) alternated form.

The automatic conversion of the untyped version of Verbənet into the typed one led us to discover and correct incoherencies for the enhancement of the resource in a virtuous circle: the untyped version is changed until the typed version is satisfactory.

The conversion program is going to be explained step by step, first in parent classes (section 4.2), second in sub-classes (section 4.3). Next we will illustrate how the frame typing allows the enhancement of the original resource by discovering and correcting incoherences (section 4.4). Before that, we need to discuss the notion of canonical frame.

---

[4]To use French Verbənet for a task such as SRL, as an initial approximation one may consider any complement to be optional.

[5]To use French Verbənet for a task such as SRL, one may consider any permutation of complements to be acceptable.

[6]The input of this program is the XML version of Verbənet available at `https://github.com/aymara/verbenet`.

Classe settle-89

- Membres de VerbəNet: accorder s' arranger s' entendre s' allier s'
- Roles :Agent[+organization][+animate], Co-Agent[+organization][+animate], Goal

Canonique	
Exemple	Luc s'est entendu avec Marie sur le prix.
Surfacique	NP V PP.co-agent PP.goal
Syntaxe	Agent V {avec} Co-Agent {sur} Goal
Sémantique	agree(result(E), Agent, Co-Agent, Goal)

Canonique avec Goal[+V-inf]	
Exemple	Luc s'est entendu avec Marie pour proposer un projet
Surfacique	NP V PP.co-agent PP.goal
Syntaxe	Agent V {avec} Co-Agent {pour} Goal[+VAgent-inf]
Sémantique	agree(result(E), Agent, Co-Agent, Goal)

Alt. Symetrique	
Exemple	Luc et Marie se sont entendus sur le prix
Surfacique	NP V PP.goal
Syntaxe	Agent<+plural> V {sur} Goal
Sémantique	agree(result(E), Agent, Goal)

Alt. Symetrique avec Goal[+V-inf]	
Exemple	Luc et Marie se sont entendus pour proposer un projet
Surfacique	NP V PP.goal
Syntaxe	Agent<+plural> V {pour} Goal[+VAgent-inf]
Sémantique	agree(result(E), Agent, Goal)

Figure 5: New Web interface for viewing Verbənet

4.1 What is a canonical frame ?

In Levin's description of English alternations, this notion is absent: there exists only the notion of two variants of an alternation which are on the same footing. It is not our intention here to enter a theoretical discussion on the topic, however, from a lexicographic and NLP perspective, it seems justified to state that verbs such as *break, cut, hit* and *touch* are "canonically" transitive and participate in various diathesis alternations (middle, conative, causative/inchoative alternations) which makes them intransitive — although some authors, e.g. (Dubois and Dubois-Charlier, 1997) for French, consider intransitive forms such as *The carafe broke* as canonical compared to the transitive causative form *Fred broke the carafe.*

One of the outcomes of this work — which is still in progress — will be to determine classes of verbs for which a canonical form can be identified and to understand why the other classes do not exhibit a canonical frame. As a prime illustration, our frame typing program gives poor results and doesn't identify a canonical frame in class 55 of aspectual verbs *(commencer (begin), continuer (continue))*, but this is not a surprise: these verbs are included in VerbNet for the sake of coverage, but they could have been excluded, much as modal and light verbs are excluded.

A second question is: should there exist only a unique canonical frame? Consider the class banish-

10.2 in Figure 6. In (Levin, 1993, p 123) it is stated that all banish verbs "allow *to* phrases as well as *from* phrases, though not simultaneously", so the second or third frame in Figure 6 cannot be considered as a sub-structure of a frame including both `Source` and `Destination` complements. Thus, there is apparently no reason to consider one as more canonical than the other, except that banish verbs are verbs "which relate to the removal of an entity, typically a person, from a location" (Levin, 1993, p 123), which seems to promote the frame with a `Source` as canonical on semantic grounds. So the idea of two canonical frames could be accepted and one of the outcomes of this work will be to understand what are the classes of verbs with two potential canonical forms and whether one of these forms can be promoted as canonical on semantic grounds.

FRAMES

NP V NP
    EXAMPLE   "The king banished the general."
    SYNTAX   AGENT V THEME
    SEMANTICS   CAUSE(AGENT, E) LOCATION(START(E), THEME, ?SOURCE) LOCATION(END(E), THEME, ?DESTINATION)
NP V NP PP.SOURCE
    EXAMPLE   "The king banished the general from the army."
    SYNTAX   AGENT V THEME {{+SRC}} SOURCE
    SEMANTICS   CAUSE(AGENT, E) LOCATION(START(E), THEME, SOURCE) NOT(LOCATION(END(E), THEME, SOURCE))
NP V NP PP.DESTINATION
    EXAMPLE   "The king deported the general to the isle."
    SYNTAX   AGENT V THEME {TO} DESTINATION
    SEMANTICS   CAUSE(AGENT, E) LOCATION(START(E), THEME, ?SOURCE) LOCATION(END(E), THEME, DESTINATION)

Figure 6: List of frames for the banish-10.2 class.

4.2   Frame typing in parent classes

The typing program identifies first the canonical frame, then the alternated frames and finally the frames with syntactic restrictions, as described below.

Canonical frame. The program which converts the untyped version into the typed one first requires the canonical frame to be identified, which raises problems discussed above. Currently, the strategy we use to automatically identify the canonical form is to spot the frame that includes all the thematic roles listed in the component **Roles** of the class (Section 2) — and which doesn't include any syntactic restrictions (written between (angle) brackets). This strategy relies on the fact that the order of complements is not coded in French Verbǝnet (Section 3).

Alterned frame. The program detects an alternated frame thanks to a set of rules designed for the set of coded alternations. For example, a rule can type a frame as **Alt. Instrument subject** (Levin, 1993, pp 80) when the subject of the canonical frame, i.e. the thematic role on the left of the symbol *V*, is replaced by the thematic role `Instrument`, see `Agent V Patient {avec} Instrument` → `Instrument V Patient`. Another rule types a frame as **Alt. Symetrique** when a `Co-Agent` (resp. `Co-Patient`) in the canonical frame is replaced by an `Agent` (resp. `Patient`) marked as `<+plural>`, see `Agent V {avec} Co-Agent {sur} Goal` → `Agent<+plural> V {sur} Goal`.

One of the main difficulties encountered in typing alternated frames is observed with cascades of alternations. This is illustrated in the paradigm in (2) from the almagate-22.2 class: (2a) gives the canonical frame, (2b) the symmetrical alternated frame, (2c) the neutral alternated frame. The difficulty in typing is for (2d) which gives the alternated form when both the symmetrical and neutral alternations apply in any order from the canonical frame.

(2)   a. **Canonique:** `Agent V Patient {avec} Co-Patient`
        Fred a associé la compagnie α avec la compagnie β (Fred associated company α with company β)
    b. **Alt. Symetrique:** `Agent V Patient<+plural>`
        Fred a associé les compagnies α et β (Fred associated companies α and β)
    c. **Alt. Neutre:** `Patient se V<+neutre> {avec} Co-Patient`

La compagnie α s'est associée avec la compagnie β (Company α associated itself with company β)

d. **Alt. Symetrique & Neutre**: `Patient<+plural> se V<+neutre>`

Les compagnies α et β se sont associées (Companies α and β associated themselves with one another)

Frame with syntactic restriction Finally, the program has to identify two frames which are identical except that in one of the frames a thematic role X has a syntactic restriction [synt], which states that the realization of X is not nominal but infinitival, for example. The two frames are then easily typed **T** and **T with X[synt]**.

4.3 Frame typing in sub-classes

For sub-classes, the frame typing program relies on the idea that the canonical frame is in the parent class. Consider the French sub-class bend-45.2.1 which includes verbs for which the non-pronominal inchoative form — named **Alternation inchoative** — is possible on top of the pronominal form *(La tige a plié / La tige s'est pliée (The rod bent))*, whereas the parent class bend-45.2 includes verbs for which only the pronominal inchoative form — named **Alternation neutre** — is possible *(La tige s'est incurvée / *La tige a incurvé (The rod curved))*.[7] As a consequence, the unique frame in the sub-class bend-45.2.1 receives the type **Alternation inchoative** which is to be understood as an alternated form of the canonical form in the parent class. More generally, if a sub-class was created because of an alternation A which is possible for only some verbs of the parent class, there is no problem with frame typing: the unique frame in the sub-class receives type **Alternation A**.

However, a sub-class may also be created for other reasons, one of them being variants in prepositions introducing complements. In French, the class correspond-36.1 includes communication verbs for which the `Theme` is introduced by the preposition *sur*, as illustrated in *Le comité a délibéré sur ce point (The committee deliberated on this issue)*. A sub-class of correspond-36.1 includes verbs that also allow the `Theme` to be introduced by the preposition *de*, as illustrated in *Le comité a discuté de ce point (The committee discussed this issue)*. The frame in the sub-class, which does not fall within alternation variants nor alternative syntactic realization (in the sense given above), has not been typed yet.

4.4 Discovering incoherencies

The automatic conversion of the untyped Verbənet version into the typed one led us to discover incoherencies. As an illustration, it has been discovered that the coding of "possessor-attribute factoring alternations" (Levin, 1993, pp 72-78) called "restructurations" in French was not satisfactory (it is not satisfactory in English either). These alternations arise because a possessor and a possessed attribute may be expressed in two different ways. As one option, they may be expressed in a single complex noun phrase whose head is the attribute modified by a genitive for the possessor *(Fred adores Jane's humour)*. Alternatively, they may be expressed separately, one as a direct argument (subject or object), and the other via a prepositional phrase *(Fred adores Jane for her humour)*. A unique syntactic function which is expressed in a complex noun phrase is thus restructured into two syntactic functions. For thematic roles, this is unusual since the complex noun phrase receives a unique thematic role while there must be two roles for the two syntactic functions in the restructured variant.

As a consequence, we chose the following solution: we use two distinct frames to code that a given thematic role, for example `Stimulus` for the object of *adorer (adore)*, is either a simple noun phrase *(Fred adores this paint)* or a complex noun phrase *(Fred adores Jane's humour)*, see (3a) and (3b). The frame with the complex noun phrase is identified with the restriction `Stimulus[+genitive]`, which requires to divide the role `Stimulus` into two parts: `Stimulus.prop` for the attribute which is the head noun and `Stimulus.poss` for the possessor expressed in a genitive phrase. These two parts are naturally used in the restructured form, see (3c) with two thematic roles assigned to the two complements. The coding for a verb such as *adorer* in the admire-31.2 class is schematized in (3), in which the non-nominal realizations of `Stimulus` are left aside. [8]

---

[7]In English, there is no sub-class bend-45.2.1 since the inchoative alternated form is compulsorily a non-pronominal form while it is pronominal and/or non-pronominal in French.

[8]In VerbNet, the role `Stimulus.prop` is named `Attribute` in the frame equivalent to (3c), and (3b) is not coded in a specific frame.

(3) a. **Canonique**: `Experiencer V Stimulus`
     Fred adore cette peinture (Fred adores this paint)
   b. **Canonique with Stimulus[+genitive]**: `Experiencer V Stimulus.prop<+genitive(Stimulus.poss)>`
      Fred adore l'humour de Jane (Fred adores Jane's humour)
   c. **Restructuration**: `Experiencer V Stimulus.poss {pour} Stimulus.prop`

      Fred adore Jane pour son humour (Fred adores Jane for her humour)

We have not yet finished our virtuous circle between the un-typed and typed versions of Verbənet but the first results we get are promising. As an illustration, 16 classes have been corrected for the coding of restructuration alternations.

5 Methods and portability for typing VerbNet-like resources in other languages

Typing frames can be done in two ways: manually or automatically. Manual typing can be a good solution for a language for which no VerbNet-like ressource exists. When starting the work from scratch, the linguist has every reason to type each frame right away so as to be guided in her work. Manual typing for a language for which a VerbNet-like ressource already exists can be time-consuming (and tiresome). This is why we choose automatic typing for French with the existing Verbənet. This automatic typing is effective in improving the resource as typing errors are more often attributable to errors in the resource itself than to the typing program.

What is the feasibility of porting a typing program from one language to another? We cannot currently answer this question since, as far as we know, French is the only language for which there is a typing program, however we do have some indication. We focus on the identification of the canonical frame (in a parent class) since it should be clear from the description of the French typing program in Section 4 that this is the most difficult point. The canonical frame in a parent class can generally be identified thanks to the fact that it is this frame that includes all the thematic roles pertinent for the class with no restriction on any thematic role (which means that all thematic roles are realized as simple noun phrases) and no role such as `Stimulus.poss` or `Stimulus.prop` (which means that no restructuration is involved, Section 4). In French, there are only a few exceptions to this principle. For example, in class appoint-29.1 *(nommer (nominate))*, the two frames include all the thematic roles and differ only by the presence of *comme (as)* in the "*as* Alternation" (Levin, 1993, p 78). For this class, we typed (somewhat arbitrarily) **Canonique** the frame without *comme (as)* and **Alt. comme** the other frame. In English, there are more exceptions to this principle. First, the "Dative and Benefactive alternations" (Levin, 1993, pp 45-49), which don't exist in French, don't change the number of thematic roles. So specific rules must be designed to spot these alternated frames. Second, two frames may differ only by the order of complements (Section 3). In this case, it is not clear what should be done.

Finally, let us examine sub-structures. As we explained in Section 3, sub-structures have not yet been coded in French Verbənet because it is not informative to code a sub-structure as acceptable without stating to which situation it corresponds. This means that when they are coded they will be simultaneously typed, e.g. `Agent V` = *Ce chien mord (This dog bites)* typed as **Alternation Characteristic property of Agent** variant of the canonical frame `Agent V Patient` = *Ce chien a mordu Jane (This dog bit Jane)*. For English, an automatic typing program from the existing VerbNet can only type *This dog bites* as a sub-structure, without any other information.

6 Conclusion

We have shown that the lack of structure/typing in the list of frames for a VerbNet class make the coding task of the linguist difficult and it can lead to incoherencies or oversights. We have proposed frame typing as a method to overcome this problem. The types are: (i) canonical, (ii) canonical with a non-nominal or complex (i.e with a genitive) nominal realization of a thematic role, (iii) alternated form of another frame where the other frame can iteratively be canonical, canonical with a non-nominal simple realization or alternated form, (iv) untyped when the typing program gives no result.

We have presented an automatic typing program for French which we believe is easily portable to other languages. The automatic conversion of the untyped Verbənet version into the typed one enabled us to discover and correct incoherencies, thus enhancing the resource in a "virtuous circle". We have not yet evaluated the effects of this enhancement, but other VerbNet-like resources could be enhanced as we have done for French.

Acknowledgements

We thank André Bittar for editing our English.

References

Marzieh Bazrafshan and Daniel Gildea. 2013. Semantic Roles for String to Tree Machine Translation. In *Proceedings of ACL conference*, pages 419–423, Sofia, Bulgaria.

Lucia Busso and Alessandro Lenci. 2016. Italian-Verbnet: A construction-based approach to Italian verb classification. In Nicoletta Calzolari, Khalid Choukri, Thierry Declerck, Sara Goggi, Marko Grobelnik, Bente Maegaard, Joseph Mariani, Helene Mazo, Asuncion Moreno, Jan Odijk, and Stelios Piperidis, editors, *Proceedings of the Tenth International Conference on Language Resources and Evaluation (LREC 2016)*, Portorož, Slovenia.

Laurence Danlos, Quentin Pradet, Lucie Barque, Takuya Nakamura, and Matthieu Constant. 2016. Un Verbenet du français. *Traitement Automatique des Langues*, 57(1):33–58.

Jean Dubois and Françoise Dubois-Charlier. 1997. *Les verbes français*. Larousse-Bordas, Paris, France.

Peter Exner and Pierre Nugues. 2011. Using semantic role labeling to extract events from Wikipedia. In *Proceedings of the Workshop on Detection, Representation, and Exploitation of Events in the Semantic Web (DeRiVE 2011). Workshop in conjunction with the 10th International Semantic Web Conference (ISWC 2011)*, pages 38–47, Bonn, Germany.

Maurice Gross. 1975. *Méthodes en syntaxe*. Hermann, Paris.

Karin Kipper, Anna Korhonen, Neville Ryant, and Martha Palmer. 2006. Extending VerbNet with novel verb classes. In *Proceedings of LREC*, Genoa, Italy. Citeseer.

Karin Kipper-Schuler. 2005. *VerbNet: A broad-coverage, comprehensive verb lexicon*. Ph.D. thesis, University of Pennsylvania.

Beth Levin. 1993. *English verb classes and alternations: a preliminary investigation*. University Of Chicago Press.

Ahmed Hamza Osman, Naomie Salim, Mohammed Salem Binwahlan, Rihab Alteeb, and Albaraa Abuobieda. 2012. An improved plagiarism detection scheme based on semantic role labeling. *Applied Soft Computing*, 12(5):1493–1502.

Quentin Pradet, Laurence Danlos, and Gaël De Chalendar. 2014. Adapting VerbNet to French using existing resources. In *Proceedings of the Ninth International Conference on Language Resources and Evaluation (LREC 2014)*, Reykjavík, Iceland.

Carolina Scarton, Magali Sanches Duran, and Sandra Maria Alusio. 2014. Using cross-linguistic knowledge to build VerbNet-style lexicons: Results for a (Brazilian) Portuguese VerbNet. In Jorge Baptista, Nuno Mamede, Sara Candeias, Ivandré Paraboni, Thiago A. S. Pardo, and Maria das Graças Volpe Nunes, editors, *Computational Processing of the Portuguese Language*. Springer International Publishing.

Dan Shen and Mirella Lapata. 2007. Using Semantic Roles to Improve Question Answering. In *Proceedings of EMNLP-CoNLL*, pages 12–21, Prague, Czech Republic.

Mihai Surdeanu, Sanda Harabagiu, Johns Williams, and Paul Aarseth. 2003. Using predicate-argument structures for information extraction. In *Proceedings of the ACL Conference*, pages 8–15, Sapporo, Japan.

Juliette Thuilier. 2012. *Contraintes préférentielles et ordre des mots en français*. Ph.D. thesis, Université Paris-Diderot.

Boyi Xie, Rebecca J. Passonneau, Leon Wu, and Germán G. Creamer. 2013. Semantic Frames to Predict Stock Price Movement. In *Proceedings of the ACL conference*, pages 873–883, Sofia, Bulgaria.

Enriching a Valency Lexicon by Deverbative Nouns

Eva Fučíková   **Jan Hajič**   **Zdeňka Urešová**

Charles University, Faculty of Mathematics and Physics
Institute of Formal and Applied Linguistics
Prague, Czech Republic
{fucikova,hajic,uresova}@ufal.mff.cuni.cz

Abstract

In this paper, we present an attempt to automatically identify Czech deverbative nouns using several methods that use large corpora as well as existing lexical resources. The motivation for the task is to extend a verbal valency (i.e., predicate-argument) lexicon by adding nouns that share the valency properties with the base verb, assuming their properties can be derived (even if not trivially) from the underlying verb by deterministic grammatical rules. At the same time, even in inflective languages, not all deverbatives are simply created from their underlying base verb by regular lexical derivation processes. We have thus developed hybrid techniques that use both large parallel corpora and several standard lexical resources. Thanks to the use of parallel corpora, the resulting sets contain also synonyms, which the lexical derivation rules cannot get. For evaluation, we have manually created a gold dataset of deverbative nouns linked to 100 frequent Czech verbs since no such dataset was initially available for Czech.

1 Introduction

Valency is one of the central notions in a "deep" syntactic and semantic description of language structure. In most accounts, verbs are in the focus of any valency (or predicate-argument) theory, even if it is widely acknowledged that nouns, adjectives and even adverbs can have valency properties (Panevová, 1974; Panevová, 1994; Panevová, 1996; Hajičová and Sgall, 2003). There have been created many lexicons that contain verbs and their predicate-argument structure and/or valency, in some cases also subcategorization information or semantic preferences are included.

Creating such a lexicon is a laborious task. On top of the sheer volume of such a lexicon (to achieve good coverage of the given language), the biggest difficulty is to keep consistency among entries that describe verbs with the same or very similar behavior. The same holds for derivations; in most cases, no attempt is made to link the derivations to the base verbs in the lexicon (with NomBank (Meyers et al., 2004) being an exception, linking nouns to base verbs in the English PropBank (Kingsbury and Palmer, 2002)).

Valency information (number and function of the arguments) is shared between the base verb and its deverbatives, undergoing certain transformations in defined cases.[1] Moreover, especially in richly inflective languages, the subcategorization information (morphosyntactic surface expression of the arguments) can be derived by more or less deterministic rules from the verb, the deverbative relation and the verb's arguments' subcategorization (Kolářová, 2006; Kolářová, 2005; Kolářová, 2014). These rules, for example, transform the case of Actor (Deep subject) from nominative to genitive as the appropriate subcategorization for the deverbative noun, or delete the Actor altogether from the list of arguments in case of the derivation *teach → teacher* (*učit → učitel*).

It is thus natural to look for ways of organizing the valency or predicate-argument lexicons in such a way that they contain the links between the underlying verb and its deverbatives, which is not only

---

[1]Throuhgout the rest of the paper, we will use the term *deverbative nouns* or *deverbatives* since the term *derivations* might imply regular prefixing or suffixing processes, which we go beyond.

Proceedings of the Workshop on Grammar and Lexicon: Interactions and Interfaces,
pages 71–80, Osaka, Japan, December 11 2016.

natural, but if successful, would help the consistency of the grammatical properties between the verb and its deverbatives.

The goal of this study is to automatically discover deverbative nouns related to (base) verbs, using primarily parallel corpora, but also existing lexicons (mainly as an additional source and for comparison). The use of a parallel corpus should give us those deverbatives which would otherwise be hard to find using only monolingual resources. However, it is not our goal here to fully transfer the valency information from the base verb - as mentioned in the previous paragraph, that work is being done separately and we assume its results (i.e., the transfer rules) can then be applied relatively easily if we are successful in discovering and linking the appropriate nouns to the base verb.

In order to evaluate and compare the resulting automatic systems, evaluation (gold-standard) data had to be developed, due to the lack of such a resource. The language selected for this project is Czech, a richly inflectional language where derivations can be related to the word from which they are derived by regular changes (stemming with possible phonological changes, suffixing, prefixing) or - as is often the case - by more or less irregular processes.

There are many types (and definitions) of event/deverbative nouns. We are using the more general term *deverbative* throughout here, to avoid possible narrow interpretation of "event". For the purpose of our study and experiments, a deverbative noun is defined as a noun which in fact describes a state or event and can be easily paraphrased using its base verb without substantial change in meaning. For example, *Po úderu do jeho hlavy utekl.* (lit. *After hitting him in the head he ran away.*) can be paraphrased as *Poté, co ho udeřil do hlavy, utekl.* (lit: *After he hit him in the head, he ran away.*). The same noun can be used as a deverbative noun or entity-referring (referential) noun in different contexts; in Czech, however, this is rarer as the noun itself would be different for the two cases. For example, *stavba* (lit: *building*) in *Při stavbě domu jim došly peníze.* (lit: *During the building of the house, they ran out of money.*) is an event noun, while in *Tato stavba* [= budova] *se prodala levně.* (lit: *This building sold cheaply.*) it refers to an entity; here, even in Czech the same noun is used. However, another Czech derivations, *stavění* (from the same base verb, *stavět*) can only be used as event noun, and *stavení* only as a referential one. We also use the term *derivation* in a very broad sense, not only describing the very regular and productive derivation such as English *-ing* (Czech: *-ění, -a/ání, -í/ávání, -(u)tí, ...*), but also those which are much less frequent (*-ba, -nost, -ota*).

2 Related Work

Derivations, especially verbal derivations, have been studied extensively. Almost all grammars include a section on derivations, even if they use different theoretical starting points. The most recent work on Czech derivations is (Žabokrtský and Ševčíková, 2014; Ševčíková and Žabokrtský, 2014; Vidra, 2015; Vidra et al., 2015). These authors also created a resource called DeriNet (cf. Sect. 3.2). The background for their work comes from (Baranes and Sagot, 2014) and (Baayen et al., 1995). DeriNet, while keeping explicit the connection between the verb and its derivative, does not use valency as a criterion for having such a link, and therefore is broader than what we are aiming at in our study; however, we have used it as one of the starting points for the creation of the gold standard data (Sect. 4).

Event nouns, which form a major part of our definition of deverbatives, have also been studied extensively. A general approach to events and their identification in text can be found, e.g., in (Palmer et al., 2009) or (Stone et al., 2000).

NomBank (Meyers et al., 2004) is a prime resource for nominal predicate-argument structure in English. Closest to what we want to achieve here, is the paper (Meyers, 2008), where the authors also use various resources for helping to construct English NomBank; however, they do not make use of parallel resources.

For Czech, while we assume that relations between verbs and their deverbatives regarding valency structure can be described by grammatical rules (Kolářová, 2014; Kolářová, 2006; Kolářová, 2005),[2] no attempt to automatically extract deverbatives from lexicons and/or corpora has been described previously.

---

[2]We have also found similar work for Italian (Graffi, 1994).

3 The Data Available

3.1 Corpora

As one source of bilingual text, we have used the Prague Czech-English Dependency Treebank (PCEDT 2.0) (Hajič et al., 2012). The PCEDT is a 1-million-word bilingual corpus that is manually annotated and sentence-aligned and automatically word-aligned. In addition, it contains the predicate-argument annotation itself, where the verbs are sense-disambiguated by linking them to Czech and English valency lexicons. The English side builds on the PropBank corpus (Palmer et al., 2005), which annotates predicate-argument structure over the Penn Treebank (Marcus et al., 1993).

The associated valency lexicons for Czech - PDT-Vallex[3] (Urešová, 2011) and English - EngVallex[4] (Cinková, 2006) are also interlinked, forming a bilingual lexicon CzEngVallex (Urešová et al., 2016), which explicitly pairs verb senses and their arguments between the two languages.

The second corpus used was CzEng[5] (Bojar et al., 2011; Bojar et al., 2012; Bojar et al., 2016), a 15-million sentence parallel corpus of Czech and English texts. This corpus is automatically parsed and deep-parsed, verbs are automatically annotated by links to the same valency lexicons as in the PCEDT. The corpus is automatically sentence- and word-aligned.

The reason for using both a small high-quality annotated and a "noisy" (automatically annotated) but large corpus is to assess the ways they can contribute to the automatic identification of deverbatives, especially with regard to the amount of manual work necessary for subsequent "cleaning" of the certainly not quite perfect result (i.e., with regard to the recall/precision tradeoff).

3.2 Lexical Resources

In addition to corpora, we have also used the following lexical resources:

- DeriNet[6] (Vidra, 2015; Vidra et al., 2015; Žabokrtský and Ševčíková, 2014; Ševčíková and Žabokrtský, 2014), a large lexical network with high coverage of derivational word-formation relations in Czech. The lexical network DeriNet captures core word-formation relations on the set of around 970 thousand Czech lexemes. The network is currently limited to derivational relations because derivation is the most frequent and most productive word-formation process in Czech. This limitation is reflected in the architecture of the network: each lexeme is allowed to be linked up with just a single base word; composition as well as combined processes (composition with derivation) are thus not included. We have used version 1.1 of DeriNet.

- Morphological Dictionary of Czech called Morfflex CZ[7] (Hajič and Hlaváčová, 2016; Hajič, 2004), which is the basis for Czech morphological analyzers and taggers, such as (Straková et al., 2014). This dictionary has been used to obtain regular noun derivatives from verb, limited to suffix changes, namely for nouns ending in *-ní* or *-tí*, *-elnost* and *-ost*. The resulting mapping, which we call "Der" in the following text, contains 49,964 distinct verbs with a total of 143,556 nouns to which they are mapped (i.e., not all verbs map to all three possible derivations, but almost all do). While DeriNet subsumes most of Morflfex CZ derivations, it has proved to be sometimes too "permissive" and the deverbatives there often do not correspond to valency-preserving derivations.

- Czech WordNet version 1.9[8] (Pala et al., 2011; Pala and Smrž, 2004), from which all noun synsets with more than 1 synonym have been extracted (total of 3,432 synsets with 8,742 nouns); this set is referred to as "Syn" in the following text. Using WordNet is deemed a natural baseline for adding synonyms–in our case, to the deverbatives extracted from other sources.

---

[3]http://lindat.mff.cuni.cz/services/PDT-Vallex
[4]http://lindat.mff.cuni.cz/services/EngVallex
[5]http://hdl.handle.net/11234/1-1458
[6]http://hdl.handle.net/11234/1-1520
[7]http://hdl.handle.net/11234/1-1673
[8]http://hdl.handle.net/11858/00-097C-0000-0001-4880-3

4 Evaluation (Gold) Dataset Preparation

4.1 The Goal

There was no available Czech dataset for testing any particular automatic identification and extraction of deverbatives. The closest to our goals is DeriNet (Sect. 3.2), however DeriNet lists all possible derivations based on root/stem, without regard to valency (predicate-argument relations). For example, for the verb *dělit* (*divide*), DeriNet lists also *dělítko*, which is (in one rare, but possible sense) a tool for dividing things; tools used in events are not considered to share their valency, even if possible transformations are considered, as described in Sect. 1.

Two such "gold" datasets have been created: a development set, which can be used for developing the extraction rules and their optimization and tuning by both manual inspection and automatic techniques, and an evaluation set, which is used only for final "blind" evaluation of the methods developed.

An example of a set of deverbatives of the verb *klesat* (lit. *to decrease*), taken from the development dataset: *klesání, klesavost, omezování, oslabování, redukování, snižování, zmenšování* (lit. *decrease, decreaseness, limitation, weakening, reduction, lowering, diminishing*).

Each set contains 100 Czech verbs (with no overlap between the two in terms of verb senses), selected proportionally to their relative frequency in a syntactically and semantically annotated corpus, the Prague Dependency Treebank (Hajič et al., 2006), excluding verbs equivalent to *to be, to have, to do*, light and support verb senses like *close [a contract]* and all idioms (e.g. *take part*).[9]

4.2 The Annotation Process

The pre-selected sets of deverbative nouns have been extracted from several sources: PCEDT, a parallel corpus using alignments coming from an automatic MT aligner (Giza++) and the DeriNet lexicon (Sect. 3.2). To avoid bias as much as possible, these sets are intentionally much larger than we expected human annotators to create, so that the annotators would mostly be filtering out those words not corresponding to the definition of a deverbative, even if allowed to add more words as well.

Annotators had the task to amend the pre-selected list of nouns for a particular verb (actually, a verb sense, as identified by a valency frame ID taken from the Czech valency lexicon entries[10] (Urešová, 2011)) so that only deverbatives with the same or very similar meaning remain, and add those that the annotator feels are missing, based e.g. on analogies with other verb-deverbative groups and following the definition of deverbatives.

The annotation was done simply by editing a plain text file which contained, at the beginning, all the 100 verbs and for each of them, a pre-selected set of nouns, one per line. Each entry has also contained a description of the particular verb sense (meaning) used, copied form PDT-Vallex. On average, there have been pre-selected 44.1 nouns per verb. The annotators proceeded by deleting lines which contained non-deverbative nouns, and adding new ones by inserting a new line at any place in the list. The resulting average number of nouns per verb has been 6.3 per verb (in the development set).

While the development dataset has been annotated by a single annotator, the evaluation dataset has been independently annotated by three annotators, since it was expected that the agreement, as usual for such open-ended annotation, would not be very high.

4.3 Inter-Annotator Agreement (IAA)

In an annotation task where the result of each item annotation is open-ended, the classification-based measures, such as the κ (kappa) metric, cannot be sensibly used. Instead, we have used the standard F_1 measure (Eq. 1), pairwise for every pair of annotators. Precision P is the ratio of matches over the number of words annotated, and recall R is the number of matches over the other annotator's set of words.[11]

---

[9]This was easily done since the annotation in the Prague Dependency Treebank contains all the necessary attributes, such as verb senses and light/support/idiomatic use. Coverage of the 100-verb evaluation set is quite substantial, about 14%.

[10]`http://lindat.mff.cuni.cz/services/PDT-Vallex`

[11]While the direction of computation between the annotators matters for computing precision and recall (precision of one annotator vs. the other is equal to the recall of the opposite direction), the resulting F_1 is identical regardless of the direction, therefore we report only one F_1 number.

$$F_1 = 2PR/(P+R) \tag{1}$$

In Table 1, we list all three pairs of annotators of the evaluation dataset and their IAA.

	Annotators 1-2	Annotators 2-3	Annotators 1-3
F_1	0.5520	0.5402	0.5327

Table 1: Inter-Annotator Agreement on the Evaluation Dataset

While the pairwise F_1 scores are quite consistent, they are relatively low; again, it has to be stressed that this is an open-ended annotation task. Not surprisingly, if we only consider deletions in the pre-selected data, the agreement goes up (e.g., for Annotators 1-2, this would then be 0.6237).

To make the evaluation fair, we could not inspect the evaluation data manually, and despite using linguistically well-qualified annotators, a test proved that any attempt at adjudication would be a lengthy and costly process. We have therefore decided to use three variants of the evaluation dataset: one which contained for each verb only those nouns that appeared in the output of all three annotators (called *"intersection"*), second in which we kept also those nouns which have been annotated by two annotators (called *"majority"*) and finally a set which contained annotations from all three (called *"union"*). Such a triple would give us at least an idea about the intervals of both precision and recall which we could expect, should a careful adjudication be done in the future. We consider the "majority" set to be most likely closest to such an adjudicated dataset.

5 Extraction Methods and Experiments

5.1 Baseline

The baseline system uses only the "Der" lists (Sect. 3.2) that contain, for each verb from the Czech morphology lexicon, its basic, regularly formed event noun derivations. For example, for the verb *potisknout* (lit. *print on* [sth] *all over*) the derivations listed in "Der" are *potisknutí* (and its derivational variant *potištění*, both lit. *printing* [of sth] *all over*) and *potištěnost* (lit. *property/ration of being printed over*).

For each verb in the test set, all and only nouns listed for it in "Der" are added. The baseline experiment is used as the basis of the other methods and experiments described below.

5.2 Adding WordNet

On top of the regular derivations, synonyms of all the derivations are added, based on Czech WordNet-based "Syn" lists (Sect. 3.2). All synonyms listed for a particular noun are added; no hierarchy is assumed or attempted to extract.

5.3 Using Parallel Corpora

Using the parallel corpus is the main contribution; all the previous methods have been included for comparison only and as a baseline "sanity check". We use either the PCEDT or CzEng (Sect. 3.1), in addition to the baseline method; each of the two has different properties (PCEDT being manually annotated while CzEng is very large). For each base verb in the test set, the following steps have been taken:

1. For each occurrence of the Czech base verb, the aligned English verb (based on CzEngVallex pairings) was extracted.

2. All occurrences of that verb on the English side of the parallel corpus were identified.

3. All nouns that are aligned with any of the occurrence of the English verb were extracted from the Czech side.

4. The verb and the noun were subject to an additional filtering process, described below; if they passed, the noun was added to the baseline list of nouns associated with the base verb.

Filtering is necessary for several reasons: first, the annotation of the data is noisy, especially in the automatically analyzed CzEng corpus, and second, the alignment is also noisy (for both corpora, since it is automatic). Even if both the annotation and the alignment are correct, sometimes the noun extracted the way described above is only a part of a different syntactic construction, and not a true equivalent of the verb. In order to eliminate the noise as much as possible, two techniques have been devised.

5.3.1 Simple Prefix-based Filtering

As the first method, we have used an extremely simple method of keeping only those nouns that share the first letter with the base verb. The rationale is that the deverbatives are often (regular as well as irregular) derivations, which in Czech (as in many other languages) change the suffix(es) and ending(s), not the prefix. After some investigation, we could not find another simple and reliable method for identifying the stem or more logical part of the word, and experiments showed that on the PCEDT corpus, this was a relatively reliable method of filtering out clear mistakes (at the expense of missing some synonyms etc.).

This method is referred to in the following text and tables as "L1 filter".

5.3.2 Advanced Argument-based Filtering

As the experiments (Table 2 in Sect. 6) show, the L1 filter works well with the PCEDT corpus, but the results on CzEng are extremely bad, due to a (still) huge number of words (nouns) generated by the above method using such a noisy and large corpus.

To avoid this problem, we have devised a linguistically-motivated filter based on shared arguments of the base verb and the potential deverbative. We first extracted all arguments of the verb occurrence in a corpus, and then all dependents of the noun as found by the process described in Sect. 5.3.[12] The noun was added as a deverbative to the base verb only if at least one of the arguments (the same word/lemma) was found as a dependent at any occurrence of the noun.

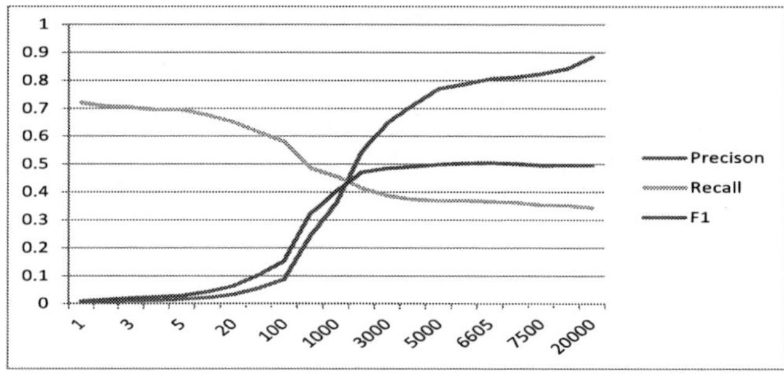

Figure 1: Recall, precision and F_1 for selected threshold values on the development dataset

However, it proved insufficient to allow the noun to be added if such sharing appeared just once - there was still too much noise, especially for CzEng. Thus we have set a threshold, which indicates how many times such a sharing should occur before we consider the noun to be a deverbative. This threshold has been (automatically) learned on the development data, and has been found to be optimal if set to 6 for the PCEDT and to 6605 for the large CzEng corpus. It has then been used in the evaluation of all the variants of the evaluation set. The effect of increasing the threshold is (as expected) that precision gradually increases (from below 1% to over 80%) while recall decreases (from slightly above 72% to below 37% at the F_1-driven optimum, Fig. 1). The F_1-optimized maximum is in fact flat and depending on the importance of recall, it could also be set at much lower point where the recall is still around 50%, which no other method came close to without dropping precision close to zero. A narrower range of precision/recall increase/decrease has been obtained on the small PCEDT corpus, with the threshold set relatively low at 6 occurrences; the highest recall (at threshold = 1) was below 53%.

---

[12]The deep level of annotation of the PCEDT and CzEng is used, which uses so-called tectogrammatical annotation (Mikulová et al., 2005). From this annotation, arguments and other "semantic" dependents can be easily extracted.

This filtering is referred to in the following text and tables as "shared arg" with the threshold as an index. "PCEDT" and "CzEng" indicate which corpus has been used for the primary noun extraction as described earlier in this section.

5.4 Combination with WordNet

The systems based on the parallel-corpus-based method have been also combined with the WordNet method; nouns extracted by the baseline method are always included.

6 Evaluation and Results

The measure used has been F-measure (F_1), see Eq. 1. The design of the experiments has intentionally been wide to assess how either high recall or high precision can be obtained; depending on the use of the resulting sets of deverbatives, one may prefer precision (P) or recall (R); therefore, for all experiments, we report, in addition to the standard F_1 measure, also both P and R.

All experiments have been evaluated on all three versions of the evaluation dataset (see Sect. 4 for more details on the evaluation dataset properties and the preparation process). We also report results on the development dataset, just as a sanity check. The results are summarized in Table 2.

Experiment	Measure	development dataset	intersection eval. data	union eval. data	majority eval. data
baseline	R	.3402	.3470	.1843	.3214
	P	.9151	.3720	.9640	.7920
	F_1	.4960	.3591	.3094	.4573
+WordNet	R	.3471	.3657	.1934	.3312
	P	.8519	.3415	.8815	.7108
	F_1	.4932	.3532	.3172	.4518
+parallel	R	.4417	.4664	.2798	*.4302*
(PCEDT,	P	.4909	.2090	.6120	.4431
L1 filter)	F_1	.4650	.2887	.3841	.4366
+parallel	R	.4801	*.5075*	*.3150*	*.4659*
(CzEng,	P	.0196	.0082	.0247	.0172
L1 filter)	F_1	.0377	.0160	.0458	.0332
+parallel	R	.4156	*.4701*	.2492	.4107
(PCEDT,	P	.6998	.3158	.8170	.6341
shared arg.$_6$)	F_1	.5215	**.3778**	.3820	**.4985**
+parallel	R	.3663	.3806	.2064	.3442
(CzEng,	P	.8066	.3269	.8654	.6795
shared arg.$_{6605}$)	F_1	.5038	.3517	.3333	.4569
+WordNet	R	.4211	*.4813*	.2584	*.4188*
+parallel (PCEDT,	P	.6703	.2959	.7752	.5917
shared arg.$_6$)	F_1	.5173	.3665	**.3876**	.4905
+WordNet	R	.3731	.4067	.2194	.3604
+parallel (CzEng,	P	.7619	.3079	.8107	.6271
shared arg.$_{6605}$)	F_1	.5009	.3505	.3454	.4577

Table 2: Summary of results of all experiments

The best F_1 scores are in **bold**, the best and second best (and close) recall scores are in *italics*.

To interpret the table, one has to take into account the ultimate goals for which the discovered deverbatives will be used. If the goal is to acquire all possible nouns which could possibly be deverbatives, and select and process them manually to extend, say, an existing noun valency / predicate argument lexicon, recall R will be more important than precision or the equal-weighted F_1 score. On the other hand, if the results are to be used, e.g., as features in downstream automatic processing or in NLP machine learning experiments, the F_1 measure, or perhaps precision P, would be preferred as the main selection criterion. It is clear that there are huge differences among the tested extraction methods, and thus all possible needs can be served by selecting the appropriate method.

Regardless of the use of the results, we can see several general trends:

- The baseline method, which used only a limited number of regular derivations of the base verb (cf. Sect. 5) and no additional lexicons or corpora, is actually quite strong and it was surpassed only by the optimized parallel corpus method(s).

- WordNet does not help much, if at all, both in the basic system where it is only combined with the baseline and in the last two systems when it adds to the results of the optimized systems. The increase in recall - which was the assumed contribution of WordNet - is small and the loss in precision substantial, even as F_1 grows.

- A manually annotated corpus, not surprisingly, gets much more precise results than a large but only automatically analyzed corpus (PCEDT vs. CzEng). The precision of the results when using CzEng alone with only simple filtering is so low that the result is beyond usefulness; however, the optimized method of filtering the results through (potentially) shared arguments between the verb and its deverbative gets surprisingly high precision even if not quite matches the PCEDT's overall F_1.

- Using a large parallel corpus (CzEng) with 100s of millions words gives us the opportunity to fine-tune the desired ratio between recall and precision by using the desired weight of recall on the F-measure definition, within a very wide range.

7 Discussion, Conclusions and Future Development

We have described and evaluated several methods for identifying and extracting deverbatives from base verbs using both lexical resources and parallel corpora. For development and evaluation, we have also created datasets, each containing 100 verbs, for further improvement of these methods and in order to allow for easy replication of our experiments.[13]

The best methods have used parallel corpora, where the translation served as a bridge to identify nouns that could possibly be deverbatives of the given base verbs through back-and-forth translation alignment. Due to the noisiness of such linking, filtering had to be applied; perhaps not surprisingly, the best method uses optimized (machine-learned) threshold for considering words shared in the deep linguistic analysis of the base verb and its potential deverbative. This simple optimization used the F_1 measure as its objective function, but any other measure could be used as well, for example F_2 if recall is to be valued twice as much as precision, etc.; this is possible thanks to the wide range of recall / precision values for the possible range of the threshold.[14]

We will further explore the argument-sharing method, adding other features, such as the semantic relation between the verb/deverbative and their arguments, in order to lower the filtering threshold and therefore to help increase recall while not hurting precision (too much). Using additional features might require new machine learning methods as well.

Finally, we will also independently check and improve our test datasets; while the "majority" voting which we have used in our experiments as the main evaluation set is an accepted practice, we would like to further improve the quality of the datasets by thoroughly checking whether the valency transformation rules as described especially in (Kolářová, 2006; Kolářová, 2005) do hold for the verb-noun pairs recorded in the datasets, amending them as necessary.

A natural continuation would be to test the methods developed on other languages, primarily English, even if the morphosyntactic transformations between a verb and a noun are not as rich as for inflective languages (such as Czech which we have used here).

We believe that for one of the intended uses of the described method, namely extending a valency lexicon of nouns with new deverbatives linked to their base verbs, the system could be used in its current state as a preprocessor suggesting such nouns for subsequent manual checking and selection; the argument sharing method optimization can be then used to balance the right ratio between desired high recall and bearable precision.

---

[13]The development and evaluation datasets will be freely available under the CC license, and the code will be also available as open source at http://lindat.cz.

[14]Upper bound for recall was at over 72% by using CzEng, see the discussion about optimization in Sect. 5.3.2.

Acknowledgments

This work has been supported by the grant No. DG16P02B048 of the Ministry of Culture of the Czech Republic. In addition, it has also been using language resources developed, stored and distributed by the LINDAT/CLARIN project of the Ministry of Education of the Czech Republic (projects LM2010013 and LM2015071). We would like to thank the reviewers of the paper for valuable comments and suggestions.

References

Harald R. Baayen, Richard Piepenbrock, and Leon Gulikers. 1995. *The CELEX Lexical Database. Release 2 (CD-ROM)*. Linguistic Data Consortium, University of Pennsylvania, Philadelphia, Pennsylvania.

Marion Baranes and Benoît Sagot. 2014. A language-independent approach to extracting derivational relations from an inflectional lexicon. In *Proceedings of the Ninth International Conference on Language Resources and Evaluation (LREC'14)*, Reykjavik, Iceland, May.

Ondřej Bojar, Zdeněk Žabokrtský, Ondřej Dušek, Petra Galuščáková, Martin Majliš, David Mareček, Jiří Maršík, Michal Novák, Martin Popel, and Aleš Tamchyna. 2011. Czech-English Parallel Corpus 1.0 (CzEng 1.0). LINDAT/CLARIN digital library at Institute of Formal and Applied Linguistics, Charles University in Prague.

Ondřej Bojar, Zdeněk Žabokrtský, Ondřej Dušek, Petra Galuščáková, Martin Majliš, David Mareček, Jiří Maršík, Michal Novák, Martin Popel, and Aleš Tamchyna. 2012. The Joy of Parallelism with CzEng 1.0. In *Proceedings of the 8th International Conference on Language Resources and Evaluation (LREC 2012)*, pages 3921–3928, İstanbul, Turkey. European Language Resources Association.

Ondřej Bojar, Ondřej Dušek, Tom Kocmi, Jindřich Libovický, Michal Novák, Martin Popel, Roman Sudarikov, and Dušan Variš. 2016. CzEng 1.6: Enlarged Czech-English Parallel Corpus with Processing Tools Dockered. In Petr Sojka et al., editor, *Text, Speech, and Dialogue: 19th International Conference, TSD 2016*, number 9924 in Lecture Notes in Computer Science, pages 231–238. Masaryk University, Springer International Publishing.

Silvie Cinková. 2006. From PropBank to EngValLex: Adapting the PropBank-Lexicon to the Valency Theory of the Functional Generative Description. In *Proceedings of the 5th International Conference on Language Resources and Evaluation (LREC 2006)*, pages 2170–2175, Genova, Italy. ELRA.

G. Graffi. 1994. *Sintassi*. Le strutture del linguaggio. Il Mulino.

Jan Hajič and Jaroslava Hlaváčová. 2016. MorfFlex CZ 160310. LINDAT/CLARIN digital library at Institute of Formal and Applied Linguistics, Charles University in Prague.

Jan Hajič, Eva Hajičová, Jarmila Panevová, Petr Sgall, Ondřej Bojar, Silvie Cinková, Eva Fučíková, Marie Mikulová, Petr Pajas, Jan Popelka, Jiří Semecký, Jana Šindlerová, Jan Štěpánek, Josef Toman, Zdeňka Urešová, and Zdeněk Žabokrtský. 2012. Announcing Prague Czech-English Dependency Treebank 2.0. In *Proceedings of the 8th LREC 2012)*, pages 3153–3160, Istanbul, Turkey. ELRA.

Jan Hajič. 2004. *Disambiguation of Rich Inflection (Computational Morphology of Czech)*. Karolinum.

E. Hajičová and P. Sgall. 2003. Dependency Syntax in Functional Generative Description. *Dependenz und Valenz–Dependency and Valency*, 1:570–592.

Jan Hajič, Jarmila Panevová, Eva Hajičová, Petr Sgall, Petr Pajas, Jan Štěpánek, Jiří Havelka, Marie Mikulová, Zdeněk Žabokrtský, Magda Ševčíková Razímová, and Zdeňka Urešová. 2006. *Prague Dependency Treebank 2.0*. Number LDC2006T01. LDC, Philadelphia, PA, USA.

P. Kingsbury and M. Palmer. 2002. From Treebank to Propbank. In *Proceedings of the 3rd International Conference on Language Resources and Evaluation (LREC-2002)*, pages 1989–1993. Citeseer.

Veronika Kolářová. 2005. *Valence deverbativních substantiv v češtině (PhD thesis)*. Ph.D. thesis, Univerzita Karlova v Praze, Matematicko-fyzikální fakulta, Praha, Czechia.

Veronika Kolářová. 2006. Valency of Deverbal Nouns in Czech. *The Prague Bulletin of Mathematical Linguistics*, (86):5–20.

Veronika Kolářová, 2014. *Special valency behavior of Czech deverbal nouns*, chapter 2, pages 19–60. Studies in Language Companion Series, 158. John Benjamins Publishing Company, Amsterdam, The Netherlands.

Mitchell P. Marcus, Beatrice Santorini, and Mary Ann Marcinkiewicz. 1993. Building a Large Annotated Corpus of English: The Penn Treebank. *COMPUTATIONAL LINGUISTICS*, 19(2):313–330.

Adam Meyers, Ruth Reeves, Catherine Macleod, Rachel Szekely, Veronika Zielinska, Brian Young, and Ralph Grishman. 2004. The NomBank Project: An Interim Report. In *In Proceedings of the NAACL/HLT Workshop on Frontiers in Corpus Annotation*, pages 70–77, Boston. Association for Computational Linguistics.

A. Meyers. 2008. Using Treebank, Dictionaries and GLARF to Improve NomBank Annotation. In *Proceedings of The Linguistic Annotation Workshop, LREC 2008*, Marrakesh, Morocco.

Marie Mikulová, Alevtina Bémová, Jan Hajič, Eva Hajičová, Jiří Havelka, Veronika Kolářová, Markéta Lopatková, Petr Pajas, Jarmila Panevová, Magda Razímová, Petr Sgall, Jan Štěpánek, Zdeňka Urešová, Kateřina Veselá, Zdeněk Žabokrtský, and Lucie Kučová. 2005. Anotace na tektogramatické rovině Pražského závislostního korpusu. Anotátorská příručka. Technical Report TR-2005-28, ÚFAL MFF UK, Prague, Prague.

Karel Pala and Pavel Smrž. 2004. Building Czech WordNet. *Romanian Journal of Information Science and Technology*, 7(2-3):79–88.

Karel Pala, Tomáš Čapek, Barbora Zajíčková, Dita Bartůšková, Kateřina Kulková, Petra Hoffmannová, Eduard Bejček, Pavel Straňák, and Jan Hajič. 2011. Czech WordNet 1.9 PDT. LINDAT/CLARIN digital library at Institute of Formal and Applied Linguistics, Charles University in Prague.

Martha Palmer, Daniel Gildea, and Paul Kingsbury. 2005. The Proposition Bank: An Annotated Corpus of Semantic Roles. *Computational Linguistics*, 31(1):71–106.

Martha Palmer, Jena D. Hwang, Susan Windisch Brown, Karin Kipper Schuler, and Arrick Lanfranchi. 2009. Leveraging lexical resources for the detection of event relations. In *Learning by Reading and Learning to Read, Papers from the 2009 AAAI Spring Symposium, Technical Report SS-09-07, Stanford, California, USA, March 23-25, 2009*, pages 81–87.

Jarmila Panevová. 1974. On verbal Frames in Functional Generative Description. *Prague Bulletin of Mathematical Linguistics*, 22:3–40.

Jarmila Panevová. 1994. Valency frames and the meaning of the sentence. *The Prague School of Structural and Functional Linguistics*, 41:223–243.

Jarmila Panevová. 1996. More remarks on control. *Prague Linguistic Circle Papers*, 2(1):101–120.

Magda Ševčíková and Zdeněk Žabokrtský. 2014. Word-Formation Network for Czech. In Nicoletta Calzolari, Khalid Choukri, Thierry Declerck, Hrafn Loftsson, Bente Maegaard, and Joseph Mariani, editors, *Proceedings of the 9th International Conference on Language Resources and Evaluation (LREC 2014)*, pages 1087–1093, Reykjavík, Iceland. European Language Resources Association.

Matthew Stone, Tonia Bleam, Christine Doran, and Martha Palmer. 2000. Lexicalized grammar and the description of motion events *. In *TAG+5 Fifth International Workshop on Tree Adjoining Grammars and Related Formalisms*. Paris, France.

Jana Straková, Milan Straka, and Jan Hajič. 2014. Open-source tools for morphology, lemmatization, POS tagging and named entity recognition. In *Proceedings of 52nd Annual Meeting of the Association for Computational Linguistics: System Demonstrations*, pages 13–18, Stroudsburg, PA, USA. Johns Hopkins University, Baltimore, MD, USA, Association for Computational Linguistics.

Zdeňka Urešová, Eva Fučíková, and Jana Šindlerová. 2016. CzEngVallex: a bilingual Czech-English valency lexicon. *The Prague Bulletin of Mathematical Linguistics*, 105:17–50.

Zdeňka Urešová. 2011. *Valenční slovník Pražského závislostního korpusu (PDT-Vallex)*, volume 1 of *Studies in Computational and Theoretical Linguistics*. UFAL MFF UK, Prague, Czech Republic.

Jonáš Vidra, Zdeněk Žabokrtský, Magda Ševčíková, and Milan Straka. 2015. Derinet v 1.0, http://lindat.cz.

Jonáš Vidra. 2015. Implementation of a search engine for derinet. In Jakub Yaghob, editor, *Proceedings of the 15th conference ITAT 2015: Slovenskočeský NLP workshop (SloNLP 2015)*, volume 1422 of *CEUR Workshop Proceedings*, pages 100–106, Praha, Czechia. Charles University in Prague, CreateSpace Independent Publishing Platform.

Zdeněk Žabokrtský and Magda Ševčíková. 2014. DeriNet: Lexical Network of Derivational Word-Formation Relations in Czech.

The Grammar of English Deverbal Compounds and their Meaning

Gianina Iordăchioaia
University of Stuttgart
Stuttgart, Germany
gianina
@ifla.uni-stuttgart.de

Lonneke van der Plas
University of Malta
Valletta, Malta
lonneke.vanderplas
@um.edu.mt

Glorianna Jagfeld
University of Stuttgart
Stuttgart, Germany
glorianna.jagfeld
@gmail.com

Abstract

We present an interdisciplinary study on the interaction between the interpretation of noun-noun deverbal compounds (DCs; e.g., *task assignment*) and the morphosyntactic properties of their deverbal heads in English. Underlying hypotheses from theoretical linguistics are tested with tools and resources from computational linguistics. We start with Grimshaw's (1990) insight that deverbal nouns are ambiguous between argument-supporting nominal (ASN) readings, which inherit verbal arguments (e.g., *the assignment of the tasks)*, and the less verbal and more lexicalized Result Nominal and Simple Event readings (e.g., *a two-page assignment)*. Following Grimshaw, our hypothesis is that the former will realize object arguments in DCs, while the latter will receive a wider range of interpretations like root compounds headed by non-derived nouns (e.g., *chocolate box)*. Evidence from a large corpus assisted by machine learning techniques confirms this hypothesis, by showing that, besides other features, the realization of internal arguments by deverbal heads outside compounds (i.e., the most distinctive ASN-property in Grimshaw 1990) is a good predictor for an object interpretation of non-heads in DCs.

1 Introduction

Deverbal compounds (DCs) are noun-noun compounds whose head is derived from a verb by means of a productive nominalizing suffix such as *-al, -ance, -er, -ion, -ing*, or *-ment*, and whose non-head is usually interpreted as an object of the base verb, as illustrated in (1). *Root compounds* differ from DCs in that they need not be headed by deverbal nouns and their interpretation may vary with the context.[1] For instance, a root compound like *chocolate box* may refer to a box with chocolate or one that has chocolate color etc, depending on the context, while others like *gear box* have a more established meaning. DCs have been at the heart of theoretical linguistic research since the early days of generative grammar precisely due to their special status between lexicon and grammar (Roeper and Siegel, 1978; Selkirk, 1982; Grimshaw, 1990; Ackema and Neeleman, 2004; Lieber, 2004; Borer, 2013, among others). As compounds, they are new lexemes, i.e., they should be part of the lexicon, and yet, their structure and interpretation retain properties from argument-supporting nominals (ASNs) and correlated verb phrases, which suggests that they involve some grammar (cf. (2)).

(1)   house ren**tal**, title insur**ance**, oven-clean**er**, crop destruc**tion**, drug traffick**ing**, tax adjust**ment**

(2)   a.   crop destruction – destruction of crops – to destroy crops

       b.   tax adjustment – adjustment of taxes – to adjust taxes

Rooted in the long debate on synthetic compounds (see Olsen (2015) for an overview), two types of analyses have been proposed to DCs. What we call *the grammar-analysis* posits a grammar component

---

[1]Grimshaw (1990) argues that compounds headed by zero-derived nouns, e.g., *bee sting, dog bite*, are root compounds, since they do not preserve verbal event structure properties. In this paper, we will propose that even some of the DCs that are headed by suffix-based deverbal nouns form root compounds if their heads lack verbal properties and exhibit a more lexicalized meaning: cf. ASN vs. Result Nominal interpretation and the discussion in Section 2.1.

Proceedings of the Workshop on Grammar and Lexicon: Interactions and Interfaces,
pages 81–91, Osaka, Japan, December 11 2016.

in their structure and draws correlations between DCs and ASNs (or VPs), as in (2) (Roeper and Siegel, 1978; Grimshaw, 1990; Ackema and Neeleman, 2004, most notably). *The lexicon-analysis* argues that DCs are just like root compounds and derive their meaning from the lexical semantics of the nouns, whether derived or not (e.g., Selkirk 1982, Lieber 2004). The various implementations take different theory-driven shapes, but the baseline for our study is the question whether DCs retain properties from ASNs (and, implicitly, VPs) or behave like root compounds.

The main property that DCs share with ASNs and VPs is the realization of an argument as the non-head, more precisely, the internal argument of the original verb, which in the VP usually appears as a direct object: see *crop* and *tax* in (2). Importantly, unlike ASNs, which may realize both external and internal arguments as prepositional/genitive phrases, DCs have a reduced structure made up of two nouns, which can host only one argument besides the head (see (3)).

> (3)   a.   The **hurricane** destroyed the **crops**.
>
>   b.   the destruction of the **crops** by the **hurricane**
>
>   c.   **crop** destruction

For grammar-analyses it is crucial to argue that the argument realized in DCs must be the lowest one in the VP, namely, the internal/object argument (see the first sister principle of Roeper and Siegel (1978) and the thematic hierarchy in Grimshaw (1990)). Subject/external arguments are known to be introduced by higher/more complex event structure (Kratzer, 1996) and, given that DCs cannot accommodate the full event structure of the original verb, it must be the lowest component that includes the object. However, the main challenge to these analyses is that, indeed, we find DCs whose non-heads come very close to receiving a subject interpretation, as exemplified in (4). In view of this evidence, Borer (2013) offers a syntactic implementation of the lexicon-analysis, in which all DCs are root compounds and their (external or internal) argument interpretation should be resolved by the context.[2]

> (4)   **hurricane** destruction, **teacher** recommendation, **government** decision, **court** investigation

In this paper, we challenge Borer (2013) as the most recent lexicon-analysis by showing that high ASN-hood of a head noun predicts an object interpretation of the non-head. Our methodology draws on evidence from a large corpus of naturally occurring text. This realm of information is analysed using simple machine learning techniques. We designed extraction patterns tailored to the properties that are associated with ASNs to collect counts for the selected deverbal heads. These counts are used as features in a logistic regression classifier that tries to predict the covert relation between heads and non-heads. We find that a frequent realization of the internal argument (i.e., high ASN-hood) with particular deverbal nouns is indeed a good predictor for the object relation in compounds headed by these nouns. This confirms Grimshaw's claim and our hypothesis that DCs involve some minimal grammar of the base verb, which compositionally includes only the internal/object argument. Non-object readings are obtained with heads that do not preserve ASN-properties and implicitly build root compounds. The theoretical implication of this study is that compounds headed by deverbal nouns are ambiguous between real argumental DCs, as in (2), and root compounds, as in (4).

2   Previous work

In this section we introduce the linguistic background for our study and review previous work on interpreting deverbal compounds from the natural language processing literature.

2.1   Linguistic background

In this paper we build on two previous contributions to the theoretical debate on DCs: Grimshaw (1990) and Borer (2013). The former supports a grammar-analysis, the latter a lexicon-analysis.

---

[2]As is well-known, since Chomsky (1970), linguistic theories on word formation have been split between 'lexicalist' and 'syntactic'. The former assume that words have lexical entries and derivation is done by lexical rules, while the latter take word formation to follow general syntactic principles. This distinction is in fact orthogonal to the lexicon- vs. grammar-analyses of DCs that we refer to here, in that ironically Grimshaw (1990) is a lexicalist theory that posits grammar (i.e., event structure) in DCs, while Borer (2013) is a syntactic theory that denies the influence of any grammar principles in the make-up of DCs.

Grimshaw (1990) introduces a three-way distinction in the interpretation of deverbal nouns: Argument-supporting Nominals (ASNs; in her terminology, *complex event nominals*), Result Nominals, and Simple Event Nominals. The main difference is between ASNs and the other two categories in that only ASNs inherit event structure from the base verb and, implicitly, accommodate verbal arguments. Result Nominals are more lexicalized than ASNs; they refer to the result of the verbal action, often in the shape of a concrete object. Simple Event Nominals are also lexicalized but have an event/process interpretation like some non-derived nouns such as *event* or *ceremony*. The deverbal noun *examination* may receive a Result Nominal (RN) reading, synonymous to *exam*, when it doesn't realize arguments, as in (5a), or it may have an ASN reading, when it realizes the object, as in (5b). The predicate *was on the table* selects the RN reading, this is why, it is incompatible with the ASN. When the external/subject argument is realized in an ASN, the internal/object argument must be present as well (see (5c)); otherwise, the deverbal noun will receive a Result or Simple Event reading (see Grimshaw 1990: 53 for details).

(5)   a.   The examination/exam was on the table.   (RN)

      b.   The examination **of the patients** took a long time/*was on the table.   (ASN)

      c.   The (**doctor's**) examination of the patients (**by the doctor**) took a long time.   (ASN)

Given that in Grimshaw's (1990) work Result Nominals and Simple Event Nominals pattern alike in not realizing argument structure and display similar morphosyntactic properties in contrast to ASNs, we refer to both as RNs, i.e., as more lexicalized and less compositional readings of the deverbal noun. Grimshaw (1990) enumerates several properties that distinguish ASNs from RNs, which we summarize in Table 1, a selection from Alexiadou and Grimshaw (2008). We come back to these properties in Section 3.4.

Property	ASN-reading	RN-reading
Obligatory internal arguments	Yes	No
Agent-oriented modifiers	Yes	No
By-phrases are arguments	Yes	No
Aspectual *in/for*-adverbials	Yes	No
Frequent, constant require plural	No	Yes
May appear in plural	No	Yes

Table 1: Morphosyntactic properties distinguishing between ASNs and RNs

Within this background, Grimshaw argues that DCs are headed by ASNs and fundamentally different from root compounds. In her approach, this means that the heads of DCs inherit event structure from the base verb, which accommodates argument structure like the ASNs in (5b-5c). Importantly, however, DCs have a reduced structure made up of two nouns, which entails that the head can realize only one argument inside the compound. In Grimshaw's approach, this predicts that the head inherits a reduced verbal event structure which should be able to accommodate only the lowest argument of the VP, namely, the object. In line with this reasoning and on the basis of her thematic hierarchy, Grimshaw argues that arguments other than themes (realized as direct objects) are excluded from DCs. These include both prepositional objects realizing goals or locations and subjects that realize external arguments, as illustrated in (6).

(6)   a.   **gift**-giving to children vs. ***child**-giving of gifts (to give gifts **to children**)

      b.   **flower**-arranging in vases vs. ***vase**-arranging of flowers (to arrange flowers **in vases**)

      c.   **book**-reading by students vs. ***student**-reading of books (**Students** read books.)

In her discussion of DCs, Grimshaw (1990) does not address the properties from Table 1 on DC heads to show that they behave like ASNs. Borer (2013) uses some of these properties to argue precisely against the ASN status of DC heads. We retain two of her arguments: the lack of aspectual modifiers and argumental *by*-phrases. Borer uses data as in (7) to argue that, unlike the corresponding ASNs, DCs disallow aspectual *in-/for*-adverbials and fail to realize *by*-phrases (contra Grimshaw's (6c)).

(7) a. the demolition of the house **by the army** *in two hours* (ASN)

  b. the maintenance of the facility **by the management** *for two years* (ASN)

  c. the house demolition (***by the army**) (**in two hours*) (DC)

  d. the facility maintenance (***by the management**) (**for two years*) (DC)

For Borer, the unavailability of aspectual modifiers indicates that event structure is entirely missing from DCs, so they cannot be headed by ASNs. Her conclusion is that DCs are headed by RNs and behave like root compounds. Thus the object interpretation of their non-head is just as valid as a subject or prepositional interpretation, depending on the context of use. In support of this, she quotes DCs as in (4) above, whose non-heads are most likely interpreted as subjects.

In our study, we will show that the presence of *of*-phrases that realize the internal argument with head nouns outside compounds is a good predictor for an object interpretation of the non-head in DCs, supporting Grimshaw's approach. Moreover, the appearance of a *by*-phrase in DCs – which pace Borer (2013) is well attested in the corpus – seems to be harmful to our model, which shows us that the *by*-phrase test is not very telling for the structure and interpretation of DCs.[3]

2.2 Interpretation of DCs in natural language processing literature

Research on deverbal compounds (referred to with the term *nominalizations*) in the NLP literature has focused on the task of predicting the underlying relation between deverbal heads and non-heads. Relation inventories range from 2-class (Lapata, 2002) to 3-class (Nicholson and Baldwin, 2006), and 13-class (Grover et al., 2005), where the 2-class inventory is restricted to the subject and direct object relations, the 3-class adds prepositional complements, and the 13-class further specifies the prepositional complement.

Although we are performing the same task, our underlying aim is different. Instead of trying to reach state-of-the-art performance in the prediction task, we are interested in the contribution of a range of features based on linguistic literature, in particular, morphosyntactic features of the deverbal head. Features used in the NLP literature mainly rely on occurrences of the verb associated with the deverbal head and the non-head in large corpora. The idea behind this is simple. For example, a verb associated with a deverbal noun – such as *slaughter* from *slaughtering* – is often seen in a direct object relation with a specific noun, such as *animal*. The covert relation between head and non-head in *animal slaughtering* is therefore predicted to be direct object. To remedy problems related to data sparseness, several smoothing techniques are introduced (Lapata, 2002) as well as the use of Z-scores (Nicholson and Baldwin, 2006). In addition to these statistics on verb-argument relations, Lapata (2002) uses features such as the suffix and the direct context of the compound.

Apart from the suffix, the features used in these works are meant to capture encyclopaedic knowledge, usually building on lexicalist theoretical approaches that list several covert semantic relations typically available in compounds (cf. most notably, Levi 1978; see Fokkens 2007, for a critical overview). The morphosyntactic features we use are fundamentally different from the syntactic relations used in this NLP literature and described above (cf. also Rösiger et al. (2015), for German). Our features are head-specific and rely on insights from linguistic theories that posit an abstract structural correlation between DCs and the compositional event structure of the original verb, as mirrored in the behavior of the derived nominals (as ASNs or RNs).

In addition, our selection of DCs is different. We carefully selected a balanced number of DCs based on the suffixes *-al*, *-ance*, *-ing*, *-ion*, and *-ment* within three different frequency bands. These suffixes derive eventive nouns which should allow both object and subject readings of their non-heads in compounds, unlike *-ee* and *-er*, which are biased for one or the other. Moreover, previous studies also included zero-derived nouns, which we excluded because they mostly behave like RNs (Grimshaw, 1990).

3 Materials and methods

This section presents the corpora and tools we used, the methods we adopted for the selection of DCs, the annotation effort, the feature extraction, as well as the machine learning techniques we employed.

---

[3]We haven't included aspectual adverbials in our study for now, because acceptability judgements on ASNs usually decrease in their presence and we expect them to be very rare in the corpus.

Frequency	ING	ION	MENT	AL	ANCE
High	spending	production	enforcement	proposal	insurance
	building	protection	development	approval	performance
	training	reduction	movement	withdrawal	assistance
	bombing	construction	treatment	arrival	clearance
	trafficking	consumption	punishment	rental	surveillance
Medium	killing	supervision	deployment	renewal	assurance
	writing	destruction	replacement	burial	disturbance
	counseling	cultivation	placement	survival	dominance
	firing	deprivation	assignment	denial	acceptance
	teaching	instruction	adjustment	upheaval	tolerance
Low	weighting	demolition	reinforcement	retrieval	defiance
	baking	anticipation	realignment	acquittal	reassurance
	chasing	expulsion	empowerment	disapproval	endurance
	measuring	obstruction	mistreatment	rebuttal	remembrance
	mongering	deportation	abandonment	dispersal	ignorance

Table 2: Samples of the suffix-based selection of deverbal head nouns

3.1 Corpus and tools

For the selection of DCs and to gather corpus statistics on them, we used the Annotated Gigaword corpus (Napoles et al., 2012) as one of the largest general-domain English corpora that contains several layers of linguistic annotation. We used the following available automatic preprocessing tools and annotations: sentence segmentation (Gillick, 2009), tokenization, lemmatization and POS tags (Stanford's CoreNLP toolkit[4]), as well as constituency parses (Huang et al., 2010) converted to syntactic dependency trees with Stanford's CoreNLP toolkit. The corpus encompasses 10M documents from 7 news sources and more than 4G words. As news outlets often repeat news items in subsequent news streams, the corpus contains a substantial amount of duplication. To improve the reliability of our corpus counts, we removed exact duplicate sentences within each of the 1010 corpus files, resulting in a 16% decrease of the corpus size.

3.2 Selection of deverbal compounds

We selected a varied yet controlled set of DCs from the Gigaword corpus. We first collected 25 nouns (over three frequency bands: low, medium, and high) for each of the suffixes *-ing*, *-ion*, *-ment*, *-al* and *-ance*. These suffixes usually derive both ASNs and RNs, unlike zero-derived nouns like *attack*, *abuse*, which, according to Grimshaw (1990), mostly behave like RNs. We excluded nouns based on the suffixes *-er* and *-ee* because they denote one participant (subject, respectively, object) of the verb, implicitly blocking this interpretation on the non-head (cf. *police$_{subj}$ trainee – dog$_{obj}$ trainer*). The base verbs were selected to allow transitive uses, i.e., both subjects and objects are in principle possible.[5] For illustration, Table 2 offers samples of five deverbal nouns per each frequency range and suffix. For each such selected noun we then extracted the 25 most frequent compounds that they appeared as heads of, where available.[6] After removing some repetitions we ended up with a total of 3111 DCs.

3.3 Annotation effort

We had all DCs annotated by two trained American English speakers, who were asked to label them as OBJ, SUBJ, OTHER, or ERROR, depending on the relation that the DC establishes between the verb from which its head noun is derived and the non-head. For instance, DCs such as in (2) would be labeled as OBJ, while those in (4) would be SUBJ. OTHER was the label for prepositional objects (e.g., *adoption*

---

[4]http://nlp.stanford.edu/software/corenlp.shtml

[5]*Arrive* is the only intransitive verb we included, but it is unaccusative, so it realizes an internal argument.

[6]Some deverbal nouns were not so productive in compounds and appeared with fewer than 25 different non-heads. To ensure cleaner results, in future work we aim to balance the dataset for the number of compounds per each head noun.

counseling 'somebody counsels somebody on adoption') or attributive uses in compounds (e.g., *surprise arrival* 'an arrival that was a surprise'). ERROR was meant to identify the errors of the POS tagger (e.g., *face abandonment* originates in 'they face$_V$ abandonment'). We allowed the annotators to use multiple labels and let them indicate the preference ordering (using '>') or ambiguity (using '–').

We used the original annotations from both annotators to create a final list of compounds and the labels that they both agreed on. We kept the multiple labels for ambiguous cases and selected only the preferred reading, when there was one. We labeled them as OBJ, NOBJ, DIS(agreement between annotators), AMBIG, or ERROR. If one annotator indicated ambiguity and the other selected only one of the readings, we selected the reading available to both. We found only two cases of ambiguity where both annotators agreed. We removed the fully ambiguous DCs together with the 163 errors and the 547 cases of disagreement.[7] This left us with 2399 DCs that we could process for our purposes. To allow for multi-class and binary classification of the data, we kept two versions: one in which OTHER and SUBJ were conflated to NOBJ, and one in which we kept them separate. In this paper, we focus on the binary classification. The resulting data set was skewed with OBJ prevailing: 1502 OBJ vs. 897 NOBJ.

3.4 Extracting features for ASN-hood

To determine how the ASN-hood of DC heads fares in predicting an OBJ or NOBJ interpretation of the non-head we constructed 7 indicative patterns mostly inspired by Grimshaw's ASN properties in Table 1, for which we collected evidence from the Gigaword corpus. They are all summarized in Table 3 with illustrations.

The feature *suffix* is meant to show us whether a particular suffix is prone to realizing an OBJ or NOBJ relation in compounds (Grimshaw, for instance, was arguing that *ing*-nominals are mostly ASNs, predicting a preference for OBJ in DCs). The features from 2 to 4 are indicative of an ASN status of the head noun when it occurs outside compounds. As shown in Table 1, Grimshaw argued that ASNs appear only in the singular (see feature 2. *percentage_sg_outside*). In the same spirit, we counted the frequency of *of*-phrases (feature 3) when the head is in the singular. The occurrence with adjectives is very infrequent, so we counted them all together under feature 4. *sum_adjectives*. For *frequent* and *constant* we again counted only the singular forms, given that Grimshaw argued that these may also combine with RNs in the plural. As agent-oriented modifiers, *intentional*, *deliberate*, and *careful* are only expected with ASNs. The features 5. *percentage_sg_inside* and 6. *percentage_by_sg_inside* test ASN-hood of the head noun when appearing inside compounds. Remember that Grimshaw documented *by*-phrases in DCs (see (6c), contra Borer's (7c-7d)). We didn't consider the parallel realization of *of*-phrases *inside* compounds, since there is no theoretical claim on them and they would have produced too much noise, given that the object argument that *of*-phrases realize would typically appear as a non-head in DCs.[8]

The rationale behind checking the ASN-properties of DC heads when they appear outside and inside DCs is that deverbal nouns exhibit different degrees of ambiguity between ASNs and RNs with tendencies towards one or the other, which would be preserved in compounds and reflected in the OBJ/ NOBJ interpretation. Our last individual feature 7. *percentage_head_in_DC* indicates the frequency of the head in compounds and is meant to measure whether the noun heads that appear very frequently in compounds exhibit any preference for an OBJ or NOBJ relation. If such a relation associates with a high preference of the head to appear in compounds, this tells us that this relation is typical of DCs.

3.4.1 Technical details of the feature extraction method

For the *inside_compound* features we collected the compounds by matching the DCs in the corpus with the word form of the non-head and the lemma of the head and required that there be no other directly preceding or succeeding nouns or proper nouns. Conversely, the *outside_compound* features apply to head nouns appearing without any noun or proper noun next to them. We determined the grammatical number of a noun (compound) by its POS tag (the POS tag of its head).

---

[7] We will base our studies on the agreed-upon relations only. However, for the sake of completeness and for showing that the task is well-defined we computed the simple inter-annotator agreement excluding the error class and the negligible class for ambiguous cases. It amounts to 81.5%.

[8] We also discarded *by*-phrases outside compounds, since they would have to be considered in combination with an *of*-phrase (Grimshaw, 1990, cf. (5c)), and we wanted to focus on individual features in relation to the head noun.

Feature label	Description and illustration
1. *suffix*	The suffix of the head noun: AL (rent**al**), ANCE (insur**ance**), ING (kill**ing**), ION (destruct**ion**), MENT (treat**ment**)
2. *percentage_sg_outside*	Percentage of the head's occurrences as singular outside compounds.
3. *percentage_of_sg_outside*	Percentage of the head's occurrences as singular outside compounds which realize a syntactic relation with an *of*-phrase. (e.g., *assignment* **of** *problems*).
4. *sum_adjectives*	Percentage of the head's occurrences in a modifier relation with one of the adjectives *frequent, constant, intentional, deliberate,* or *careful.*
5. *percentage_sg_inside*	Percentage of the head's occurrences as singular inside compounds.
6. *percentage_by_sg_inside*	Percentage of the head's occurrences as singular inside compounds which realize a syntactic relation with a *by*-phrase. (e.g., task assignment **by** teachers)
7. *percentage_head_in_DC*	Percentage of the head's occurrences within a compound out of its total occurrences in the corpus.

Table 3: Indicative features

We counted a noun (or DC) as being in a syntactic relation with an *of-phrase* or *by-phrase*, if it (respectively, its head) governs a collapsed dependency labeled 'prep_of'/'prep_by'. As we were interested in prepositional phrases that realize internal, respectively, external arguments, but not in the ones appearing in temporal phrases (e.g., 'by Monday') or fixed expressions (e.g., 'by chance'), we excluded phrases headed by nouns that typically appear in these undesired phrases. We semi-automatically compiled these lists based on a multiword expression lexicon[9] and manually added entries. The lists comprise 161 entries for *by*-phrases and 53 for *of*-phrases. To compute the feature *sum_adjectives* we counted how often each noun appearing outside compounds governs a dependency relation labeled 'amod' where the dependent is an adjective (POS tag 'JJ') out of the lemmas *intentional, deliberate, careful, constant,* and *frequent.*

3.5 Using Machine Learning techniques for data exploration

The features listed in Table 3 are a mix of numerical (2 to 7) and categorical features (1). The dependent variable is a categorical feature that varies between one of the two annotation labels, OBJ and NOBJ. Thus, in order to test our hypotheses that the features in Table 3 are useful to predict the relation between the deverbal head and the non-head, we trained a Logistic Regression classifier[10] using these features.

The resulting model was tested on a test set for which we ensured that neither compounds, nor heads[11] were seen in the training data. To this end, we randomly selected two mid-frequency heads for each suffix and removed these from the training data to be put in the test data. We selected these for this initial experiment, because we expect mid-frequency heads to lead to most reliable results. High-frequency heads may show higher levels of idiosyncrasy and low-frequency heads may suffer from data sparseness. Since our goal is not to determine the realistic performance of our predictor, but to measure the contribution of features, this bias is acceptable. In future experiments, we plan to investigate the impact of frequency, which is not in the scope of the present study. This resulted in a division of roughly 90% training and 10% testing data.[12] Because the data set resulting from the annotation effort is skewed, and our selection of test instances introduces a different proportion of OBJ and NOBJ in the test and training sets, we balanced both sets by randomly removing instances with the OBJ relation from the training and test sets until both classes had equal numbers. The balanced training set consisted of 1614 examples,

---

[9]http://www.cs.cmu.edu/ ark/LexSem/

[10]We used version 3.8 for Linux of the Weka toolkit (Hall et al., 2009) and experimented with several other classifiers, focusing on those that have interpretable models (Decision Tree classifier, but also SVMs and Naive Bayes). All underperformed on our test set. However, the Decision Tree classifier also selects *percentage_head_in_DC* and *percentage_of_sg_outside* as the strongest predictors, just like the Logistic Regression classifier we are reporting on in Table 4.

[11]As can be seen in Table 3 the features are all head-specific.

[12]Multiple divisions of training and test data would lead to more reliable results, but we have to leave this for future work.

Features	Accuracy
All features	66.7%
All features, except *sg_percentage_outside*	66.7%
All features, except *sum_adjectives*	66.7%
All features, except *sg_percentage_inside*	66.7%
All features, except *percentage_head_in_DC*	46.7%†
All features, except *percentage_of_sg_outside*	56.1%†
All features, except *suffix*	61.7%†
All features, except *percentage_by_sg_inside*	71.1%†
Percentage_head_in_DC, *percentage_of_sg_outside*, and *suffix* combined	**76.1%**†

Table 4: Percent accuracy in ablation experiments. † indicates a statistically significant difference from the performance when including all features

and the test set of 180 examples. We ran ablation experiments to determine the individual contribution of each feature and combined the top-n features to see the predictive potential of the model.

4 Discussion of results

Our main concern was to determine whether our morphosyntactic head-related features have any predictive power. For this we compared the results using these features with a random baseline that lacked any information.[13] When using all features from Table 3, the classifier significantly outperforms[14] the random baseline (50%) with a reasonable margin (66.7%), showing that our features driven by linguistic theory have predictive power.

The ablation experiments in Table 4 shed light on the contribution of each feature.[15] The experiments show that *percentage_head_in_DC* has a high contribution to the overall model when it comes to predicting the relation between the deverbal head and the non-head, as its removal leads to a large drop in performance. The second strongest feature is *percentage_of_sg_outside*, and third comes *suffix*. One feature is actually harmful to the model: *percentage_by_sg_inside*, as its removal improves the accuracy of the classifier. The remaining features seem unimportant as their individual removal does not lead to performance differences. The best result we get on this task is 76,1%, when combining just the top-3 features (*percentage_head_in_DC*, *percentage_of_sg_outside*, and *suffix*). Although our test set is small, the performances indicated with the dagger symbol (†) lead to a statistically significant difference from the performance when including all features.

After inspecting the coefficients of the model, we are able to determine whether higher values of a given feature are indicating higher chances of an OBJ or NOBJ relation. Higher values of both *percentage_head_in_DC* and *percentage_of_sg_outside* lead to higher chances of predicting the OBJ class. For the categorical feature in our model, *suffix*, some point in the direction of a NOBJ interpretation (*-ance* and, less strongly, *-ment*), while others point in the direction of OBJ (*-ion* and, less strongly, *-al*), or do not have much predicting power as in the case of *-ing*.

From a theoretical point of view, these results have several implications. First, a high percentage of occurrences of the head inside compounds (i.e., *percentage_head_in_DC*) predicts an OBJ reading, which means that OBJ is the default interpretation of non-heads in DCs. Although this feature is not related to ASN-hood and previous linguistic literature does not mention it, we find it highly relevant as it defines the profile of DCs, in that deverbal heads that typically occur in compounds show a tendency to trigger an

---

[13] While stronger baselines would be needed to test the practical use of these features as compared to features used in the NLP literature, the random baseline is perfectly suitable to determine the predictive power of head features in theory.

[14] Significance numbers for these experiments in which training and test data are fixed were computed using a McNemar test with $p < .05$, because it makes relatively few type I errors (Dietterich, 1998).

[15] We realize that ablation does not lead to a complete picture of the strength of the features and their interplay. In addition, we tested several feature selection procedures by running the AttributeSelectedClassifier in Weka, because this allowed us to provide a separate test set. The best of these procedures (CfsSubsetEval) prefers subsets of features that are highly correlated with the class while having low inter-correlation and resulted in a non-optimal score of 70.3%. In future work, we would like to experiment with regularization to see which of the features' weights will be set to 0.

Head noun	Percentage_head_in_DC	OBJ
laundering	94.80%	95.45%
mongering	91.77%	100%
growing	68.68%	95.23%
trafficking	61.99%	100%
enforcement	53.68%	66.66%

Table 5: Head nouns with high compoundhood

Head noun	*Of*-phrases	OBJ
creation	80.51%	72.72%
avoidance	70.40%	100%
obstruction	65.25%	90.47%
removal	63.53%	92%
abandonment	55.90%	90%

Table 6: Head nouns with frequent *of*-phrases

OBJ interpretation of the non-head. This supports Grimshaw's claim that DCs structurally embed event structures with internal arguments.

Second, the next most predictive feature we found is the presence of an *of*-phrase realizing the internal argument of the head/verb (i.e., *percentage_of_sg_outside*), which again indicates an OBJ reading. In Grimshaw's approach, the realization of the internal argument is most indicative of the ASN status of a deverbal noun. This finding provides the strongest support for Grimshaw's claims and proves our hypothesis that high ASN-hood of the head triggers an OBJ interpretation of the non-head in DCs.

Tables 5 and 6 illustrate some examples related to these two most predictive features. Table 4 shows the five noun heads that present the highest percentage of appearance in a compound context and the percentage of OBJ readings among its compounds. Table 5 illustrates the five nouns heads that present highest percentage of *of*-phrases outside compounds and the corresponding percentage of OBJ readings.[16]

Third, the *suffix* feature is also predictive, with *-ion* and *-ance* indicating strong affinity for OBJ, respectively, NOBJ, and *-ing* being undetermined. These findings need further investigation, since the theoretical literature usually takes the suffixes *-ion*, *-ment*, *-ance*, and *-al* to be very similar. Should one wonder whether our overall results were not foreseeable given the selection of the suffixes in our dataset, we can name at least two reasons why this cannot be the case. First, the suffixes *-ing*, *-ion*, *-ment*, *-ance*, and *-al* all allow both OBJ and NOBJ readings and in terms of ASN-properties they all exhibit the ambiguity that Grimshaw describes. If any, then *-ing* should theoretically show a preference for OBJ, according to both Grimshaw's (1990) and Borer's (2013) approaches. Grimshaw takes *-ing* to mostly introduce ASNs, while Borer extensively argues that *-ing* lexically contributes an external argument, leaving only the internal argument available to be filled by the non-head in a compound. Thus, both approaches predict a preference for OBJ readings in DCs with *-ing*, while this suffix came out as undetermined between the two readings in our experiment. This means that the suffix that theoretically should have triggered the most foreseeable results, did not do so. Second, if the selection of the suffixes had had a decisive influence on the results, we would have expected the *suffix* feature to have more predictive power than it does and to trigger more unitary readings. But, as shown above, our results are mixed: while *-ion* prefers OBJ, *-ance* favors NOBJ. Within this background, more careful inspection of the data and further study on the individual suffixes would be necessary before we can conclude anything on the influence of each suffix.

Finally, we would like to comment on the noise that the feature *percentage_by_sg_inside* introduces into our model. Remember that the theoretical debate is unsettled as to whether *by*-phrases are possible in DCs. With (6c), Grimshaw indirectly states that they are possible, while Borer explicitly argues the opposite (see (7c-7d)). While theoretical analyses except for Borer (2013) show no clear stand, the fact that our model found this feature to be noisiest might be an indicator that *by*-phrases do not play a crucial role in the structure and interpretation of DCs.

Comparisons to performances in the NLP literature for the task of relation prediction make little sense at this time. The evaluation data in previous work are less carefully selected and cover a wider range of DC types (including zero-derived nominals and nouns ending in *-er* or *-ee*, among others). They used different statistical methods for prediction and different features. Moreover, it was not our aim to

---

[16]Note that despite having balanced the dataset for suffixes and number of compounds at the beginning, after the manual annotation some noun heads presented more errors than others as well as more disagreement among the annotators. This means that our final dataset is not so balanced as we initially designed it, but we will seek to do this in future work. In these tables we only included the nouns heads that were represented by at least 20 compounds in our final dataset.

reach state-of-the-art performance for a particular application. Our aim has been theoretical in nature and focused on understanding whether features of the head reported in the linguistic literature have predictive power, as well as determining which of these features are strongest.

For the sake of completeness, we would like to give the performance numbers reached by previous work. In the two-class prediction task, Lapata (2002) reaches an accuracy of 86.1% compared to a baseline of 61.5%, i.e, 24,6% above the baseline. The accuracy we achieve is 26,1% above the lower baseline of 50%.[17] Moreover, given the approach we used to discover useful indicators – that is, by means of a prediction task, in line with previous NLP work – it should be relatively easy to compare these results with previous studies in future work. We could test how our features based on the head compare with their encyclopaedic features for the prediction task, by evaluating our methods on their test sets and/or by incorporating their encyclopaedic features into our models for a direct comparison.

5 Conclusions

In this study, we identified two properties of deverbal noun heads with high predictive power in the interpretation of DCs: a head's predilection for DC-contexts and its frequent realization of internal arguments outside DCs. The latter is the most distinctive ASN-property that Grimshaw (1990) uses in her disambiguation of deverbal nouns, confirming her claim and our assumption that DCs have some event structure hosting internal arguments.

For the theoretical debate between the presence or absence of grammar in DCs, this means that we have two categories of DCs: some are part of the grammar and some should be part of the lexicon. On the one hand, we have DCs whose heads have ASN-properties and realize OBJ non-heads as predicted by the grammar-analysis (e.g., *drug trafficking*, *money laundering*, *law enforcement*). These DCs are part of the grammar and their OBJ interpretation can be compositionally derived from their event structure, so they do not need to be listed in the lexicon. On the other hand, DCs whose heads behave like RNs and realize NOBJ non-heads do not involve any event structure, so they cannot be compositionally interpreted and should be listed in the lexicon. Without previous (lexical) knowledge of the respective compound, one would interpret *adult supervision* or *government announcement* as involving an object by default, which would be infelicitous, since these compounds have a lexicalized NOBJ (i.e., subject-like) interpretation.

From a computational perspective, these experiments are a first attempt at trying to discover the complex set of dependencies that underlie the interpretation of deverbal compounds. Further work is necessary to determine the interdependence between the individual features, as well as to find out why adjectives and suffixes do not yield better results. Subsequently, taking into account the picture that arises from these additional experiments, we would like to compare our model based on head-dependent features with models that stem from NLP research and focus on encyclopaedic knowledge gathered from large corpora.

Acknowledgements

We thank our three anonymous reviewers for insightful and stimulating comments, which resulted in an improved and hopefully clearer version of our paper. Our work has been supported by the German Research Foundation (DFG) via a research grant to the Projects B1 *The Form and Interpretation of Derived Nominals* and D11 *A Crosslingual Approach to the Analysis of Compound Nouns*, within the Collaborative Research Center (SFB) 732, at the University of Stuttgart. We are also grateful to Katherine Fraser and Whitney Peterson for annotating our database and to Kerstin Eckart for technical support with respect to the Gigaword Corpus.

---

[17]Remember that we eventually balanced our dataset for 50% OBJ and 50% NOBJ compounds (cf. Section 3.5). Note that, given the biased interpretation of suffixes such as *-er* and *-ee*, including them into our dataset would have resulted in better accuracy and a higher predictive power for the *suffix* feature. But unlike, for instance, in Lapata (2002), we excluded this potential aid from our study, since we aimed to determine the morphosyntactic features of the head that are most relevant for the prediction task.

References

Peter Ackema and Ad Neeleman. 2004. *Beyond Morphology*. Oxford University Press, Oxford.

Artemis Alexiadou and Jane Grimshaw. 2008. Verbs, nouns, and affixation. In Florian Schäfer, editor, *Working Papers of the SFB 732 Incremental Specification in Context*, volume 1, pages 1–16. Universität Stuttgart.

Hagit Borer. 2013. *Taking Form*. Oxford University Press, Oxford.

Noam Chomsky. 1970. Remarks on nominalization. In Roderick A. Jacobs and Peter S. Rosenbaum, editors, *Readings in English transformational grammar*, pages 184–221. Waltham, MA: Ginn.

Thomas G Dietterich. 1998. Approximate statistical tests for comparing supervised classification learning algorithms. *Neural computation*, 10(7):1895–1923.

Antske Sibelle Fokkens. 2007. A hybrid approach to compound noun disambiguation. MA-thesis. Universität des Saarladens, Saarbrücken.

Dan Gillick. 2009. Sentence boundary detection and the problem with the u.s. In *Proceedings of Human Language Technologies: The 2009 Annual Conference of the North American Chapter of the Association for Computational Linguistics, Companion Volume: Short Papers*, NAACL-Short '09, pages 241–244, Stroudsburg, PA, USA. Association for Computational Linguistics.

Jane Grimshaw. 1990. *Argument Structure*. MIT Press, Cambridge, MA.

Claire Grover, Mirella Lapata, and Alex Lascarides. 2005. A comparison of parsing technologies for the biomedical domain. *Journal of Natural Language Engineering*, 11:01:27–65.

Mark Hall, Eibe Frank, Geoffrey Holmes, Bernhard Pfahringer, Peter Reutemann, and Ian H. Witten. 2009. The weka data mining software: An update. *SIGKDD Explorations*, 11(1):10–18.

Zhongqiang Huang, Mary Harper, and Slav Petrov. 2010. Self-training with products of latent variable grammars. In *Proceedings of the 2010 Conference on Empirical Methods in Natural Language Processing*, EMNLP '10, pages 12–22, Stroudsburg, PA, USA. Association for Computational Linguistics.

Angelika Kratzer. 1996. Severing the external argument from its verb. In Johan Rooryck and Laurie Zaring, editors, *Phrase Structure and the Lexicon*, pages 109–137. Kluwer Academic Publishers.

Mirella Lapata. 2002. The disambiguation of nominalizations. *Journal of Computational Linguistics*, 28:3:357–388.

Judith N. Levi. 1978. *The Syntax and Semantics of Complex Nominals*. Academic Press, New York.

Rochelle Lieber. 2004. *Morphology and Lexical Semantics*. Cambridge University Press, Cambridge.

Courtney Napoles, Matthew Gormley, and Benjamin Van Durme. 2012. Annotated gigaword. In *Proceedings of the Joint Workshop on Automatic Knowledge Base Construction and Web-scale Knowledge Extraction*, AKBC-WEKEX '12, pages 95–100, Stroudsburg, PA, USA. Association for Computational Linguistics.

Jeremy Nicholson and Timothy Baldwin. 2006. Interpretation of compound nominalisations using corpus and web statistics. In *Proceedings of the Workshop on Multiword Expressions: Identifying and Exploiting Underlying Properties*, pages 54–61, Sydney, Australia.

Susan Olsen. 2015. Composition. In Peter O. Müller et al., editors, *Word-Formation: An International Handbook of the Languages of Europe*, volume I, pages 364–386. De Gruyter.

Thomas Roeper and Muffy Siegel. 1978. A lexical transformation for verbal compounds. *Linguistic Inquiry*, 9:199–260.

Ina Rösiger, Johannes Schäfer, Tanja George, Simon Tannert, Ulrich Heid, and Michael Dorna. 2015. Extracting terms and their relations from german texts: Nlp tools for the preparation of raw material for e-dictionaries. In *Proceedings of eLex 2015*, pages 486–503. Herstmonceux Castle, UK.

Elisabeth O. Selkirk. 1982. *The Syntax of Words*. MIT Press, Cambridge, MA.

Encoding a syntactic dictionary into a super granular unification grammar

Sylvain Kahane
MoDyCo, CNRS/Université Paris Ouest
sylvain@kahane.fr

François Lareau
OLST, Université de Montréal
francois.lareau@umontreal.ca

Abstract

We show how to turn a large-scale syntactic dictionary into a dependency-based unification grammar where each piece of lexical information calls a separate rule, yielding a super granular grammar. Subcategorization, raising and control verbs, auxiliaries and copula, passivization, and tough-movement are discussed. We focus on the semantics-syntax interface and offer a new perspective on syntactic structure.

1   Introduction

The encoding of large-scale syntactic dictionaries into formal grammars has been achieved many times since the 1990s. This paper presents the encoding of a large-scale syntactic dictionary in a dependency grammar (DG) characterized by extreme granularity. The first main contribution of this paper lies in the fact that each specification in the dictionary calls a separate rule. All rules are expressed in the same basic unification-based formalism in the form of elementary structures *à la* Tree Adjoining Grammar (TAG). The second contribution is that our syntactic dependency structure is richer than the usual representations in most DGs. It appears as a directed acyclic graph (DAG) from the point of view of the semantics-syntax interface, but as a proper tree for the syntax-text interface.

The formal framework in question, Polarized Unification Grammar (PUG), has been presented in various papers (Kahane, 2006; Kahane and Lareau, 2005; Lareau, 2008; Kahane, 2013), but the description of the lexicon in PUG has never been formally discussed. To see whether PUG could handle a wide range of lexico-syntactic phenomena, we built a formal lexicon-grammar interface on top of *Lexique des formes fléchies du français* (Lefff), a large-scale syntactic dictionary of French (Sagot, 2010). For the sake of clarity, we translated the entries discussed here into English and adapted some notations (without modifying the dictionary's architecture).

Unlike other unification-based grammars (Shieber, 1986; Francez and Wintner, 2011), PUG makes linguistic structure more apparent: we do not combine abstract feature structures, but geometrical structures such as graphs and trees. We have only one abstract mechanism, polarization, to control the combination of rules, so we do not need *ad hoc* features to do that. All the features in our structures correspond to lexical information that could not be suppressed in any framework. Thus, model artifacts are minimal.

Elementary PUG structures can combine to obtain less granular descriptions equivalent to TAG elementary trees. But unlike TAG, PUG uses the same mechanism for the combination of elementary pieces of information than for whole lexical units. In other words, it expresses both TAG's grammar and meta-grammar (Candito, 1996; de La Clergerie, 2010) in the same formalism, which allows us to consider at the same time very fine-grained rules and rules with a larger span (routines, for instance).

In this paper, we focus on the semantics-syntax interface, including the mismatches between these two levels of representation, i.e., what generative grammar models in terms of movement. In our dependency-based approach, it is not words or constituents that are moved around, but rather the dependencies themselves, i.e., the relations between words (or constituents).

Proceedings of the Workshop on Grammar and Lexicon: Interactions and Interfaces,
pages 92–101, Osaka, Japan, December 11 2016.

2   Lexical description

Le*fff*'s entries are divided into six fields, as illustrated below:

```
WANT; V; 'want'; (1=subj:N|ProNom, 2=obj:N|ProAcc, 3=comp:to-Vinf);
CtrlObjComp:to-Vinf; passive.
```

This entry contains the following information:

1. the lemma, WANT;
2. the part of speech V;[1]
3. the meaning, 'want';[2]
4. the subcategorization frame, giving for each semantic argument its syntactic realization; e.g., the third argument (3) realizes as an infinitive verb (Vinf) being a complement (comp) marked by TO;
5. control and raising features: CtrlObjComp:to-Vinf indicates that the object of WANT is controlled by (the "subject" of) the **comp:to** infinitive verb;
6. redistributions, such as passive voice for verbs or tough-movement for adjectives.

We slightly enriched the Le*fff* in three ways:

- We introduced an explicit numbering of semantic actants, useful for an interface with semantic description. It corresponds to the order in which actants are listed in the subcategorization frame.
- We slightly modified some entries for a better account of the distinction between control and raising, as well as tough-movement.
- We added entries for some lexical units that have a grammatical use, such as auxiliaries, that we encoded in Le*fff*'s format.

3   Model architecture

Our approach is based on Meaning-Text Theory (MTT), which views a linguistic model as a device that associates meanings to texts (Mel'čuk, 2016). Meanings are represented as graphs of predicate-argument relations between semantemes (i.e., signifieds of linguistic signs). We do not consider the phonological module here, so our texts are just strings of wordforms. Between meaning and form, we consider an intermediate level of representation, a syntactic dependency graph. Fig. 1 illustrates the full representation of sentence (1).

(1)   *She slept.*

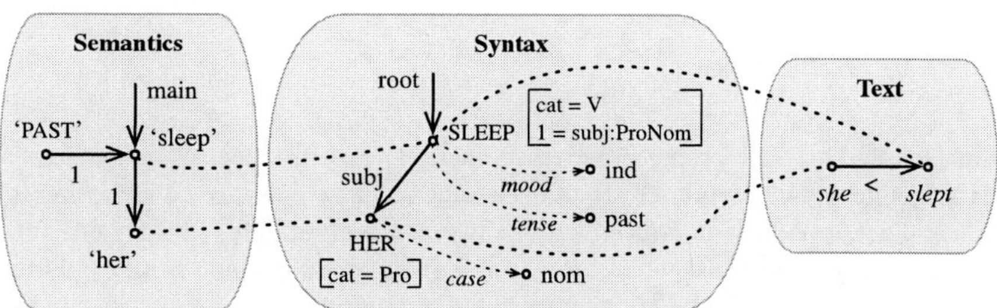

Figure 1: The three linguistic representations of (1)

The semantic representation contains two main kinds of objects: semantic nodes, labeled by semantemes (e.g., the lexical semanteme 'sleep' or the grammatical semanteme 'PAST') and semantic dependencies, labeled by a number r linking a predicate to its r-th argument. In addition to semantemes and predicate-argument relations, there is one pointer labeled "main" that flags one semanteme as the most salient; it corresponds roughly to the rheme's dominant node (Mel'čuk, 2001).

A syntactic representation comprises three kinds of objects: lexical nodes, labeled by lexical units (e.g., SLEEP), grammatical nodes, labeled with grammemes and linked to lexical units (e.g., "past" which

---

[1]Morphosyntactic subclasses, such as the conjugation group for verbs, are not considered here.

[2]Le*fff*'s entries do not contain this information; by default, we just recopy the lemma. We add it manually for grammatical words like BE_copula and BE_progressive (§5.2 and §5.3). Ideally, this field would distinguish senses and give a definition.

is a *tense*), and syntactic dependencies, labeled with syntactic functions (e.g., **subj**). All objects can bear features, such as "[cat=V]" on SLEEP.

A text representation contains two kinds of objects: nodes labeled by wordforms (e.g., *slept*), and linear precedence relations labeled "<".

Fig. 1 also shows another kind of object, correspondence links, represented by undirected dashed lines between nodes corresponding to the same linguistic sign across levels.[3] In the following sections, we will focus on the semantics-syntax interface.

4   The formal grammar

PUG generates a set of finite structures by combining elementary structures. A structure is a set of objects that are linked to three kinds of elements: 1) other objects (e.g., a dependency is linked to its source and target nodes), 2) atomic values (labels or feature values), or 3) polarities. All objects of elementary structures are polarized; this simple mechanism ensures that all necessary rules have been triggered without imposing any order on the combination of the rules (Kahane, 2006). The same rules are used for both analysis and synthesis, and the model allows incremental application strategies.

Polarities differ from atomic values in the way they combine. When two (elementary) structures combine, at least one object of a structure must be unified with an object of the other structure (as with TAG substitution, whereby the root of one tree is unified with a leaf of the other tree). When two objects are unified, all the elements linked to them must also be combined: objects and values are unified while polarities combine by a special operation called the product. We consider two polarity values in this paper: □ (white, unsaturated, or active), and ■ (black, saturated, or inactive). Only □ can combine with other polarity values, and it is the identity element of the product: $□ \times □ = □$; $□ \times ■ = ■$; $■ \times ■ = \perp$. Polarities should be interpreted as follows: white objects are unsaturated (they absolutely must combine with a non-white object and a final structure derived by the grammar must not contain any white object), while black objects are the elements of the structure constructed by the grammar. Objects are polarized by associating them to one of these two values via a function.

The grammar is modular: each module has its own polarizing function and also uses the polarities of adjacent modules to trigger their application (Kahane and Lareau, 2005). We consider here three levels (semantics, syntax and text) and two interfaces (semantics-syntax and syntax-text), giving us five modules. Instead of explicitly plotting the polarizing functions in our figures, we use five different geometric shapes, each associated with one module, as sketched in Fig. 2.

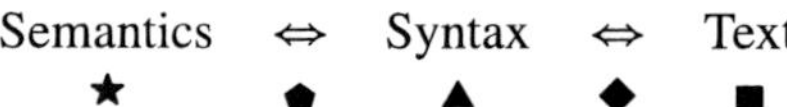

Semantics   ⇔   Syntax   ⇔   Text
★   ⬟   ▲   ◆   ■

Figure 2: Modules of the grammar

We refer to modules by their proper polarizing function. For instance, G★ is the semantic module, which builds semantic graphs, while G⬟ is the semantics-syntax interface, which links semantic and syntactic objects. Each module is interfaced with its two adjacent modules (or only one for the modules at the ends of the pipeline). In consequence, a rule of a given module handles three polarities: the main polarity (the one proper to its module) and two articulation polarities (the ones of the adjacent modules). Generally, when an object's main polarity is saturated, its articulation polarities are white; they are used to trigger rules from adjacent modules, which are the only rules that saturate these polarities. We use black articulation polarities only when there are mismatches between two levels (e.g., with raising, when a semantic dependency does not correspond to a syntactic dependency linking the same lexical units). Indeed, an object with a black articulation polarity, being already saturated, does not trigger rules from the adjacent module. A rule always contains at least one object with a black main polarity. Objects with a white main polarity are used to specify the context and are not articulated.

Each object in a rule is typed and belongs to a specific level of representation. They all bear at least two polarities: ★ □ for semantic objects, □ ▲ ◇ for syntactic objects, and ◇ ■ for a surface object. Correspondence links, which will be introduced below, belong only to an interface and bear only the

---

[3]Dependencies also correspond pairwise, but links between them are not necessary for the implementation of this grammar.

interface polarity, ⬟ or ◆. To make our figures more legible, we only show the black polarities. But keep in mind that, for instance, a syntactic object drawn with only ▲ in a rule actually also bears ◯ and ◇, since a syntactic object has always these (and only these) three polarities.

5 Encoding the lexicon

5.1 Lexicalization and government patterns

Let us start with the basic sentence (1) to show how modules are articulated. This first fragment of the grammar contains about twenty rules, which seems a lot for such a simple sentence. But most of these rules constitute the heart of the grammar and would be re-used for almost any sentence. The rules relating to specific lexical units' idiosyncrasies are directly derived from our lexical resource by instantiating a few very generic patterns. As we will show in the following sections, we do not need lots of additional rules to handle much more complex phenomena. For now, let us look at the following two lexical entries:

```
SLEEP; V; 'sleep'; ⟨1=subj:N|ProNom⟩; ∅; ∅.

HER; Pro; 'her'; ⟨∅⟩; ∅; ∅.
```

Our first module, $G^\star$ (Fig. 3), builds the semantic graph and calls $G^\bullet$. All objects constructed by these rules bear ★, while context objects bear ☆ (not shown). Remember that each ★ object is interfaced with $G^\bullet$ by bearing ◯ as an articulation polarity (not plotted here). The rule $R^\star_{\text{main}}$ is the initial rule, marking one of the semantic nodes as the most communicatively salient meaning (which is normally realized as the syntactic root). $R^\star_{\text{sleep}}$ indicates that 'sleep' is a unary predicate; this is trivially derived from the subcategorization frame of SLEEP, which states that this lexeme has only one argument.

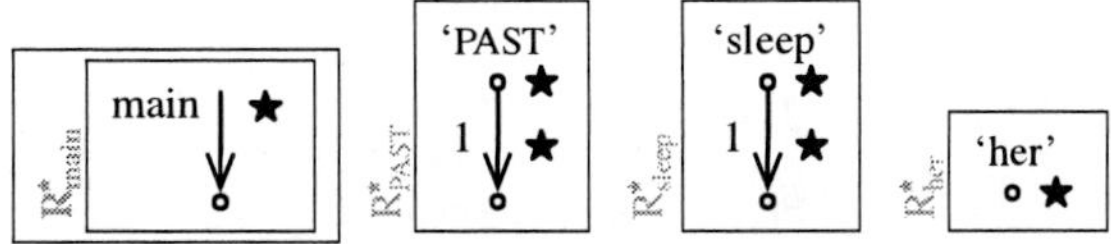

Figure 3: A fragment of $G^\star$

The next module, $G^\bullet$ (Fig. 4), ensures the lexicalization and arborization of the semantic representation.[4] The left part of the rule contains semantic objects (bearing ☆, not plotted here), while the right part contains syntactic objects (bearing △, also hidden). Semantic and syntactic objects that correspond to each other are linked by a correspondence link object. The objects constructed by a rule bear ⬟, while the others bear ◯ (implicit). The two ◯ correspondence links of $R^\bullet_{\text{1=subj:ProNom}}$ (represented by dashed lines) ensure that the governors and dependents of the semantic and syntactic dependencies will be put in correspondence by a lexicalization rule that saturates them. $R^\bullet_{\text{main}}$ indicates that the main verb can have the indicative mood (there could be competing rules to allow different roots). $R^\bullet_{\text{past}}$ indicates that 'PAST' is realized by a grammeme. The dotted link labeled *tense* is a function linking the grammatical object to the lexical node and is not an object itself (and therefore is not polarized).

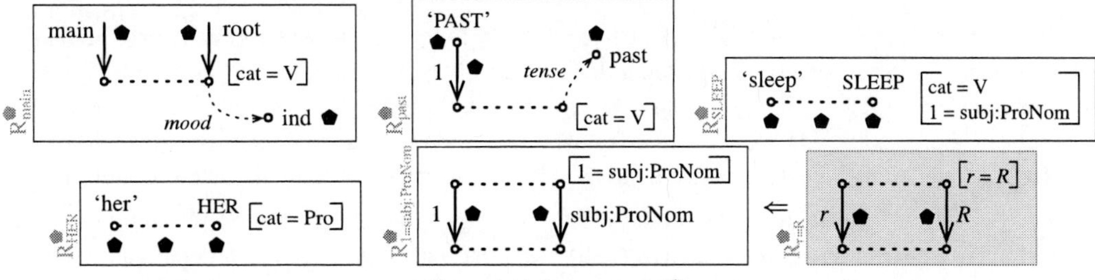

Figure 4: A fragment of $G^\bullet$

The lexical rules $R^\bullet_{\text{SLEEP}}$ and $R^\bullet_{\text{HER}}$ are directly induced by the dictionary: the meaning and lemma fields provide the labels for the semantic and syntactic nodes, the part of speech field provides the value for the "cat" attribute, and the subcategorization frame provides a list of features that are recopied as is

---

[4]We chose to present the grammar in the perspective of synthesis, from meaning to text, but this model is completely reversible and is compatible with various procedures, the cohesion of structures being completely ensured by polarization.

on the syntactic node. If present, control and redistribution features are also attached to the syntactic node and used as explained in §5.2. The actancial rule $R^{\bullet}_{1=subj:ProNom}$ instantiates the generic pattern $R^{\bullet}_{r=R}$ (grayed out). The syntactic dependency **subj:ProNom** is a "temporary" object and $R^{\bullet}_{1=subj:ProNom}$ only makes sense when combined with $R^{\blacktriangle}_{subj:ProNom}$, presented below.

The module $G^{\blacktriangle}$ (Fig. 5) verifies the well-formedness of syntactic structures. The lexical rules of $G^{\blacktriangle}$ have been reduced to the minimum here, just to verify the general constraints related to parts of speech.[5] Grammatical rules verify that the grammemes *ind*, *past*, and *nom* appear in the right context. $R^{\blacktriangle}_{subj:ProNom}$ expresses the fact that **subj:ProNom** is indeed a subject dependency (**subj**), the dependent of which is a pronoun (*Pro*) with the nominative case (*Nom*). This is realized by "replacing" **subj:ProNom** with **subj**. In fact, there is no replacement, as both dependencies actually remain in the syntactic structure (both are syntactic objects), but only **subj:ProNom** is active for $G^{\bullet}$ (it bears ○), while **subj** is active for $G^{\blacklozenge}$ (it bears ◇). This amounts to considering deep and surface functions (Fillmore, 1968; Blake, 2002). A dependency labeled by a surface function is validated by a rule such as $R^{\blacktriangle}_{subj}$, which sends it to $G^{\blacklozenge}$ just by leaving the articulation polarity ◇ white. Consequently, the syntactic dependencies built by $G^{\blacktriangle}$ form a DAG, from which only a subtree receives ◇ and thus is visible to $G^{\blacklozenge}$ and interfaced with the text.[6]

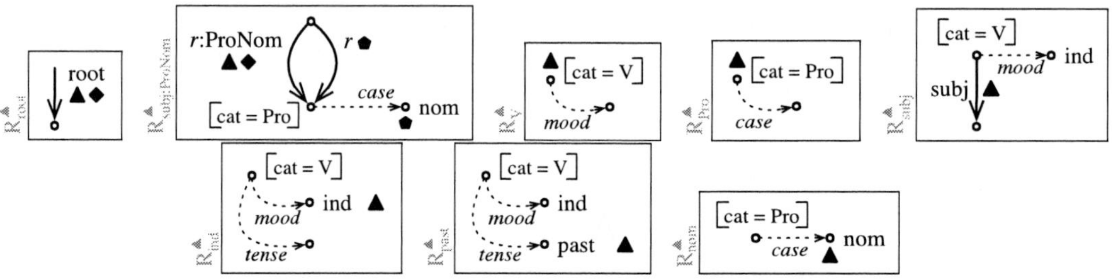

Figure 5: A fragment of $G^{\blacktriangle}$

The module $G^{\blacklozenge}$ (Fig. 6) ensures the linearization of the syntactic tree. $R^{\blacklozenge}_{subj}$ indicates that the subject can precede its governor without constraints. $R^{\blacklozenge}_{slept}$ indicates that the indicative past form of SLEEP is *slept* and $R^{\blacklozenge}_{she}$ indicates that the nominative form of HER is *she*. See (Kahane and Lareau, 2016) for a more detailed description of $G^{\blacklozenge}$, including rules for non-projective cases.

The module $G^{\blacksquare}$, which verifies that the output of $G^{\blacklozenge}$ is a string, is trivial and not discussed here.

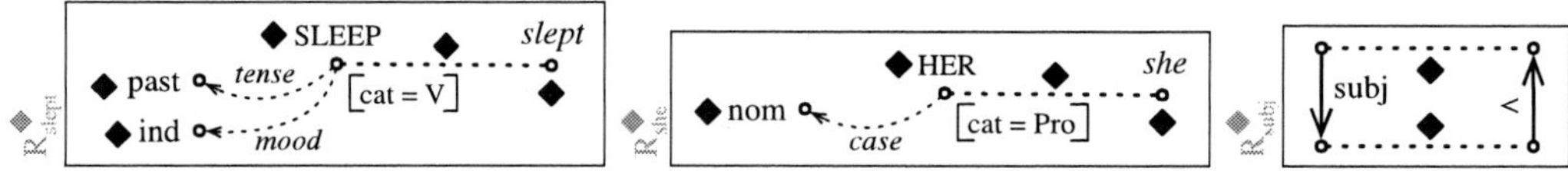

Figure 6: A fragment of $G^{\blacklozenge}$

5.2 Modification

Adjectives have at least one actant, which receives the **subj** fonction. However, it can never be realized as a subject on the adjective because a **subj** dependency can only be validated by $G^{\blacktriangle}$, which requires it to be headed by a verb (see $R^{\blacktriangle}_{subj}$, Fig. 5). In other words, the **subj** relation on the adjective must be "moved". Two solutions are possible: 1) the adjective is attributive and becomes a dependent of its first semantic actant ($R^{\blacktriangle}_{mod}$), or 2) the adjective is predicative and becomes the dependent of the copula ($R^{\blacktriangle}_{BE_{copula}}$), its subject becoming the subject of the copula ($R^{\blacktriangle}_{RaisSubjAux}$). The copula has no semantic contribution. Its lexical entry says that it has an adjective (Adj) or a past participle (Ved) as a dependent with the **aux** relation and that BE has the same semantic correspondent as its dependent. The rule $R^{\blacktriangle}_{RaisSubjAux}$ saturates a **subj** dependency (thus making it inert for $G^{\blacklozenge}$) and "replaces" it by a new **subj** relation (which receives ● because it must not be interfaced with the semantic level). The triggering of $R^{\blacktriangle}_{RaisSubjAux}$ is only possible

---

[5]More specific constraints can be verified, such as the fact that a syntactic actant is obligatory, by introducing the corresponding syntactic dependency with △.

[6]It is very easy to write a PUG grammar to check that a structure is a proper tree (Kahane, 2006). We do not present this part of the syntactic module here.

if the verb has the feature "[RaisSubjAux]", which comes from the dictionary and is just recopied on the node. Its value is a boolean; by convention, its presence means it is "True", while its absence means "False". The same goes for the control and raising features in §5.3.

```
RED; Adj; 'red'; (1=subj:N|ProNom); Ø; Ø.

BE_copula; V; Ø; (0=aux:Adj|Ved); RaisSubjAux; Ø.
```

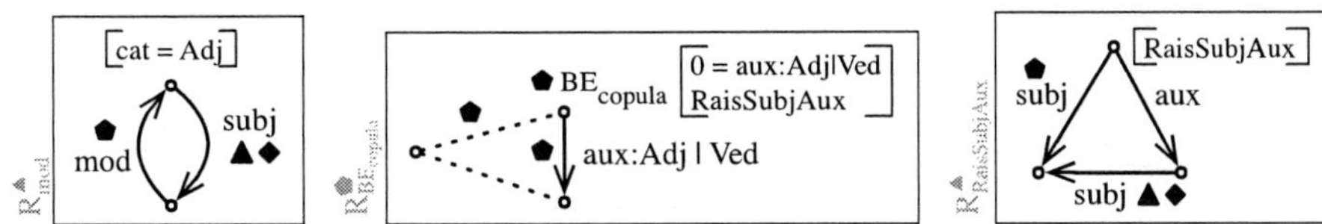

Figure 7: Adjectival modifiers

The rule $R_{BE_{copula}}$, as shown above, is in fact the combination of two simpler rules: a lexicalization rule that says BE_copula has no specific semantic contribution, and a rule that activates the "0=aux:Adj|Ved" instruction by mapping a single semanteme to a configuration of lexemes that jointly express that meaning (i.e., one is semantically empty):

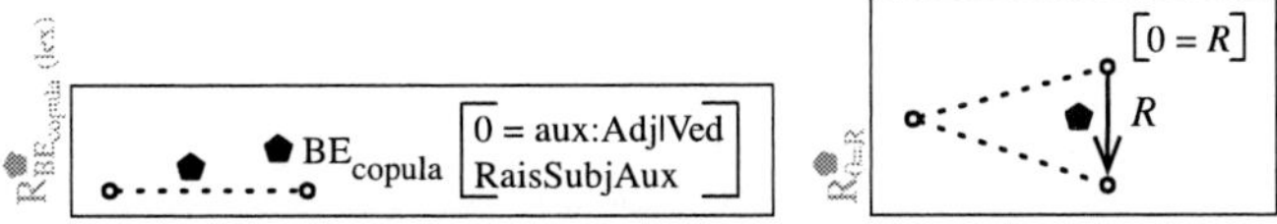

Figure 8: Decomposition of $R_{BE_{copula}}$

5.3 Control and raising

All verbs have a **subj** dependency, even infinitives and participles, but for these the **subj** dependency will not be active for G♦. This is achieved by rules of control and raising, which say that the **subj** dependency of the infinitive is realized on another verb. SEEM is a classical example of a raising verb; it has only one actant, which is realized as its complement (Fig. 9). Its subject can be an expletive ((2-b), $R^{\bullet}_{IT_{expletive}}$) or the subject of its verbal dependent ((2-a), $R^{\blacktriangle}_{RaisSubjComp:to\text{-}Vinf}$).

```
SEEM; V; 'seem'; (1=comp:to-Vinf|that-Vind); RaisSubjComp:to-Vinf; Ø.
```

(2) a. *Ann seems to sleep.*
     b. *It seems that Ann is sleeping.*

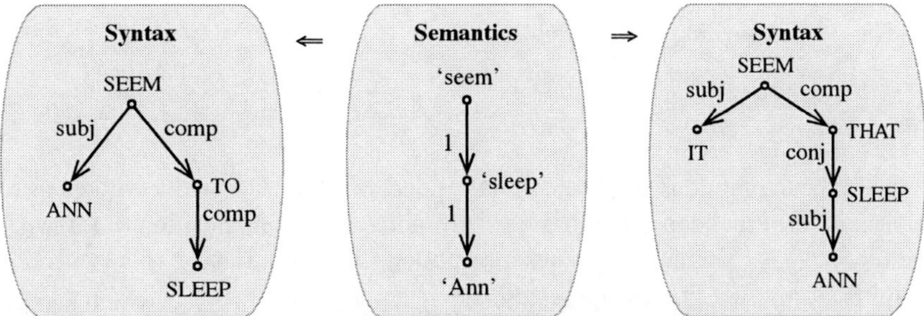

Figure 9: The simplified semantic and syntactic representations of (2).

A specification such as "[2=comp:to-Vinf]" will be expressed in three steps: a G♦ rule associates the semantic **2** dependency to a syntactic **comp:to-Vinf** dependency ($R^{\bullet}_{r=R}$), which is first "replaced" by a **comp:to** dependency with a dependent that is a verb (V) with an infinitive mood (inf) ($R^{\blacktriangle}_{comp:to\text{-}Vinf}$), and then the **comp:to** dependency is "replaced" by a configuration with TO ($R^{\blacktriangle}_{comp:to}$). Even if as a result, **comp:to** is not active anymore for any of the interface modules G♦ and G♦, it is still part of the syntactic representation built by G▲ and it can be called as a needed context by the rules of raising and control.

Unlike SEEM, WANT controls its subject, which it shares with its verbal dependent. Therefore, contrary

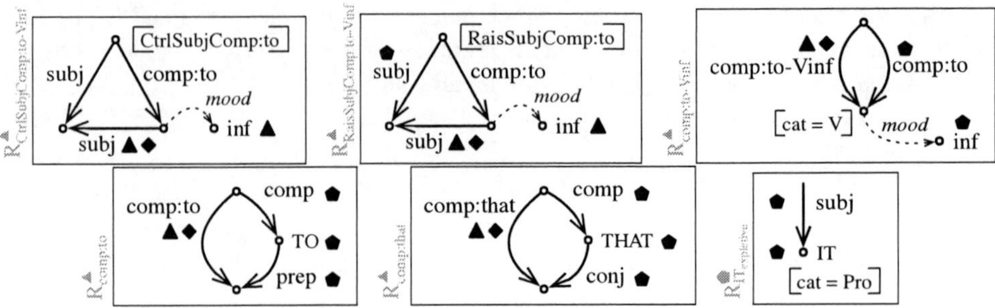

Figure 10: Rules for control and raising

to $R^{\blacktriangle}_{\text{RaisSubjComp:to-Vinf}}$, $R^{\blacktriangle}_{\text{CtrlSubjComp:to-Vinf}}$ does not block the semantic correspondence of the **subj** (cf. ♠ on **subj** in $R^{\blacktriangle}_{\text{RaisSubjComp:to-Vinf}}$). Such rules are in fact $G^{\blacktriangle}$ rules validating the infinitive grammeme.

Tense-aspect-mood auxiliaries can also be described as raising verbs, such as the English progressive, which is a unary predicate expressed by the auxiliary BE imposing the gerundive form (Ving) on its unique actant and raising its subject:

```
BEprogressive; V; 'PROGRESSIVE'; ⟨1=aux:Ving⟩; RaisSubjAux:Ving; ∅.
```

5.4   Redistributions

In PUG, redistributions are dependency rewriting rules. For instance, the passive voice promotes the object to the subject position ($R^{\blacktriangle}_{\text{passiveObj}}$). The marker of this redistribution is the past participle, so such a rule can also be interpreted as a rule realizing this mood grammeme. As can be seen in Fig. 11, the **obj** dependency becomes inactive for $G^{\blacklozenge}$ and is replaced by a **subj** dependency inactive for $G^{\blacklozenge}$ but still active for $G^{\blacktriangle}$. The $R^{\blacktriangle}_{\text{passiveObj}}$ can be combined with another rule, $R^{\blacktriangle}_{\text{passiveSubj}}$, which demotes the subject to an agent complement (**comp:by**). The **obj** with a separate dependent ensures that the **subj** to be demoted is not an object that had been promoted by another rule.

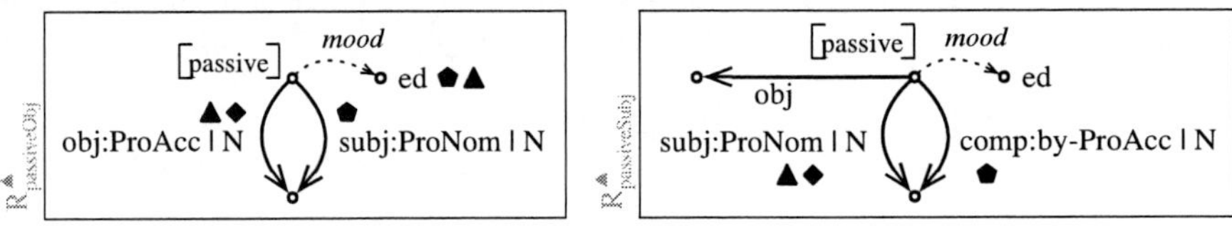

Figure 11: Passive

5.5   Tough-movement

Tough-movement is an interesting case of redistribution.

(3)   a.   *The book is easy to read.*
       b.   *a book easy to read*

We consider that in the expressions in (3) the initial subject of EASY has been demoted as a complement and that the object of its verbal dependent has been promoted in the **subj** position of EASY (Fig. 12). This is done by the rule $R^{\blacktriangle}_{\text{tough-mvt}}$, which combines a demotion rule and a raising rule (where an **obj** and not a **subj** is raised). The infinitive is not validated by $R^{\blacktriangle}_{\text{tough-mvt}}$, but by $R^{\blacktriangle}_{\text{inf-*ONE}}$, which suppresses the **subj** dependency but allows it to correspond to a general meaning 'one', as in *One reads the book*.

```
EASY; Adj; 'easy'; ⟨1=N|ProNom|Ving|to-Vinf|that-Vind⟩; ∅; tough-mvt.
```

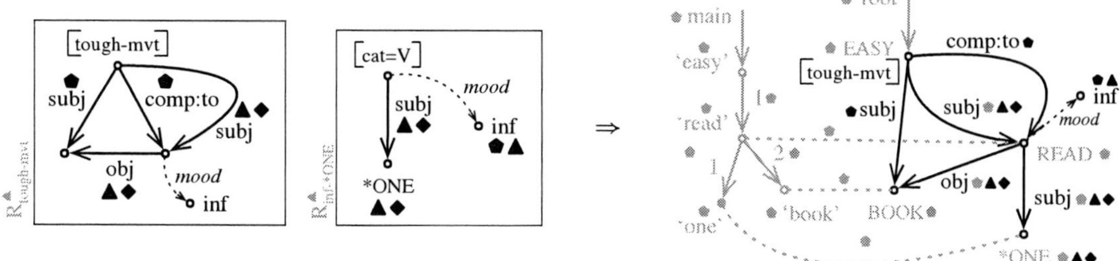

Figure 12: Tough-movement

6 Conclusion

The implementation of a dictionary as a formal grammar has been achieved in many frameworks (TAG, Lexical Functional Grammar (LFG), Head-driven Phrase Structure Grammar (HPSG), etc.). The dictionary we consider here has been used by TAG and LFG parsers for French (Boullier and Sagot, 2005; de La Clergerie, 2010). Implementing this dictionary in a new formal grammar is not challenging in itself. What should be interesting in our work is the fact that our grammar is very granular and each piece of information from the dictionary yields a separate rule. Moreover, the rules coming from the dictionary and the rules associated with grammatical items are quite similar in essence. It results from it that there is no real frontier between lexicon and grammar: what we obtain is a list of correspondence rules in the spirit of the *constructicon* of CxG (Goldberg, 1995; Fillmore et al., 2012), i.e., a dictionary describing both lexical units and more abstract constructions, such as dependencies, control and redistribution patterns, etc. That is, we have a grammar that describes linguistic signs, regardless of their lexical or grammatical nature. The cost of this granularity is that it is harder to implement, since PUGs must consider more possible object unifications than simple unification grammars. We are working on heuristics that will speed up unification in an implementation that is underway.

Another important point is that our grammar allows to understand some divergences in the literature concerning the nature of the syntactic structure. If we consider that the syntactic structure is the one containing all the objects with ▲, then our structure is richer than that of most frameworks; it contains various substructures considered by other formal grammars, *à la* (Hudson, 2007) (Fig. 13).

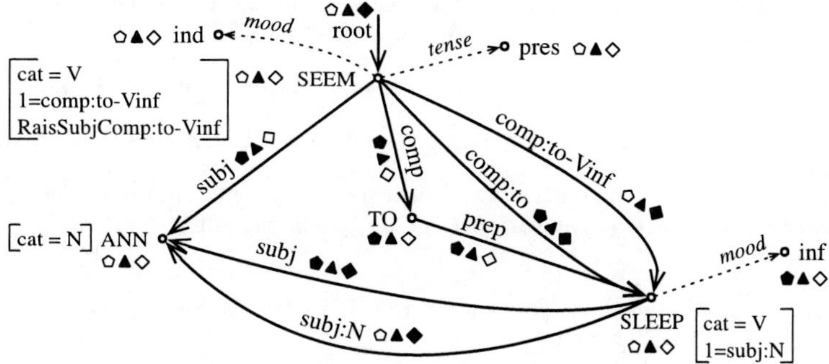

Figure 13: The whole syntactic structure of (2-a) produced by G▲

- The substructure that is interfaced with the text by G◆ (objects that bear ◇) is a surface syntactic tree, as considered by many dependency grammars. This structure contains both lexical nodes and grammatical nodes and has exactly one node per "syntaxeme" (lexeme or grammeme). Such a structure is more or less equivalent to a surface constituency tree in X-bar tradition, containing both lexical and functional projections.
- The substructure that is interfaced with the semantic graph by G⬮ (objects that bear ○) is a deep syntactic tree (Mel'čuk, 2012). This dependency structure contains only full words (e.g., TO is not part of this structure). It is a DAG, rather than a tree, some nodes having potentially two governors (in case of control, for instance).

- The whole structure can be compared to a phrase structure with movements (Graf, 2012; Stabler, 1997). A word can have several governors corresponding to several steps in the construction of the structure (cf. raising rules, for instance), which means that the same word occupies several positions alternatively. It is also comparable to the dependency structures considered by Word Grammar (WG) (Hudson, 2007) or Functional Generative Description (FGD) (Sgall et al., 1986).

Note that in PUG, "movements" do not duplicate the nodes in a structure. The number of nodes we consider never exceeds the number of syntaxemes. What we multiply are the dependencies between nodes, each encoding a syntactic combination of two items, which would be encoded in phrase structure trees by a new binary branching (Kahane and Mazziotta, 2015). In other words, we can involve a lexeme in various combinations without having to duplicate it, thus avoiding coindexation and movement.

References

Blake, B. (2002). *Relational grammar*. Routledge.

Boullier, P. and Sagot, B. (2005). Efficient and robust lfg parsing: Sxlfg. In *Proceedings of the Ninth International Workshop on Parsing Technology*, pages 1–10. Association for Computational Linguistics.

Candito, M.-H. (1996). A principle-based hierarchical representation of ltags. In *Proceedings of the 16th conference on Computational linguistics-Volume 1*, pages 194–199. Association for Computational Linguistics.

de La Clergerie, E. V. (2010). Building factorized tags with meta-grammars. In *The 10th International Conference on Tree Adjoining Grammars and Related Formalisms-TAG+ 10*, pages 111–118.

Fillmore, C. J. (1968). The case for case. In Bach, E. and Harms, R. T., editors, *Universals in Linguistic Theory*, pages 1–88. Holt, Rinehart, and Winston.

Fillmore, C. J., Lee-Goldman, R., and Rhodes, R. (2012). The framenet constructicon. In Boas, H. C. and Sag, I. A., editors, *Sign-based construction grammar*, pages 309–372. CSLI Publications, Stanford.

Francez, N. and Wintner, S. (2011). *Unification grammars*. Cambridge University Press, Cambridge.

Goldberg, A. E. (1995). *Constructions: A construction grammar approach to argument structure*. University of Chicago Press.

Graf, T. (2012). Movement-generalized minimalist grammars. In Béchet, D. and Dikovsky, A. J., editors, *LACL 2012*, volume 7351 of *Lecture Notes in Computer Science*, pages 58–73.

Hudson, R. (2007). *Language networks: the new Word Grammar*. Oxford University Press.

Kahane, S. (2006). Polarized Unification Grammars. In *Proceedings of Coling-ACL 2006*, Sydney.

Kahane, S. (2013). Predicative adjunction in a modular dependency grammar. In *Proceedings of the Second International Conference on Dependency Linguistics (DepLing 2013)*, pages 137–146, Prague. Charles University, Matfyzpress.

Kahane, S. and Lareau, F. (2005). Meaning-Text Unification Grammar: modularity and polarization. In *Proceedings of MTT 2005*, pages 163–173, Moscow.

Kahane, S. and Lareau, F. (2016). Word ordering as a graph rewriting process. In Foret, A., Morrill, G., Muskens, R., Osswald, R., and Pogodalla, S., editors, *Formal Grammar: 20th and 21st International Conferences, FG 2015, Barcelona, Spain, August 2015, Revised Selected Papers. FG 2016, Bozen, Italy, August 2016, Proceedings*, pages 216–239. Springer, Berlin/Heidelberg.

Kahane, S. and Mazziotta, N. (2015). Syntactic polygraphs. a formalism extending both constituency and dependency. In *Proceedings of the 14th Meeting on the Mathematics of Language (MoL)*, Chicago, USA. Association for Computational Linguistics.

Lareau, F. (2008). *Vers une grammaire d'unification Sens-Texte du français: le temps verbal dans l'interface sémantique-syntaxe*. Ph.d. thesis, Université de Montréal / Université de Paris 7.

Mel'čuk, I. A. (2001). *Communicative organization in natural language: the semantic-communicative structure of sentences*. Studies in language companion series. John Benjamins, Amsterdam/Philadelphia.

Mel'čuk, I. A. (2012). *Semantics: From Meaning to Text*, volume 1 of *Studies in Language Companion Series*. John Benjamins, Amsterdam/Philadelphia.

Mel'čuk, I. A. (2016). *Language: From Meaning to Text*. Ars Rossica, Moscow/Boston.

Sagot, B. (2010). The lefff, a freely available and large-coverage morphological and syntactic lexicon for french. In *7th international conference on Language Resources and Evaluation (LREC 2010)*.

Sgall, P., Hajičová, E., Panevová, J., and Mey, J. L. (1986). *The meaning of the sentence in its semantic and pragmatic aspects*. D. Reidel/Kluwer Academic, Dordrecht/Boston Hingham.

Shieber, S. M. (1986). *An Introduction to Unification-Based Approaches to Grammar*. CSLI Publications, Stanford, CA.

Stabler, E. (1997). Derivational minimalism. In *International Conference on Logical Aspects of Computational Linguistics*, pages 68–95. Springer.

Identification of Flexible Multiword Expressions with the Help of Dependency Structure Annotation

Ayaka Morimoto, Akifumi Yoshimoto, Akihiko Kato,
Hiroyuki Shindo, and Yuji Matsumoto
Graduate School of Information Science
Nara Institute of Science and Technology
8916-5 Takayama, Ikoma, Nara, 630-0192, Japan
`{morimoto.ayaka.lw1, akifumi-y, kato.akihiko.ju6,`
`shindo, matsu}@is.naist.jp`

Abstract

This paper presents our ongoing work on compilation of English multi-word expression (MWE) lexicon and corpus annotation. We are especially interested in collecting flexible MWEs, in which some other constituents can intervene the expression such as "a number of" vs "a large number of" where a modifier of "number" can be placed in the expression while inheriting the original meaning. We first collect possible candidates of flexible English MWEs from the web, and annotate all of their occurrences in the Wall Street Journal portion of OntoNotes corpus. We make use of word dependency structure information of the sentences converted from the phrase structure annotation. This process enables semi-automatic annotation of MWEs in the corpus and simultaneously produces the internal and external dependency representation of flexible MWEs.

1 Introduction

Multiword Expressions (MWEs) are roughly defined as those that have "idiosyncratic interpretations that cross word boundaries (or spaces)" (Sag, 2002), and are classified into the following categories:

- Lexicalized phrases

    - fixed expressions: Those with fixed word order and forms (e.g. *with respect to*).
    - semi-fixed expressions: Those with lexical variation such as inflection, etc. (e.g. *keep up with, kept up with*).
    - syntactically flexible expressions: Those with a wide range of syntactic variability (e.g. some of the internal words in an MWE can have a modifier).

- Institutionalized phrases

    - Phrases that are syntactically compositional but semantically specific (e.g. *traffic light*).

In this paper we mainly focus on English syntactically flexible multi-word expressions, since they are less investigated than other types of MWEs. There are a number of MWEs that grammatically behave as single lexical items belonging to some specific parts-of-speech, such as adverbs, determiners, prepositions, subordinate conjunctions, and so on. Other than MWEs with those functions, we also consider multi-word verbs such as *take into consideration*, but not multi-word nouns. The reason we do not consider multi-word nouns is that most of them are syntactically not flexible, meaning they do not allow to have modifiers within them. MWEs have specific grammatical functionalities and can be regarded as an important part of an extended lexicon.

The objective of our work is to construct a wide coverage English syntactically flexible MWE lexicon, to describe their structures in dependency structures with possible modifiers within them, and to annotate their occurrences in the Wall Street Journal portion of OntoNotes corpus (Pradhan et al., 2007).

There have been some attempts for constructing English MWE lexicon. An English fixed MWE lexicon and a list of phrasal verbs are presented in (Shigeto et al., 2015) and (Komai et al., 2015). They

Proceedings of the Workshop on Grammar and Lexicon: Interactions and Interfaces,
pages 102–109, Osaka, Japan, December 11 2016.

also annotated the occurrences of those expressions in Penn Treebank. While most of English dictionaries for human use include a large list of multi-word expressions and idioms, to the best of our knowledge, there has been no comprehensive lexicon of English flexible MWEs constructed that is usable for NLP tasks.

The main contributions of our work are the following:

1. We constructed a large scale syntactically flexible English multi-word lexicon by collecting them from various web sites that list MWEs.

2. Through annotation of collected MWEs in OntoNotes corpus, we identified possible modifiers that can appear within the expressions.

Our current work has clear limitation that we cannot know how flexible those expressions are that do not appear in a form of flexible usage in OntoNotes. So, the first contribution is still ongoing. But, for the second contribution, we try to annotate all the occurrences of flexible MWEs in OntoNotes. In the following sections, we first describe related research, then explain how we collected English flexible MEWs and the method we used to annotate the occurrences of MWEs in OntoNote. We also give some statistics concerning with our experiments.

2   Related Works

Corpus annotation of MWEs hasn't been done in large scale in English. On the other hand, in French there is a large scale MWE annotated corpus (Abeillé et al., 2003), which includes 18,000 sentences annotated with 30,000 MWEs. In English, (Schneider et al., 2015) constructed an MWE-annotated corpus on English Social Web Corpus with all types pf English MWEs. However, the size of the corpus is small (3,800 sentences). This is the first and only corpus that has annotation of syntactically flexible English MWEs.

For English fixed and semi-flexible MWEs there are some works on construction of lexicons and on annotation on a large scale corpus. (Shigeto et al., 2015) and (Kato et al., 2016) annotated the Wall Street Journal portion of OnteNotes with fixed functional MWEs. The size of the corpus is 37,000 sentences and the number of annotated MWEs is 6,900. In the former work they constructed an English fixed MWE lexicon and annotated the spans of all occurrences of MWEs in the corpus. The latter work annotated and modified dependency structure of the sentences in accordance with their functionality. A specific type of English MWEs, phrasal verbs, are annotated on the same corpus by (Komai et al., 2015), in which they annotated 22,600 occurrences of phrasal verbs in 37,000 sentences.

PARSEME (PARSing and Multi-word Expressions) Project[1] is a project devoted to the issue of Multiword Expressions in parsing and in linguistic resources in multi-lingual perspective. A comprehensive introduction of the project is found in (Savary et al., 2015). A detailed survey of MWEs in Treebanks is found in (Rosén et al., 2016).

3   Collection of English Flexible Multi-word Expressions

For collecting English flexible MWE candidates, we explored ALL IN ONE English learning site[2] and the index of the English Idiom dictionary by Weblio[3]. Both sites provide useful information for English learners such as dictionaries, examples and useful expressions. In addition, we explored the entiries in Wiktionary[4] that contain white space(s) within the expressions whose part-of-speech are either Verb, Adjective, Adverb, Preposition, or Conjunction.

All of those collected 16,339 MWE candidates. Then, we counted the corpus occurrences of those expressions using Web 1T 5-gram(LDC2006T13)[5]. By ordering them according to the occurrence frequencies, we collected top 3,000 expressions. We then deleted all the MWEs already known as fixed

---

[1] http://typo.uni-konstanz.de/parseme/
[2] http://www.allinone-english.com/A13E/phrases-table-A-K.html, /phrases-table-L-Z.html
[3] http://ejje.weblio.jp/cat/dictionary/eidhg
[4] https://en.wiktionary.org/wiki/Wiktionary:Main_Page
[5] https://catalog.ldc.upenn.edu/ldc2006t13

MWEs or phrasal verbs based on the lexicons constructed by previous works, (Shigeto et al., 2015) and (Komai et al., 2015). This results in 2,927 MWEs, which are our starting candidate flexible MWEs. At this stage, we do not know they are really flexible MWEs. Moreover, even if a candidate MWE is known as a flexible MWE, we do not know how flexible it is, that is, what kind of modifications it can involve.

4 Identification and Annotation of MWEs with Dependency Structure

4.1 Overview and objective

One of our objectives is to construct an English flexible MWE lexicon with the information of the degree of flexibility. Here, we only focus on flexibility concerning modification within the expression. For example, an MWE "a number of" can be used as "a growing number of" or "a very large number of". Finding those occurrences and their syntactic uniformity, we can guess that "a number of" can involve a word that modifies "number" in the expression[6]. To know correct syntactic structure of candidate MWEs, we make use of the Wall Street Journal portion of OntoNotes Release 5.0 (LDC2013T19) and converted all the phrase structure trees into dependency structure trees (those based on Stanford dependency[7]). The reason we used dependency tree rather than phrase structure trees is that the phrase structures in Peen Treebank are not uniform on their structure and phrase names. The same MWEs or the phrases that include them are in places annotated in slightly different phrase structures or with different phrase names. When they are converted into dependency structures, they become quite uniform.

Another objective is to annotate all the occurrences of MWEs in OntoNotes both in fixed or flexible forms. For all the possible occurrences of an MWE, that is, the occurrences of not only the exact appearances of the MWE but also the appearances that have one or more words intervened in the expression, we made annotation. With the help of dependency information obtained from the phrase structure tree, we semi-automatically annotated correct occurrences of MWEs. The same forms of some MWEs can be in literal usage. So, we are going to manually check all the annotation results before making them open to public.

The following subsections explain how we conducted the semi-automatic annotation of MWE candidates.

4.2 Extraction of Dependency Structure that Cover MWEs

This section describes the method for extracting dependency tree fragments that cover candidate MWEs. We used the Wall Street Journal portion (wsj_00-24) of OntoNotes after converting the phrase structure trees into Stanford dependency trees.

We took the following steps:

1. For each candidate MWE, we first extract all the sentences in OntoNotes that include the MWE in a flexible form. Fo example, in the case of "a number of", we extract all the sentences contain "a", "number" and "of" in this ordering. This process extracts quite a large number of sentences, but captures all sentences that potentially include the MWE.

2. We convert all the sentences into Stanford dependency (de Marneffe and Manning, 2008)[8].

3. For each sentence, we extract the minimal dependency subtree that covers the all the words comprising the MWE. An example of an extracted subtree is shown in Figure 1.

4. Within the subtree, there can be some other words or subtree that do not comprise the MWE. In the above case, the subtree consisting of "division heads" is an example. In such a case, we leave only the head of the subtree and delete all other children. Then we replace all the words that do not comprise the MWE with the POS labels. In the above example, we obtain the tree that represents a flexible usage of the MWE, "*a JJ number of NN*" (shown in Figure 2).

---

[6]The example "a very large number of" includes two words between "a" and "number", while only "large" modifies "number".

[7]http://nlp.stanford.edu/software/stanford-dependencies.shtml

[8]We designated "-conllx -basic -makeCopulaHead - keepPunct" as an option for the conversion command

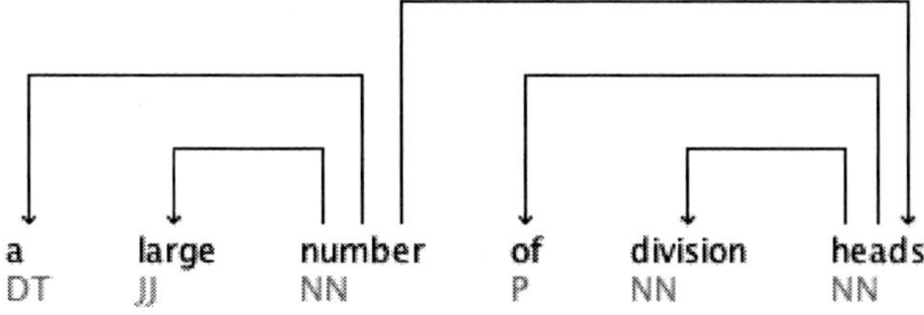

Figure 1: Minimal dependency subtree that covers "a number of"

Figure 2: Representation of flexible usage of "a number of'

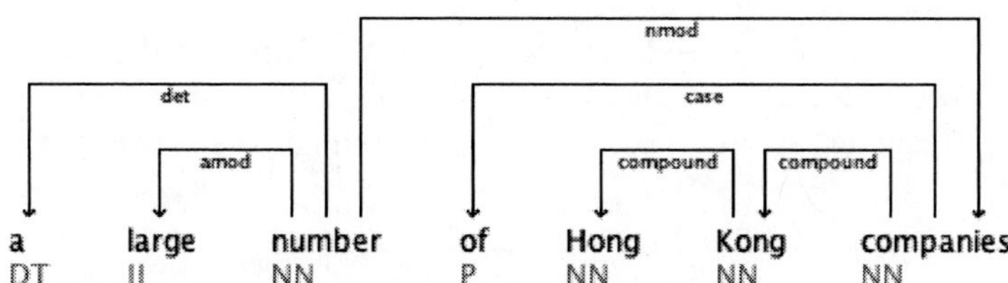

Figure 3: Another Minimal Dependency Subtree of "a number of"

Figures 3, 4, and 5 show three occurrences of "a number of" in different forms (all the figures show the minimal subtrees that include this MWE).

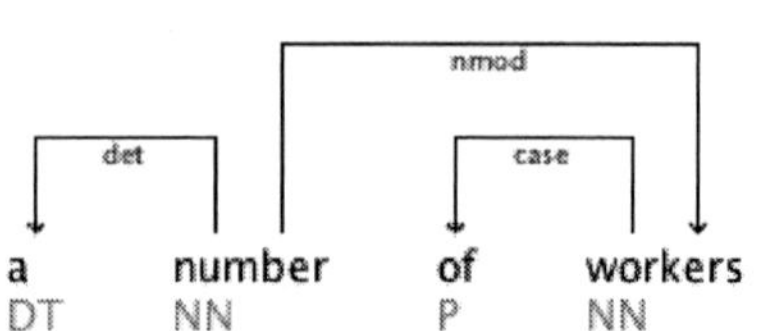 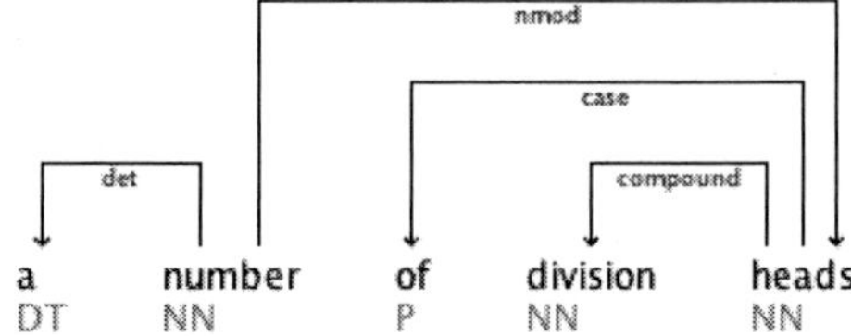

Figure 4: Subtree of "a number of workers ..."   Figure 5: Subtree of "a number of division heads ..."

After the procedure described above, we obtain isomorphic trees with only difference of existence of modifiers within the expression, e.g., the tree in Figure 3 includes a JJ as a modifier of "number". From those trees we can obtain the dependency tree shown in Figure 6 as a flexible MWE so that "number" can have an internal modifier. In the figure, *1 is a wild card to be defined as a JJ or an empty element in the current case, but will be eventually defined as $\{\epsilon, JJ, NN, VBG, VBN\}$ and *2 is defined as $\{NN, SYM\}$ since words with those POS tags appear at the corresponding positions in some examples.

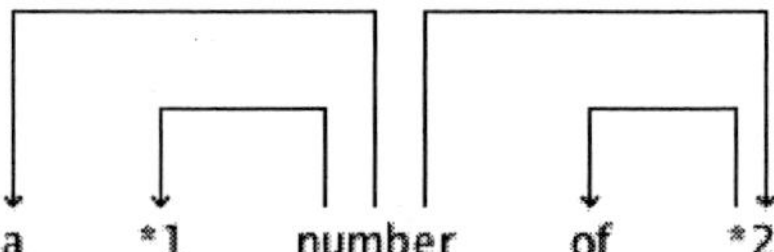

Figure 6: Representation of flexible MWE "a number of"

For each candidate MWE, we run the above procedure and obtain all possible subtrees. Some of the subtrees are from the fixed form of the MWE, i.e., in the original sentences there are no extra words intervening the expression. Still, they do not necessarily produce the same subtree. Within those subtrees, we pick up the smallest one, and assume it as the dependency structure of the MWE in the usage of its fixed form and call it as the canonical tree of the MWE. We assume all the other cases as non-MWE usages of the expression. We extract all the subtrees extracted from flexible occurrences and compare them with the canonical tree. If they are isomorphic except for the structure stemming from additional words that appear within the MWE, we regard them as the true flexible usage of the MWE. For all the subtrees that are not the same as the canonical tree nor isomorphic to the canonical tree are regarded as false cases, meaning they are not the true usage of the MWE.

For the 2927 MWE candidates we collected, we looked for all the fixed and flexible occurrences of them in the total of 37,015 sentences. Only 1871 MWEs have at least one occurrence in the corpus. We then obtained 26,358 minimal subtrees, and 14,146 unique minimal subtrees. We summarize them in Table 1.

Number of MWE types	1871
Number of Minimal Subtrees	26,358
Number of Unique Subtrees	14,146

Table 1: Dependency Subtrees of MWEs obtained from OntoNotes

Those figures suggest and we confirmed that most of the false occurrences of MWEs are unique.

5 Automated Annotation of MWEs

By comparing the subtrees for each MWE, we apply the above mentioned process for identifying positive usages of the MWE and for obtaining the dependency tree representation of the MWE.

For each MWE candidate, the instances that correspond to the canonical dependency trees and those that produce its isomorphic dependency trees are regarded as positive and true usages of the MWE. We cannot make any decision on the MWEs that appear only once in the corpus. In the following analysis, we excluded those MWEs.

When we decided that the canonical usages and their isomorphic usages are positive usages of MWEs, we found 1,194 positive fixed cases (i.e., canonical usages), 1,704 positive flexible cases (i.e., isomorphic to canonical form), and 11,248 negative cases. Table 2 summarizes them.

label	count
Positive Fixed MWEs	1194
Positive Flexible MWEs	1704
Negative cases	11,248

Table 2: The number of Fixed and Flexible MW and examples

5.1 Some Problematic Examples

In this section, we show some examples that are difficult to discriminate based on the structure uniformity with canonical usages. Figure 7 shows a positive usage (i.e., the canonical usage) of "a certain". Figure 8 shows a negative occurrence of this MWE. The dependency tree in Figue 8 is isomorphic to that in Figure 7 except for the existence of an adverb "almost" within the expression as a parent of "certain". Although our procedure cannot identify the latter case as a negative example, it is clear that the head NN's in the trees are at different positions in the latter expression. The head NN in the canonical usage appears to the right of "certain", while the head NN in the negative case appears to the left of "certain". Taking the relative positons of head or modifiers into consideration solves this problem. We are going to investigate if this is true in all other cases.

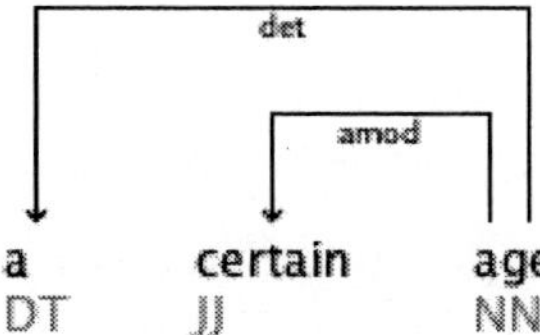

Figure 7: Canonical Subtree of "a certain"

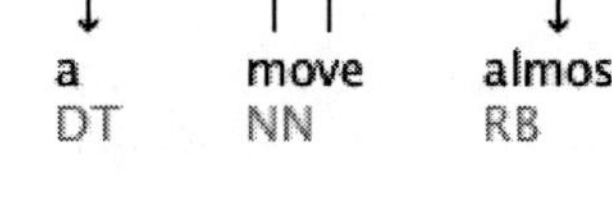

Figure 8: Negative Subtree of "a certain"

Another problematic and difficult case is shown in Figures 9 and 10. Figure 9 shows the canonical usage of "a couple of", and Figure 10 shows a variation of this MWE. Since the minimal subtree extracted from the latter example is not isomorphic to the former subtree, we cannot recognize this as a positive usage. On the other hand, if we like to regard the latter case as an admissible variation of the MWE "a couple of", we need to find better ways for identifying these types of positive usages where an extra element is not necessarily a modifier (child) of a component of an MWE.

6 Conclusion and Feature work

We presented our ongoing project of English flexible multi-word expression lexicon construction and corpus annotation. We especially described a method of flexible MWE lexicon construction and their

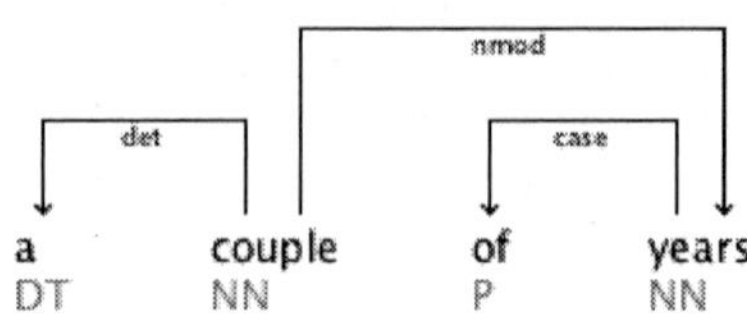

Figure 9: Subtree of "a couple of"

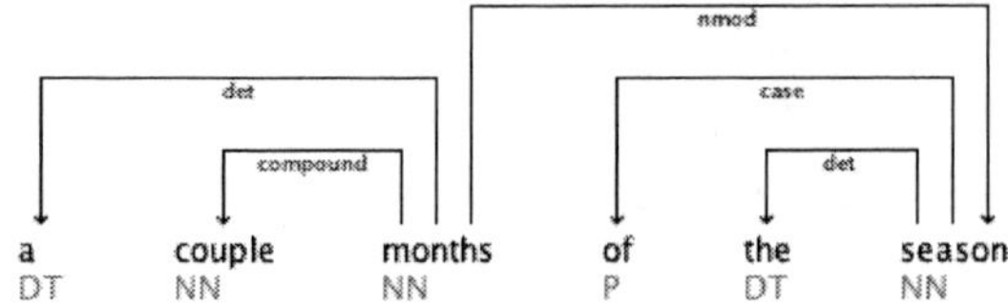

Figure 10: Subtree of "a couple month of"

annotation on a part of OntoNotes corpus. Our method enables semi-automatic annotation of flexible MWEs and also produces dependency structure representations of flexible MWEs.

While the method can achieve high recall of annotating positive occurrences in treebank, we need manual checking for those cases where the extracted minimal dependency subtrees are close but a slightly different from the canonical subtrees. Another problem we need to pursue is that the coverage of candidate MWEs is not wide enough. As we show in the experiments, within the MWE candidates we collected, only one third of them appear in the OntoNotes corpus. Furthermore, many of them show one or a small number of occurrences.

For the future work, we will try to collect far larger number of occurrences of the candidate MWEs in a large scale corpus, parse all the extracted sentences in dependency structure, and apply the method presented in this paper to those parsed results. Although the parsing accuracy is not 100%, handling a large number of examples hopefully provides results with high confidence.

Acknowledgement

This work was supported by CREST, JST, and JSPS KAKENHI Grant Number 15K16053.

References

Anne Abeillé, Lionel Clément, and François, Toussenel. 2003. *Building a Treebank for French.* In Treebanks : Building and Using Parsed Corpora. pages 165 – 188. Springer.

Marie Candito and Matthieu Constant. 2014. *Strategies for Contiguous Multiword Expression Analysis and Dependency Parsing.* Proc. of ACL, pages 743 – 753.

Matthieu Constant and Joakim Nivre. 2016. *A Transition-Based System for Joint Lexical and Syntactic Analysis.* In Proceedings of the 54th Annual Meeting of the Association for Computational Linguistics, pages 161 – 171.

de Marneffe, Marie-Catherine and Manning Christopher D. 2008. *The Stanford typed dependencies representation..* In Proceedings of the Coling workshop on Cross-Framework and CrossDomain Parser Evaluation, pages 1 – 8.

Akihiko Kato, Hiroyuki Shindo, Yuji Matsumoto 2016. *Construction of an English Dependency Corpus incorporating Compound Function Words.* Proceedings of the Tenth International Conference on Language Resources and Evaluation (LREC 2016), pages 1667 – 1671.

Masayuki Komai, Hiroyuki Shindo, Yuji Matsumoto. 2015. *An Efficient Annotation for Phrasal Verbs using Dependency Information.* In Proceedings of the 29th Pacific Asia Conference on Language, Information and Computation (PACLIC), Posters, pages 125 – 131.

Sameer S. Pradhan, Eduard Hovy, Mitch Marcus, Martha Palmer, Lance Ramshaw, and Ralph Weischedel. 2007. *OntoNotes: A unified relational semantic representation.* Proc. of ICSC, pages 517 – 526, Washington, DC, USA.

Victoria Rosén, Koenraad De Smedt, Gyri Smørdal Losnegaard, Eduard Bejček, Agata Savary and Petya Osenova 2016. *MWEs in Treebanks: From Survey to Guidelines.* Proc. of LREC-2016, pages 2323 – 2330, Portoro ž , Slovenia.

Ivan A. Sag, Timothy Baldwin, Francis Bond, Ann Copestake, and Dan Flickinger. 2002. *Multiword Expressions: A Pain in the Neck for NLP*. In Proceedings of the Third International Conference on Intelligent Text Processing and Computational Linguistics (CICLing 2002), pages 1 − - 15, Mexico City, Mexico.

Agata Savary, Manfred Sailer, Yannick Parmentier, Michael Rosner, Victoria Rosén, Adam Przepiórkowski, Cvetana Krstev, Veronika Vincze, Beata Wójtowicz, Gyri Smørdal Losnegaard, Carla Parra Escartín, Jakub Waszczuk, Matthieu Constant, Petya Osenova, Federico Sangati. 2015. *PARSEME − PARSing and Multiword Expressions within a European multilingual network*. Proceedings of the 7th Language & Technology Conference (LTC 2015), Pozna ń , Poland.

Nathan Schneider, Spencer Onuffer, Nora Kazour, Emily Danchik, Michael T. Mordowanec, Henrietta Conrad, and Noah A. Smith. 2014. *Comprehensive annotation of multiword expressions in a social web corpus*. Proceedings of LREC-2014, pages 455 − 461, Reykjavik, Iceland.

Yutaro Shigeto, Ai Azuma, Sorami Hisamoto, Shuhei Kondo, Tomoya Kose, Keisuke Sakaguchi, Akifumi Yoshimoto, Frances Yung, Yuji Matsumoto. 2013. *Construction of English MWE Dictionary and its Application to POS Tagging*. Proceedings of the 9th Workshop on Multiword Expressions (MWE 2013), pages 139 − 144.

Natalia Silveira, Timothy Dozat, Marie-Catherine de Marneffe, Samuel R. Bowman, Miriam Connor, John Bauer and Christopher D. Manning. 2014. *A Gold Standard Dependency Corpus for English*. In Proceedings of the Ninth International Conference on Language Resources and Evaluation (LREC-2014).

A new look at possessive reflexivization: A comparative study between Czech and Russian

Anna Nedoluzhko

Charles University, Faculty of Mathematics and Physics

Institute of Formal and Applied Linguistics

Prague, Czech Republic

nedoluzko@ufal.mff.cuni.cz

Abstract

The paper presents a contrastive description of reflexive possessive pronouns "svůj" in Czech and "svoj" in Russian. The research concerns syntactic, semantic and pragmatic aspects. With our analysis, we shed a new light on the already investigated issue, which comes from a detailed comparison of the phenomenon of possessive reflexivization in two typologically and genetically similar languages. We show that whereas in Czech, the possessive reflexivization is mostly limited to syntactic functions and does not go beyond the grammar, in Russian it gets additional semantic meanings and moves substantially towards the lexicon. The obtained knowledge allows us to explain heretofore unclear marginal uses of reflexives in each language.

1   Introduction

It is generally known that a comparison of the performance of a phenomenon in different languages brings more knowledge about this phenomenon. The fact that a cross-lingual study brings more knowledge about how a phenomenon functions in each separate language under comparison is less trivial, but also challenging. Our research here contributes to the latter claim: we compare possessive pronouns in Czech and Russian by addressing statistics obtained from the parallel English-Czech-Russian corpus PCEDT-R (Novák et al., 2016) as well as existing (mostly) monolingual theoretical knowledge with the aim to learn more about this type of pronouns in each language separately. Taking into account existing variety of means to express the notion of possessivity, we concentrate on reflexive possessive pronouns "svůj" in Czech and "svoj" in Russian.

In occasional references, the rules of the use of reflexive pronouns are observed as similar or the same (cf. Panevová, 1986; Čmejrková, 2003). Indeed, a shallow observation proves this assumption. Both in Czech and in Russian, the reflexive possessive "svůj/svoj" is basically coreferential with the subject. Situations where it is not the case are thoroughly described in the literature and, again, a shallow observation of research papers on this topic proves the similarity. However, there can be found a number of sentences, where a very frequent conventional use of Russian "svoj" cannot be translated as such into Czech, as can be seen in Example (1). Also, the statistics obtained from PCEDT_R (see Section 3) provides a significant difference in the frequency of the use of possessive pronouns and the distribution between personal and reflexive possessive pronouns in Czech and Russian.

(1)   RU: *U každogo učenogo jesť **svoja** biblioteka.* - CZ: *Každý vědec má ***svou/vlastní*** knihovnu.* [lit. Each scientist has self's/own library.]

The analysis of these discrepancies shows that it is meaningful to compare possessives in Czech and Russian according to the following aspects:

a)   Syntactic rules and tendencies for the use of reflexive possessives (possibility of the use of "svůj/svoj" with antecedents in direct or indirect cases, occurrences of reflexive possessives in the nominative case, the use and referential qualities of nominal groups with reflexive possessives in sentences with embedded explicit and implicit predications, etc.);

b)   Semantics and functions of reflexive possessives (i.e. we should answer the question if

Proceedings of the Workshop on Grammar and Lexicon: Interactions and Interfaces,
pages 110–119, Osaka, Japan, December 11 2016.

"svůj/svoj" has its own meaning, if it may change the meaning of a nominal group it is used with, or if it is just the formal means of possessive reflexivization);

c) Pragmatic factors of the use of personal and reflexive possessive pronouns;
d) Competition of personal (*můj, tvůj, náš, váš, jeho, její, jejich* in Czech, *moj, tvoj, naš, vaš, jego, jeje, ich* in Russian) and reflexive possessives, co-occurrence in specific contexts and comparison of these contexts for Czech and Russian, also with respect to pragmatic factors;
e) Optionality of possessives, possibility to omit possessive pronouns, or, on the contrary, to insert them to the places where they have not been used by the speaker;
f) Distribution between spoken and written discourse, sociolinguistic and historical factors for Czech and Russian, etc.

Due to extensiveness of the topic, this paper primarily addresses the first three aspects, namely syntactic, semantic and partially pragmatic factors of the use of reflexive possessive pronouns.

We believe that our findings are interesting both from the theoretical and computational perspectives. From the perspective of computational linguistics, searching for rules of expressing possessivity helps us find and verify specific features in text that can be further used as background knowledge for the improvement of multilingual tools for coreference and anaphora resolution. From the theoretical point of view, our research contributes to contrastive comparative analysis of typologically related languages. The knowledge acquired by such comparison not only gives us the typologically relevant information in general but also an opportunity to know more about each separate language.

2   Theoretical Background

The use and distribution of personal and reflexive possessive pronouns are analyzed in scientific literature both for Czech and for Russian, but mostly separately. To our knowledge, the only study concerning both languages in detail is Bílý (1981), who explains the choice of pronouns on the background of the theory of FSP, applying the notion of communicative dynamism.

For Czech, the description of personal and reflexive possessive pronouns begins with Svoboda (1880) and is further addressed in a number of theoretical studies and grammars (Gebauer, 1890; Trávníček, 1951; Daneš—Hausenblas, 1962; Grepl—Karlík, 1986; Daneš et al., 1987, etc). These studies formulate the basic rule of coreference of the reflexive possessive "svůj" with the subject (Gebauer, 1890) and point out an ambiguous reference of reflexive possessives in sentences with embedded predications.

The study of reflexive possessives in Russian goes back to Peškovskij (1914). After a longer time period, the cases of oblique control of Russian possessives were addressed within the binding theory by Timberlake (1980) and Rappoport (1986).

The most intensive research, both for Czech and for Russian, begins independently in 1980s. The shallow and deep syntactic criteria for the use of personal and reflexive possessives in Czech have been formulated within the theory of Functional Generative Description (Hajičová et al., 1985; Panevová 1980, 1986) and it was later developed by Čmejrková (1998, 2002, 2003, 2005, 2006, 2011), who used pragmatic criteria to explain the concurrence of personal and reflexive possessives in literary and colloquial Czech.

The research of possessivity and reflexivization for Russian continued in the semantic and pragmatic directions. Yokoyama—Klenin (1976) and Yokoyama (1980) analyze possessive pronouns within the theory of empathy (Kuno, 1975). Padučeva (1983, 1985) considers additional meanings of a reflexive possessive "svoj" which largely conform to the list of the meanings presented in the Dictionary of Russian (Ožegov—Švedova, 1997). Semantic functions and non-canonical control of Russian possessives is further addressed in Brykina (2009) and Fed'ko (2007).

Coreference resolution of reflexive pronouns is generally considered an easy task, particularly for English. Usually a principle that the reflexive pronoun refers to the subject in the same clause is followed (Mitkov 2002). However, this task may be more challenging for other languages, especially for those with free word order for which syntactic parsers perform worse. For example, in their error analysis of coreference resolvers for Russian, Toldova et al. (2016) report the maximum resolution accuracy on reflexive pronouns to be 80%. Even for English, the strict syntax-driven approach starts to fail if applied on more complicated texts, as reported on split antecedent coreference resolution on a patent material (Burga et al., 2016).

3 What data show

The analysis performed in this study is inspired by statistical results obtained from the three-language parallel corpus **PCEDT-R** (Novák et al., 2016) and presented in Nedoluzhko et al. (2016). The corpus contains 50 journalist texts (1078 sentences), manually translated from English into Czech and Russian. The corpus is provided with rich morphological, shallow syntactic and tectogrammatical annotation, it also contains manual annotation of word alignment for Czech and English pronouns. The Russian part was automatically aligned with the Czech part of PCEDT using GIZA++ (Och and Ney, 2000), which was run on a large amount of parallel Czech-Russian data. The resulting triples containing possessive units (in at least one of the languages used) have been manually annotated and analyzed from the perspective of each language separately. The absolute numbers of the mapping of 238 English possessive pronouns in PCEDT-R are briefly presented in Table 1.

238 English possessive pronouns	Personal possessives	Reflexive possessives	External possession[1]	No possessive
Czech	92	80	12	54
Russian	112	83	8	35

Table 1: Counterparts of English possessive pronouns in Czech and Russian.

The statistics of the correspondences of English possessive pronouns to their Czech and Russian counterparts showed the tendency of Czech and Russian to use possessive pronouns less frequently than in English. Moreover, Nedoluzhko et al. (2016) observed that the numbers differ significantly for Czech and for Russian. In Russian, 15% of English pronouns remain unexpressed, whereas in Czech this number comes up to 23%. The more frequent use of possessives in Russian texts raise the suspicion that it could be influenced by lower translation quality, but the comparison with original texts from the Prague Dependency Treebank for Czech (PDT 3.0; Bejček et al., 2013) and the Russian Treebank (RTB; Boguslavsky et al., 2000) proved that the difference between the frequency of pronouns in original and translated texts in Czech is even higher than in Russian.

As concerns the distribution of personal and reflexive possessives, the data show a moderate but statistically significant prevalence of personal possessives over reflexive ones in both languages, and in Czech reflexive possessives are significantly more frequent than in Russian.

Another finding obtained from the parallel data is a similar optionality of possessives in Czech and Russian. Out of the translations of English possessive pronouns, about 20% were marked as optional in both languages. However, we observe a substantial difference in optionality of expressing possessivity between personal and reflexive possessives in both languages: Reflexive possessives can be omitted more frequently.

4 Syntactic rules for reflexive possessives

The basic "school-grammar" rule for the use of reflexive possessive pronouns was formulated for Czech (Gebauer, 1890) and for Russian (Peškovskij, 1914) in a similar way: a reflexive pronoun refers to the subject of the sentence (Example 2). The moderate difference can be observed in the modality of the rule: It is formulated rather prescriptively for Czech and more descriptively for Russian.[2]

(2) CZ: *Petr ztratil **svou** peněženku* – RU: *Petr poterjal **svoj** košelek.* [lit. Peter lost self's wallet.]

---

[1] See, e.g., the English possessive pronoun *their* translated with the external dative reflexive *si* into Czech: *Glenn and Sharon Beebe of Cincinnati had sued the company in 1981 after installing Burlington carpets in **their** office.* – CZ: *Společnost zažalovali Glenn a Sharon Beebeovi z Cincinnati v roce 1981 poté, co si koberce Burlington položili do kanceláře.*

[2] This difference mostly concerns the attitude on this issue in general during the research period, not primarily the studies of J. Gebauer (1890) and A. Peškovskij (1914).

Reference to antecedents in indirect cases is restricted to a close set of Russian verbs (Padučeva, 1983).[3] As for Czech, the use of "svůj" referring to an antecedent in an indirect case is unacceptable for singular subjects (Example 3 and 4a) but, interestingly, it sounds somewhat better in distributive contexts (Example 4b)[4]:

(3) RU: *Jemu tošno ot* **svojej** *bespomosčnosti.* – CZ: *Je mu špatně ze* ***své*** *bezmoci.* [lit. He feels sick because of self's helplessness.]

(4a) CZ: **Petrovi je líto* ***svého*** *mládí.* [lit. Petr feels sorry for self's youth.]

(4b) CZ: *[?]Každému je líto* ***svého*** *mládí.*[lit. Everybody feels sorry for self's youth.]

In a simple sentence like Example (2), the speaker, as well as the interpreter, is able to process sentences demanding reflexivization unambiguously. Differences occur when sentences contain embedded predications (Example 5). It is not clear then, which subject (i.e. the subject of the main clause or the subject of the embedded predication) triggers reflexivization.

(5) CZ: *Profesor požádal asistenta přednést* **svůj** *referát.* – RU: *Professor poprosil assistenta pročitať* **svoj** *doklad.* [lit. The professor asked the assistant to read self's report.]

The interpretation of sentences like (5) evoked intensive discussion which began with J. Gebauer and A. Peškovskij (such cases are even referred to as so called 'Peškovskij sentences'), continued with Trávníček (1951), Daneš—Hausenblas (1962), Růžička (1973), Bílý (1981), Timberlake (1980), Rappoport (1986), Panevová (1980, 1986), Hajičová et al. (1985, 2002) and it is still addressed in the recent studies of Feďko (2007), Brykina (2009) and Čmejrková (2011 etc.).

There is, again, an interesting discrepancy in the modality of claims concerning referential ambiguity in 'Peškovskij sentences' for Czech and for Russian. For Russian, their ambiguity is generally accepted. For Czech, we find contradictory opinions in different studies on this topic. According to most of the authors, „svůj/svoj" in (5) is ambiguous, as it can refer to the subject of the matrix sentence (*professor*), as well as to the agent of the embedded predication (*assistant*). However, Fr. Trávníček in his Grammar of Czech (Trávníček, 1951) and even in his translation of Gebauer's Czech grammar (Trávníček, 1939) gives the prescription saying that the reflexive "svůj" must refer to the subject of the embedded predication (*assistant*). Contrarily, the prescription in school grammars is opposite: "svůj" in sentences like (5) must refer to the shallow subject of the sentence (*professor*). Panevová (1986) formulated the following syntactic hypothesis: in cases with embedded predications, „svůj" tends to refer to the Agent of the embedded structure, i.e. to *the assistant* in (5). Besides the cases with explicit embedded predications, this pattern nicely explains the acceptance of sentences with indirect cases of the deep subject in non-personal sentences like (6) for Czech.

(6) CZ: *Zátopkové se podařilo opakovat* **svůj** *úspěch* _Daneš–Hausenblas(1962)_ [lit. To Zátopková was possible to repeat self's success.]

Moreover, Panevová (1986) formulates two other syntactic tendencies for Czech, interesting from the comparative point of view. The first observation is the strong restriction to the use of reflexive possessives within the subject of the sentence (cf. impossible "svůj" in Examples 7–9 for Czech).

(7) CZ: ***Svoje*** *děti běhají po ulici.* [lit. Self's children are running on the street.]

(8) CZ: **Trhání* **svých** *zubů ve mně vzbudilo nelibé pocity.* [lit. Pulling out the self's teeth was unpleasant to me.]

(9) CZ: **Matku dojala péče o osud* **svých** *dětí.* [lit. The care for self's children affected the mother.]

However, these sentences contain additional restrictions. In (7), "svůj" is used in Nominative case, which is forbidden with the reflexive possessive in its basic function (see Section 5.1). In (8) and (9), the antecedent of "svůj" is different from the Agents of the verbal nouns used within the same subject

---

[3] This claim concerns the reflexive "svoj" in its basic purely possessive meaning. For other meanings see Section 5.

[4] Deliberately, we do not consider sentences like (6) with embedded implicit predications that determine the antecedent for the reflexivization.

(*trhání* [pulling out] in (8) and *péče* [care] in (9)). If we change the Agent and reformulate the sentence (8) to (8a) in Czech, it becomes acceptable in Czech and absolutely normal in Russian.

(8a) CZ: *Trhání ?svých zubů je dost nepříjemný úkol.* – RU: *Udalenije **svoich** zubov – zanjatije vesma neprijatnoje.* [lit. Pulling out the self's teeth is quite unpleasant.]

Surprisingly, however, the same transformation for (9) does not give an acceptable sentence in Czech, whereas in Russian it becomes fully acceptable.

(9a) CZ: *Matku vždy velice těšila péče o *své dětí.* – RU: *Mamu vsegda očeň radovala zabota o **svoich** detjach.* [lit. The care for self's children always gave joy to the mother.]

The second Panevová's restriction concerns the use of personal and reflexive possessive pronouns in matrix and embedded predications. She claims for Czech that in the embedded clause, a reflexive possessive must be used when referring to the subject in the matrix clause, and only personal possessive may be used when referring to the Agent of the embedded predication. The claim is demonstrated on Example (10). However, this delicate syntactic rule does not work for Russian, where all forms of possessive pronouns may be used with slight stylistic but not referential difference.[5]

(10) CZ: *Jan byl znepokojen chováním **svých/*jeho** dětí v **jejich/*svém** pokoji.* – RU: *Jan byl nedovolen povedenijem **svoich/jeho** detej v **svojej/ich** komnate* [lit. Jan was unhappy with the behaviour of self's/his children in self's/their room.]

5 Semantics of reflexive possessives

Most studies addressing possessive reflexivization in Czech do not concern any special lexical semantics of „svůj“, it is considered to be "lexically completely emptied" (Čmejrková, 2003:186). Uses mismatching this claim, such as Exampe (12) or (15) below are observed as a "special transformation" (Daneš – Hausenblas (1962), "implied predications […] of very low predicative quality" (Bílý, 1981), substandard expressions (Karlík et al., 1995), homonyms with the basic reflexive "svůj" (Dočekal, 2000), phrasemes (Čmejrková, 2003), etc.

On the other hand, for Russian, additional semantics of "svoj" is generally accepted and presents an issue of linguistic interest. Apart from its basic reflexive meaning, which expresses possession or a valency position ("svoj$_1$"), Padučeva (1983) distinguishes five additional meanings of "svoj" in Russian, which were later supplied by one more meaning in Brykina (2009). In what follows, we list these meanings and look for Czech equivalents for them.

- *svoj$_2$* = 'svoj$_1$'+'own' (Example 11). In Czech, "svůj" is not used in this meaning, but we meet it in phrasemes or collocations (cf. Example (12), *prosadit své/svou* [get one's way, lit. enforce self's], or *trvat na svém* [insist, lit. insist on self's]);

(11) RU: ***Svoja** kvartira lučše čem sjemnaja.* – CZ: ****Svůj** byt je lepší než nájemní.* [lit. Self's flat is better than a rented one.]

(12) CZ: ***Svá** vlast je každému nejmilejší* [lit. Self's homeland is to everybody the best.]

- *svoj$_3$* = 'svoj$_1$'+ distributive meaning (Example 1 in Section 1). Being very productive in Russian, this meaning is marginal in Czech (cf. phraseological Example 12). However, as we observed in Example (4b in Section 4), the distributive semantics can make reflexives in some forbidden contexts sound better;

- *svoj$_4$:* = 'svoj$_1$'+'specific, special' (Examples 13 and 14). In Russian, this meaning is common and productive, also with "svoj" in the nominative case (Example 13). In Czech, it is rather marginal, but yet possible in examples like (14):

---

[5] In some idiolects, the combination *svoich detej v svojej komnate* [self's children in self's room] is suppressed in the meaning 'Jan's children in children's room' or 'Jan's children in Jan's room', although othe speakers allow for these readings. However, this form is stylistically worse than other combinations, probably due to some kind of priming effect.

(13) RU: *No i zdes' kipjat **svoi** strasti.* – CZ: *Ale i tady jsou ***své** vášně.* [lit. But here, there are also self's passions.]

(14) RU: *Zdes' jesť **svoja** logika.* – CZ: *To má **svou** logiku.* [There is a certain (lit. self's) logic here.]

- *svoj₅* = 'svoj₁'+'corresponding' (Examples 15 and 16). The Czech "svůj" has this meaning in constructions with *své místo* [self's place] (Example 15) and in the proverb (16). Due to its semantics, this meaning is not very productive in Russian, but still there are more such contexts for Russian than for Czech (cf. ru. *Den'gi budut v svoje vremja* [lit. Money will come in self's time], *Delo idet svoim por'adkom* [The thing is going on as it should (lit. by self's order)] which are not possible in Czech).

(15) CZ: *Dej to na **své** místo.* – RU: *Postav' eto na **svoje** mesto.* [Put it into (self's) place.]

(16) CZ: *Všechno má **svůj** čas.* – RU: *Vsemu **svoje** vremja.* [The better day the better deed, lit. Everything has self's time.]

- *svoj₆* = 'a relative, close person' (Example 17 and 18). This meaning tends to be phraseological as it does not contain the basic reflexive meaning of "svoj₁" and does not refer to an antecedent. In Czech, this meaning could be slightly (almost not) acceptable in (18). A similar meaning is present in the Czech proverb *Svůj k svému* (Example 18) or the phrase *být svoji* [to be a married couple].

(17) RU: *V semje jego Ivan byl **svoj** čelovek.* – CZ: *V jeho rodině byl Ivan ***svůj** člověk.* [lit. In his family, Ivan was the self's (*meaning* close, dear) person.]

(18) RU: ***Svoj svojego** izdaleka vidit.* [lit. Self's see self's from far away.] – CZ: *⁇**Svůj svého** z dálky vidí.* BUT ***Svůj k svému**.* [lit. Self's to self's, meaning ca. that people of similar background should associate with one another.]

- *svoj₇:* = 'svoj₁'+'typical, characteristic' (Example 19). The reflexive "svoj" used in this meaning functions as a modifier and makes a quality modified by it definite to the interpreter. It also changes the communicative structure of the utterance: the nominal group used with "svoj" becomes contextually bound and gets an additional intonation stress (Brykina, 2009:158).

(19) RU: *On mne nadojel **svoimi** žalobami na žizň.* – CZ: *ᵗUž mě nudí **svým** stěžováním na život.* [lit. He bores me with self's complaints to his life.]

***

As we can see, the cases lacking a uniform description for Czech (like *dej to na své místo* [lit. Put it on its place], etc.) may be treated as having one of the additional meanings that are described for Russian. However, differently from Russian, they are rather marginal and may be considered to be phrasemes or collocations.

5.1 Syntax of reflexive possessive with additional meanings

Syntactic rules for the use of reflexive possessives with additional functions differ from those in its basic possessive meaning in the following respects:

(i) Reflexive possessive in its secondary meaning allows Nominative case (cf. Examples (11), (13), (14) for Russian). This is also true for Czech, but because in Czech secondary meanings of reflexives are marginal, it is mostly considered as an exception (cf. Example (12)).

(ii) Opposite to its basic meaning, reflexive possessives with additional semantics may refer to antecedents in indirect cases in Russian without any restrictions (Example 20). This is not the case of Czech. However, the better acceptability of (4b) compared to (4a) in Section 4 in distributive context is similar to it.

(20) RU: *V redakcii malo **svoich** rabotnikov.* – CZ: *V redakci je málo ***svých** (vlastních) pracovníků* [lit. There are few self's employees in the editorial board.]

(iii) The reflexive possessive in its secondary meaning in Russian allows the predicative use (Example 21):

(21) RU: *A gruď – svoja!* – CZ: *Ale prsa jsou *své!* [lit. But (her) breast is self's.]

(iv) Secondary meanings of reflexive possessives tend to be used in the focus of the sentence, in intonationally stressed positions, etc.

5.2 Animacy of the antecedent

The competition between personal and reflexive possessives in Russian may be also explained by the animacy of their antecedents. In Padučeva (1983), the author claims that „svůj" with inanimate antecedent cannot be used if it fills the valency position of Patiens, whereas with animate antecedents it is allowed, cf. Example (22) for inanimate antecedent *zakony* [laws]. Interestingly, for Czech, this form is not fully prohibited[6]. As concerns animate antecedents, Padučeva suggests the example from Dostojevsky (23), where „svůj/svoj" is allowed for both languages. However, reflexive possessive reference to Patient is common neither in Czech nor in Russian, so many other examples sound unnatural or impossible (Example 24).

(22) RU: *Zakony rasšatyvajutsja ot **ich** (*svojego) narušenija.* – CZ: *Zákony trpí ʔsvým častým porušováním.* [lit. Laws get weaker because of self's often breaking.]

(23) RU: *Dlja mnogich naš krestjanin po osvoboždenii **svojem** javilsja strannym nedoumenijem.* – CZ: *Pro mnohé se náš rolník stal po **svém** osvobození podivnou raritou.* [lit. For many people, our peasant became a strange creature after self's emancipation.]

(24) RU: *Posle *svojego ubijstva, jego vskore zabyli.* – CZ: *Po *svém zabití byl brzy zapomenut.* [lit. After self's murder, he was quickly forgotten.]

When referring to an inanimate Agent of the sentence, the reflexive possessives are freely replaceable with personal possessives in Russian (Example 25). This is not the case for referring to animate Agent in Russian, moreover this tendency does not work in Czech. In Czech, the choice between personal and reflexive possessives is made according to syntactic (Section 4) and pragmatic (Section 6) criteria, the factor of animacy is not very important.

(25) RU: *Slovo „takže" v **jego/svojem** osnovnom upotreblenii bezudarno.* – CZ: *Výraz "také" je ve **svém** (ʔʔjeho) primárním významu enklitický.* [lit. The word „also" is enclitic in its/self's meaning.]

6 Pragmatic aspects in possessive reflexivization

Yokoyama–Klenin (1976) and Yokoyama (1980) claim that the choice between personal and reflexive possessive pronouns in Russian is determined by discourse-oriented factors, namely by the degree, to which the speaker identifies with his inner self in the process of the speech performance (Yokoyama, 1980). According to the authors, the situation is different for the 1st, 2nd and 3rd persons. For the 1st and 2nd persons, reflexivization occurs when the speaker feels a distance between his inner self and the utterance, while a personal possessive is used when the speaker psychologically completely identifies himself with the antecedent. For the 3rd person, the situation is reverse.

The Yokoyama–Klenin's approach was developed primarily for Russian, but not all the examples presented by the authors sound well in Russian, cf. almost unacceptable Example (26).

(26) RU: *Nu i čto, čto on zametil, kak kakaja-to baba uronila ʔʔ**jeje** košelek.* [lit. So what, if he didn't notice that a woman dropped her wallet?]

Interestingly, Yokoyama–Klenin's approach seem to better pass for Czech than for Russian. S. Čmejrková provides a series of studies (Čmejrková, 1998, 2002, 2005, 2006, 2011), where she provides numerous reliably acceptable corpus and empirical examples supporting this approach. The author also distinguishes between pragmatic rules for the pronouns of different persons and number. So, for the concurrence of the reflexive possessive with the 1st person singular "můj" [my], she defines a number of emphatic contexts, in which there is a strong tendency to use personal possessive pronouns instead of the reflexive one. The possibility to use the reflexive increases with the increasing distance

---

[6] This sentence was presented to ten native speakers in different pragmatic contexts and it was definitely rejected only by two of them when they were explicitly asked if this sentence was grammatical. However, the sentence does not sound natural by itself, thus the language intuition could not be applied properly and the experiment is not fully legitimate.

between the speaker's inner self and the utterance: from lexicalized phrasemes like *na mou/*svou duši* [lit. *to my/*self's soul*], *na mou/*svou čest* [lit. *to my/*self's honour*] through close relatives and friends, where the use of personal possessives is very often in (especially spoken) texts (Example 27) up to all other objects of possession where the special degree of empathy with the speaker may be expressed with the personal possessive (Example 28).

(27) CZ: *Mám obavu o **moji** rodinu.* Čmejrková (2011) [lit. I'm afraid for my family.]

(28) CZ: *To je věc, kterou bych rád připomněl pro **mé** kolegy.* Čmejrková (1998) [lit. This is a thing that I would like to remind to my colleagues.]

As for Russian, this tendency exists, but it is substantially weaker than for Czech. Differently from Czech, the distribution rules for personal and reflexive possessives in the 1st and 2nd persons are not so strong in Russian, so the distinction in pragmatic aspects is also missing.

7   Conclusion

Based on parallel corpus statistics from one hand and on existing theoretical research on the other hand, we contrasted the use of reflexive possessive pronouns "svůj/svoj" in Czech and in Russian. The observed facts indicate substantial difference in the use of possessive pronouns in Czech and Russian.

In Czech, syntactic functions of the reflexive possessive pronoun „svůj" absolutely prevail, its lexical semantics is so poor that expressions containing semanticalized „svůj" are rather observed as phrasemes. Furthermore, there is a number of syntactic limitations determining the use of the reflexive possessive in Czech. Contrarily, the Russian pronoun „svoj" has a number of secondary meanings, most of them supplement the basic reflexivization function of the pronoun. Syntactic rules for the use of „svoj" in its secondary meanings differ from those when it is used only to express possessivity (common use in the nominative case, reference to antecedents in indirect cases, etc.). The limitations determining the use of the reflexive possessive in Russian include semantic ones (e.g., animacy of the antecedent). These facts indicate that the phenomenon of possessive reflexivization does not exceed the limits of grammar in Czech, whereas in Russian it goes beyond grammar towards the lexicon.

On the other hand, the obtained knowledge about frequently used additional functions of the reflexive possessive in Russian allows us to interpret the nature of marginal uses of reflexive possessives in Czech (e.g., semantic interpretation of *dej to na své místo* [*put it on self's place*]). Furthermore, it opens new issues of research leading to understanding the essence of reflexivization and passivization phenomena. In the future work, the ideas obtained from our comparison should be secondarily checked on corpus data, this time also on monolingual, and also spoken texts have to be taken into account.

A certain limitation, which makes the study of reflexive possessives especially hard, is the looseness of standards, especially in Czech and especially in sentences with embedded constructions (but not exceptionally). Judging grammatical acceptability differs significantly by speakers, the reason is both in the social–historical background (purist influences on the topic and the prescriptive character of rule for Czech that can form different idiolects and attitudes) and in the nature of the phenomenon itself.

Acknowledgements

We acknowledge the support from the Grant Agency of the Czech Republic (grant 16-05394S). This work has been using language resources developed and stored and distributed by the LINDAT/CLARIN project of the Ministry of Education, Youth and Sports of the Czech Republic (project LM2015071).

Reference

Eduard Bejček et al. 2013. *Prague Dependency Treebank 3.0.* Data/software, Charles university in Prague, MFF, ÚFAL, Prague, Czech Republic, http://ufal.mff.cuni.cz/pdt3.0/

Milan Bílý. 1981. *Intrasentential Pronominalization and Functional Sentence Perspective (in Czech, Russian, and English)*, Lund Slavonic Monographs, Slaviska Institutionen, Lund.

Igor M. Boguslavsky, Svetlana Grigorieva, Nikolai Grigoriev, Leonid Kreidlin, Nadežda Frid. 2000. Dependency Treebank for Russian: Concepts, Tools, Types of Information. *Proceedings of the 18th Conference on Computational Linguistics*. Saarbrücken, Vol 2:987–991.

Maria Brykina. 2009. *Coding the possessivity (corpus-based study of Russian)* [Jazykovyje sposoby kodirovanija possessivnosti (na materiale korpusnogo issledovanija russkogo jazyka]. Ph.D. thesis, Moscow.

Alicia Burga, Sergio Cajal, Joan Codina-Filba and Leo Wanner. 2016. Towards Multiple Antecedent Coreference Resolution in Specialized Discourse. *Proceedings of LREC 2016*. Portorož.

Czech National Corpus—Intercorp [Český národní korpus—InterCorp]. Ústav Českého národního korpusu FF UK, Prague. Cit.02.02.2016 , accessible from WWW: <http://www.korpus.cz>.

Světla Čmejrková. 1998. Syntactic and discourse aspects of reflexivization in Czech: The case of the reflexive pronoun svůj. // E. Hajičová (ed.), *Issues of Valency and Meaning. Studies in Honour of Jarmila Panevová*, Karolinum, Prague , 1998: 75–87.

Světla Čmejrková. 2002. Grammar and Pragmatics. [Gramatika a pragmatika], In: Z. Hladká and P. Karlík (eds.), *Universals and specifics* [Univerzália a specifika], Prague, 2002 (4):59–69.

Světla Čmejrková. 2003. Fortune of the possessive reflexive pronoun "svůj". [Osudy zvratného posesivního zájmena svůj]. *Naše řeč*, 86 (2003), 4:181-205.

Světla Čmejrková. 2005. Let the language be. [Nechte jazyk svému osudu.] In: Čmejrková S. and Svobodová I. (eds.) *Oratio et ratio*. Prague, 2005:79-86.

Světla Čmejrková. 2006. Is the pronoun "svůj" always on its place? [Je zájmeno "svůj" vzdy na svém místě?] In F. Štícha (ed.) *Possibilities and bounds of the Czech grammar* [Možnosti a meze české gramatiky.], Prague, Academia, 2006: 211-225.

Světla Čmejrková. 2011. Possessive reflexivization: Pronoun "svůj", its use and meaning. [Posesivní reflexivizace. Zájmeno svůj. Jeho užití a významy.] In Fr. Štícha (ed.) *Chapters from the Czech Grammar*. [Kapitoly z české gramatiky], Prague 2011: 655- 686.

Frantíšek Daneš and Karel Hausenblas. 1962. Přivlastňovací zájmena osobní a zvratná ve spisovné čeština. Personal and reflexive pronouns in Czech. *Slavica Pragensia* 4:191-202.

Frantíšek Daneš, Zdeněk Hlavsa and Miroslav Grepl. 1987. The Grammar of Czech – III. Syntax. [Mluvnice češtiny III. Syntax], Prague, Academia.

Mojmír Dočekal. 2000. Possessive reflexives in bohemistics. [Posesivní reflexivum v bohemistice]. *Collection of studies FF Brno university* [Sborník prací FF Brněnské university]. Studia minora Facultatis Philosophicae Universitatis Brunensis A 48, Brno:47–59.

Eugeny Fed'ko. 2007. *Non-canonical control of the reflexive pronoun in Russian* [Nekanonicheskij kontrol refleksivnogo mestoimenija v russkom jazyke], Master Thesis, MSU, Moscow.

Jan Gebauer. 1890. *The Czech grammar for secondary schools and pedagogical institutes*. [Mluvnice česká pro školy střední a ústavy učitelské], Prague.

Miroslav Grepl and Petr Karlík. 1986. *The syntax of Czech*. [Skladba spisovné češtiny.] Prague.

Jan Hajič, Hajičová E., Panevová J., Sgall P., Bojar O., Cinková S., Fučíková E., Mikulová M., Pajas P., Popelka J., Semecký J., Šindlerová J., Štěpánek J., Toman J., Urešová Z., Žabokrtský Z. 2012. Announcing Prague Czech-English Dependency Treebank 2.0. *Proceedings of the 8th International Conference on Language Resources and Evaluation (LREC 2012)*, European Language Resources Association, İstanbul:3153–3160.

Eva Hajičová, Jarmila Panevová, Petr Sgall. 1985. Coreference in the grammar and in the text, *PBML* 44:3–22.

Eva Hajičová, Jarmila Panevová, Petr Sgall. 2002. New level of bohemistics: Use of the annotated corpus. [K nové úrovni bohemistické práce: Využití anotovaného korpusu], *SaS* 63:241–262.

Eugene Charniak and Micha Elsner. 2009. EM works for pronoun anaphora resolution. *Proceedings of the 12th Conference of the European Chapter of the ACL (EACL 2009)*, Athens: 148 156.

Petr Karlík et al. (eds.) 1995. *A Reference Grammar of the* Czech *Language.* [Příruční mluvnice češtiny], Prague.

Susumu Kuno. 1975. Three Perspectives in the Functional Approach to Syntax. *CLS parasession on Functionalism*, 276-336.

Ruslan Mitkov. 2002. *Anaphora resolution.* Longman.

Anna Nedoluzhko, Anna Schwarz (Khoroshkina), Michal Novák. 2016. Possessives in Parallel English‑Czech-Russian Texts. *Computational Linguistics and Intellectual Technologies*, 15: 483-497.

Michal Novák, Oele Dieke, van Noord Gertjan. 2015. Comparison of Coreference Resolvers for Deep Syntax Translation. *Proceedings of the Second Workshop on Discourse in Machine Translation*, Lisbon: 17-23, 2015.

Michal Novák, Anna Nedoluzhko, Anna Schwarz (Khoroshkina). 2016. *Prague Czech-English-Russian Dependency Treebank* (PCEDT-R). Data/software, Lindat/Clarin data and tools, http://hdl.handle.net/11234/1-1791, Prague.

Franz Josef Och and Hermann Ney. 2000. Improved Statistical Alignment Models. *Proceedings of the 38th Annual Meeting of the Association for Computational Linguistics*. Stroudsburg: Association for Computational Linguistics.

Serhej I. Ožegov and Natalja Ju. Švedova. 1997. *Dictionary of Russian* [Tolkovyj slovar russkogo jazyka]. Moskva.

Elena V. Padučeva. 1983. Reflexive pronoun with indirect antecedent and the semantics of reflexivization. [Vozvratnoje mestoimenije s kosvennym antecedentom i semantika refleksivnosti], *Semiotics and informatics* [Semiotika i informatika], 21:3-33.

Elena V. Padučeva. 1985. *The statement and its relation to reality (referential mechanisms of the semantics of pronouns).* [Vyskazyvanije i jego sootnesennost s dejstvitelnostju (referencialnyje aspekty semantiki mestoimenij)], Moscow. Nauka.

Jarmila Panevová. 1986. K voprosu o refleksivnoj pronominalizacii v češskom jazyke, *Linguistische Arbeitsberichte* 54/56:44–56.

Jarmila Panevová. 1980. *Formy a funkce ve stavbě české věty*, Academia, Prague.

Alexander M. Peškovskij. 1914. *Russian syntax from scientific point of view.* [Russkij sintaksis v naučnom osveščenii.], Moscow.

Petr Piťha. 1992. *The relation of possessivization in Czech.* [Posesivní vztah v češtině], Prague.

Gilbert C. Rappoport. 1986. On Anaphor Binding in Russian. *Natural Language and Linguistic Theory*. No4: 97-120.

Rudolf Růžička. 1973. Reflexive oder nichtreflexive Pronominasierung in modernen Russischen und anderen slawischen Sprachen der Gegenwart. *Zeitschrift für Slawistik*, 17:636-779.

Václav Svoboda. 1880. Debate on the use of personal, possessive and reflexive pronouns in sentences. [Rozprava o užívání osobných, přisvojovacích a zvratných námestek v souvětích zkrácených], *Newspaper of Czech museum.* [Časopis Českého muzea] 54:124–142, 301–343.

Alan Timberlake. 1980. Oblique control of Russian reflexivization. C. Chvany and R. Brecht (eds.) *Morphosyntax in Slavic*. Columbus (Ohio), Slavica: 235-259.

Toldova, Svetlana, Ilya Azerkovich, Alina Ladygina, Anna Rojtberg and Maria Vasilyeva. 2016. Error analysis for anaphora resolution in Russian. *Proceedings of CORBON 2016.* SanDiego.

František Trávníček. 1939. *Gebauer's grammar of Czech.* [Gebaurova příruční mluvnice jazyka českého], Prague.

František Trávníček. 1951. *Grammar of Czech.* [Mluvnice spisovné češtiny], Prague.

Olga. T. Yokoyama. 1980. Studies in Russian Functional Syntax. *Harvard Studies in Syntax and Semantics III.* Harvard, 1980: 451–773.

Olga. T. Yokoyama and E. Klenin. 1976. The semantics of optional rules: Russian personal and reflexive possessives. *Sound, Sign, and Meaning*, Ann Arbor, 1976:249–267.

Modeling non-standard language

Alexandr Rosen
Institute of Theoretical and Computational Linguistics
Faculty of Arts, Charles University
Prague, Czech Republic
`alexandr.rosen@ff.cuni.cz`

Abstract

A specific language as used by different speakers and in different situations has a number of more or less distant varieties. Extending the notion of non-standard language to varieties that do not fit an explicitly or implicitly assumed norm or pattern, we look for methods and tools that could be applied to such texts. The needs start from the theoretical side: categories usable for the analysis of non-standard language are not readily available. However, it is not easy to find methods and tools required for its detection and diagnostics either. A general discussion of issues related to non-standard language is followed by two case studies. The first study presents a taxonomy of morphosyntactic categories as an attempt to analyse non-standard forms produced by non-native learners of Czech. The second study focusses on the role of a rule-based grammar and lexicon in the process of building and using a parsebank.

1 Introduction

It is often the case that instances of language use – in writing or speech of native and non-native speakers alike – do not comply with a conventional pattern specified in standard handbooks or seen as appropriate by the community of native speakers.[1] Yet the message is often intelligible and the communication is not hampered by linguistic variations. Language users are able to recover meaning from idiosyncrasies on any level of the linguistic system, such as phonetics, phonology, graphemics, morphology, syntax, semantics or pragmatics, including peculiarities occurring on multiple levels in parallel. In addition to understanding the content of the message, the hearer is often able to recognize implicit signals conveyed by any deviations from the expected and appropriate *register* and may even use various linguistic signs to make guesses about the speaker's background or covert intention.

Such abilities of the language user are in sharp contrast with the rigidity and performance of most language models. While rule-based models are very vulnerable to any unexpected phenomena and appropriate categories usable for their analysis are not readily available, stochastic models seem to be in a better position to cope with non-standard language. Apart from being more robust in general, perhaps at the cost of lower precision, various strategies can be used instead of a naively applying a model trained on 'standard' language. Reviewing a range of options, such as annotating more data, normalizing test data, deliberately corrupting training data, or adapting models to different domains, Eisenstein (2013) stresses the importance of a suitable match between the model and the domain of the text, while Plank (2016) points out that rather than to domains we should adapt our tools to text varieties in a multi-dimensional space of factors such as dialect, topic, genre, the speaker's gender, age, etc. Such models should be built using non-standard language as the training data to handle similar input. To handle code-switching and a mix of language varieties within a single text, multiple models may be needed in parallel. Alternatively, a single model can be trained on an appropriately annotated text as one of the 'domain adaptation' methods, which leads us back to the issue of a suitable taxonomy and markup of unexpected phenomena – one of the topics of this paper (see §3).

[1]The appropriateness is to a large extent determined by all sorts of contextual factors and the community may include only some privileged or elitist groups.

Proceedings of the Workshop on Grammar and Lexicon: Interactions and Interfaces,
pages 120–131, Osaka, Japan, December 11 2016.

We start with the assumption that there is an important role for a rationalist approach to language modeling in general, and to modeling of non-standard language varieties in particular. At the core of this premise is an observation that the varieties are not just random collection of unrelated phenomena, that each variety represents a system, with rules and principles partially shared with other varieties, standard or non-standard. In addition to its theoretical merit, the discovery of these rules and principles has practical benefits for many tasks in today's increasingly multilingual and globalized linguistic communities. These benefits include applications in the field of foreign language teaching, forensic linguistics, identification of the author's first language or processing of non-standard language in general for purposes of all sorts, better suited to the needs of both native and non-native speakers.[2]

We are aware of the wealth of studies targeting linguistic variability, including language development and acquisition, dialects, ethnolects, idiolects, specifics of spoken and colloquial language, and language disorders, in sociolinguistics and other fields. However, our specific aim is to explore options for extending the space of linguistic phenomena covered by existing language models beyond the limits of a standard language.

A general discussion of issues related to non-standard language (§2) is followed by two case studies. The first study (§3) presents a taxonomy of morphosyntactic categories as an attempt to analyse non-standard forms produced by non-native learners of Czech. The second study (§4) focusses on the role of a rule-based grammar and lexicon in the process of building and using a parsebank. Both topics are very partial probes into the general topic of non-standard language, but at least they target different issues, which can make the overall picture less patchy and more relevant.

2 Types of non-standard language

According to Bezuidenhout (2006), non-standard use of a language is one that "flouts a linguistic convention or that is an uncommon or novel use." The standard, conventional use is based on an explicit or implicit agreement among members of a linguistic community about the appropriate form of the language, given a specific situation.

This definition is problematic, because it may not include some common language varieties that are quite far from the standard use of a language, assumed both in traditional linguistics or in NLP, such as Twitter messages.[3] Rather than using the notion of standard as a universal yardstick, a more realistic view could be a point of reference relative to a binary opposition. It can be the prescriptive or literary norm in contrast to colloquial, dialectal, 'uneducated' or archaic use; the language as a system (*langue*, the idealized linguistic competence) in contrast to the real use of language (*parole*, linguistic performance); written in contrast to spoken varieties; native in contrast to non-native language; the language of a child in contrast to the language of an adult native speaker; the language of people without language disorders in contrast to those with such handicaps; and also expectations of the grammar writer in contrast to anything else.

Most deviations from any of the above "standards" are not random. Representative corpora of native written language show that there are regularly occurring patterns of non-standard usage, such as orthographical errors due to attraction in subject-predicate agreement.[4] There are many other regular phenomena occurring in the process of acquisition of non-native language, some of them universal or specific to the target language, some of them due to the influence of the native or some other language already known to the learner. These deviations reveal facts about the speaker, the target language and the native language and can be used in methods and tools identifying the language users and their background.

---

[2] A trivial example is represented by Czech typing assistants on portable devices. To the best of our knowledge, they do not offer any alternative to predicting standard word forms, ignoring any user preferences.

[3] While we do not agree with Plank et al. (2015) that the annotation of 'non-canonical' language is as hard (or as easy) as the annotation of newswire texts, we agree that "standard language" may be very different from what these traditional resources offer.

[4] According to Dotlačil (2016), SYN2010, the 100M Czech corpus (available at http://korpus.cz) includes 47 instances of short distance subject-predicate agreement patterns including purely orthographical errors in masculine animate past tense forms, where the *-ly* ending is used instead the correct homophonous *-li* ending.

A more practically oriented definition is offered by Hirschmann et al. (2007) in the context of annotating a learner corpus, referring to non-standard ('non-canonical') utterances as

> "[...] structures that cannot be described or generated by a given linguistic framework – canonicity can only be defined with respect to that framework. A structure may be non-canonical because it is ungrammatical, or it may be non-canonical because the given framework is not able to analyse it. For annotation purposes the reason for non-canonicity does not matter but for the interpretation of the non-canonical structures, it does. Most non-canonical structures in a learner corpus can be interpreted as errors [...] whereas many non-canonical structures in a corpus of spoken language or computer-mediated communication may be considered interesting features of those varieties."

This 'technical' view of what counts as non-standard language is more suitable to the tasks we cover in the present paper: annotating Czech as a foreign language and analyzing 'non-standard' linguistic phenomena in a parsebank of Czech. As Hirschmann et al. (2007) note, even if the interpretation of non-canonical structures differs for non-native and native speakers, many issues related to their appropriate annotation or analysis are shared by both tasks. However, we still feel the need to delineate the notion of non-standard language used here to include language varieties: (i) as used beyond the community of native speakers, (ii) of non-literary language, often widespread and representing a standard of its own kind, such as "Common Czech" (Sgall and Hronek, 1992), (iii) of spoken language, and (iv) including deviations due to the specifics of language production, i.e. performance errors of all sorts.

There are multiple ways how non-standard language can be processed, detected and diagnosed. As for learner texts, tools developed for standard language and trained on standard or non-standard language can be applied (Ramasamy et al., 2015), texts can be manually annotated (as it happens in learner corpora) and used to built stochastic models (Aharodnik et al., 2013), hand-crafted rules targeting standard and non-standard varieties can be used. While it is still true that "domain adaptation for parsing the web is still an unsolved problem" (Petrov and McDonald, 2012), it seems that designing an annotation scheme specific to non-standard (learner) language in order to build such a model brings better results (Berzak et al., 2016) than efforts to shoehorn existing annotation schemes to fit learner data (Cahill, 2015).

These results point to the need of "non-canonical categories for non-canonical data" (Dickinson and Ragheb, 2015). Such categories are not part of common linguistic wisdom. It is not clear which linguistic categories are suitable for the annotation of a non-standard text to design a tagset describing deviant word forms and syntactic structures, a taxonomy of errors at multiple levels of interpretation, an intelligibility metrics or even a specification of the influence of other languages.

The following section includes a proposal for a taxonomy of word forms, non-standard from the morphological perspective.

3   Designing categories for the morphology of Czech as a foreign language

With the increasing role of linguistic corpora, statistics and other formal analytical tools used in the field of language acquisition, demand is growing for categories applicable beyond standard language to the specific needs of the analysis of a language produced by non-native speakers. But before proceeding to the topic of a taxonomy suitable for the task of annotating such texts, we show some options of how standard assumptions about word classes could be modified. The resulting picture is actually a good starting point for an extension to non-standard language.[5]

Taxonomies of linguistic units such as morphemes, words, multiword expressions, phrases, clauses or sentences and of their properties are of critical importance to both theoretical and applied linguistics. Categories representing those units are crucial components in all rule-based and most stochastic models. The standard sets of 8–10 word classes (POS) are defined by a mix of morphological, syntactic and semantic criteria. For some POS the three criteria yield the same result, but POS such as numerals and pronouns end up as heterogeneous classes. A relative pronoun, defined by its semantic property of

---

[5]For a more detailed description of the proposed taxonomy of word classes see Rosen (2014).

referentiality to an antecedent, may have an adjectival declension pattern as its morphological property, but it can be used in its syntactic role in a nominal position.

More evidence of multiple class membership is easy to find. In Czech, the second position clitic is a category that must be lexically specified as such, but it is an auxiliary, a weak pronoun or a particle at the same time. Auxiliaries, prepositions and reflexive particles are sometimes treated as internal to a single analytical paradigm: a periphrastic verb form, a noun in "prepositional case", or inherently reflexive verb, while the rules of syntax need to access the independent functional morphemes as individual syntactic words to make sure that they obey constraints on ordering, agreement or government.

Thus, morphology, syntax and semantics take different perspectives, calling for a cross-classification of linguistic units at least along the three dimensions of morphology, syntax and semantics. Unsurprisingly, the option of cross-classification is often mentioned in literature, but it is hardly ever pursued. One of the criteria is usually adopted as the main one and others as complementary. Semantics is favored e.g. by Brøndal (1928), morphology by Saloni and Świdziński (1985, p. 95), syntax by Grzegorczykowa et al. (1998, p. 59). In theoretical linguistics, the syntactic criterion prevails: four basic lexical categories, determined by the combinations of two binary features (Chomsky, 1970), correspond to labels in a syntactic tree. The syntactic perspective is even more explicit in Jackendoff (1977, p. 31–32), or Dechaine (1993) – see Table 1. The binary features can be used to specify hyperclasses, such as −nominal for verbs and prepositions, which both assign case. However, none of the feature systems in the table is able to capture classes distinguished by all relevant properties.

	Chomsky (1970)		Jackendoff (1977)		Dechaine (1993)	
	nominal	verbal	subject	object	referential	object
Nouns	+	−	+	−	+	−
Verbs	−	+	+	+	+	+
Adjectives	+	+	−	−	−	−
Adpositions	−	−	−	+	−	+

Table 1: A syntax-based taxonomy – features determining basic lexical categories

The morphology-based classification of Saloni and Świdziński (1985), based on the presence of specific inflectional categories as properties of a POS, shows how POS correlate with sets of morphological categories. However, a single item can have more than one set of such categories, as in the Czech example (1). Like personal pronouns, possessive pronouns are marked for (i) person, number and gender to agree with their antecedents and – like adjectives – for (ii) number, gender, case to agree with the modified noun. Cross-classification allows for the former set to be appropriate for pronouns as a semantic POS, while the former set represents the properties of morphological adjectives. Czech possessive pronouns belong to both classes at the same time.

(1)   Jana   přišla, ale jejího   syna   jsem   neviděl.
      Jana$^{\text{FEM,NOM}}$ came   but her$^{\text{FEM,3RD}}_{\text{MASC,ACC}}$ son$_{\text{MASC,ACC}}$ I haven't seen
      'Jana has arrived, but I haven't seen her son.'

The cross-classification approach has been proposed e.g. by Brøndal (1928) and Komárek (1999), but rarely presented in standard reference books. To handle gerunds and other hybrid categories, Lapointe (1999) proposes dual lexical categories, determining both the external and internal syntactic properties of the item. Similarly as Combinatory Categorial Grammar (Steedman and Baldridge, 2011), this approach points to cross-classification. HPSG (Pollard and Sag, 1994) goes a step further by representing words and phrases as objects consisting of the unit's morphological, syntactic and semantic properties. The individual properties may be used as interfaces to external theories or processing modules.

To model variations in non-standard language, occurring at multiple levels of the language system, cross-classification, a multi-dimensional or multi-level system seems to be a natural choice. In the rest of this section, we will focus on the application of multidimensional taxonomy to the language of non-native speakers. The primary focus is on Czech, but most points should be relevant also to other morphologically rich languages.

It has been noted before (Díaz-Negrillo et al., 2010) that a cross-classifying scheme can be usefully applied to texts produced by foreign language learners. The scheme treats such texts as specimens of *interlanguage*, a language sui generis, approximating the target language in the process of language acquisition, to some extent independently of the target language, i.e. of the error-based approach (Corder, 1981; Selinker, 1983). The non-standard features of interlanguage can be modelled as deviations on appropriate levels.

For English, the use of an adjective in an adverbial position can be analysed as a mismatch between adverb as the syntactically appropriate category and adjective as the lexical category of the form used by the author of the text. A parallel Czech example is shown in (2), where the adjectival form *krásný* 'beautiful' is used instead of the standard adverbial form *krásně* 'beautifully'. The word can be annotated as morphological adjective and syntactic adverb.

(2)   Whitney Houston zpívala ***krásný**   → krásně.
       Whitney Houston sang   ***beautiful**$_{ADJ}$ → beautifully$_{ADV}$
       'Whitney Houston sang beautifully.'

However, in Czech as a morphologically rich language, interlanguage typically deviates not just in the use of word classes, but also in morphemics, morphology and morphosyntax. A richer taxonomy is required that the one proposed in Díaz-Negrillo et al. (2010) for English. First of all, categories such as number, gender, case are needed. In (3), *táta* 'daddy' is nominative, but its syntactic role as the object of *viděl* 'saw' requires the accusative. This represents a mismatch between morphology and syntax in the category of case. A parallel example in English would be would be (4-a)[6] or, with a mismatch in number, (4-b).

(3)   Lucka   viděla ***táta** → tátu.
       Lucy$_{NOM}$ saw   daddy$_{*NOM → ACC}$
       'Lucy saw her dad.'

(4)   a.   I must play with ***he**$_{NOM}$ → him$_{ACC}$.
       b.   The first year ***have**$_{PL}$ → has$_{SG}$ been wonderful.

In (5-a), the aspect of the content verb *napsat* 'to write' is perfective, while the auxiliary verb *bude* can only form analytical future tense with an imperfective form. A perfective verb is used in its present form to express future meaning, as in (5-b).

(5)   a.   Eva bude ***napsat**   dopis.
           Eva will   write$_{*PERF}$ letter
           'Eva will write a letter.'
       b.   Eva napíše   dopis.
           Eva writes$_{PERF}$ letter.
           'Eva will write a letter.'

Although the cross-classification idea can be applied to the analysis of all of the above examples as mismatches between morphology and syntax, it does not seem to be the most intuitive solution.

As Dickinson and Ragheb (2015) say: "While errors (i.e., ungrammaticalities) can be derived from mismatches between annotation layers, they are not primary entities. The multi-layer linguistic annotation is primarily based on linguistic evidence, not a sentence's correctness." Indeed, the annotation of (4-a) may be seen as agnostic about the fact that *he* is in a wrong case and that the accusative case can be accepted as a syntactic category. As the authors say: "the word *he* cannot simply be marked as a nominative or accusative pronoun because in some sense it is both. Thus, one may want to annotate multiple layers, in this case one POS layer for morphological evidence and one for syntactic distributional evidence (i.e., position)."

---

[6]The example is taken from Dickinson and Ragheb (2015).

Yet we see as legitimate a different claim, namely that the form is only nominative rather than both nominative and accusative. While nominative is the morphological category, the missing syntactic interpretation is that of an object, a category specific to the layer of syntax. Moreover, it is not obvious that considerations related to correctness are absent from the analysis or secondary. We prefer to see the mismatch between annotation layers on the one hand and the aspect of comparison to the target (correct) form on the other as complementary.[7]

This modification of the original cross-classifying scheme is supported by more evidence from the domain of morphology. The original proposal of Díaz-Negrillo et al. (2010) is concerned with English learner texts, assuming only standard POS labels at three layers: distribution (syntax), morphology and lexical stems. In standard language, the evidence from the three levels converges on a single POS. Mismatches indicate an error: stem vs. distribution (*they are very kind and *friendship*), stem vs. morphology (*television, radio are very *subjectives*), distribution vs. morphology (*the first year *have been wonderful*). All of these types are attested in Czech, but due to a wide range of phenomena related to morphemics and morphology, bare POS and mismatches of this type are not sufficient.

To accommodate possibly parallel deviations in orthography, morphemics and morphology the number of layers must be extended, each with categories of its own. We start from an existing taxonomy for Czech learner texts with less granular morphological categories (Rosen et al., 2014), using the following layers to analyse non-standard forms, abstracting from other issues of syntax, semantics or pragmatics. Each of the layers is specified by its relevant linguistic category (stem, paradigm, case, number, gender, etc.) and possibly by an error label. The first two items are actually not layers in the linguistic sense but rather specifications from a different viewpoint.

- Formal: missing or redundant character, character metathesis, etc.

- Location: identification of the part of the form where the deviation occurs, such as stem, prefix, derivational suffix or inflectional ending

- Orthography: including word boundaries, capitalization, punctuation

- Morphemics: the form includes a non-existing morpheme or a morpheme incompatible with other morphemes present in the form, problems in palatalization, epenthesis or other processes

- Morphology: improper use of a morphological category or word class, also due to agreement or government

In the practical task of manual annotation, it is often difficult to decide what the cause of a specific deviation is. If this is the case, there are two possible strategies: (i) to specify the deviation as occurring at a level where the analysis requires a more sophisticated judgment, i.e. morphosyntax in preference to orthography; or (ii) to specify the deviation in parallel on all relevant levels. We opt for the latter solution, which leaves the decision open for additional analysis and fits well in the concept of cross-classification. In any case, the choice is alleviated by the option of automatic identification of some error types, given a corrected ("emended") form, or even by using a tool suggesting corrections. Actually, the automatic identification always produces at least a formal identification, such as missing or redundant character.

In addition to the layered annotation of the original form, an ill-formed word is assigned a target hypothesis (corrected form) and its analysis, corresponding to the annotation of the original form. Additional categories, such as syntactic function, can also be specified. The two annotation poles – one for the ill-formed and one for the corrected word – are seen as a pattern, a type of mismatch between the annotation layers and the two poles. For a simple case such as (3), the pattern is shown in Table 2.[8] A taxonomy of such patterns can be built and references to more or less abstract patterns can be used as tags. A more abstract pattern in Table 3 represents all cases where a nominative form is used instead of an accusative form.

---

[7] As Dickinson and Ragheb (2015) also say "There are two main wrinkles to separating linguistic annotation from error annotation, however: 1) annotation categories could employ a notion of grammatical correctness to define; and 2) the decision process for ambiguous cases could reference a sentence's correctness."

[8] In a fully specified pattern, morphological analysis includes all relevant categories, including lemma.

	original	target
formal	replacement of a single character	
location	inflectional suffix	
orthography	*a*	*u*
morphology	nominative noun	accusative noun

Table 2: A pattern for *táta* in (3) (*Lucka viděla *táta*)

	original	target
location	inflectional suffix	
morphology	nominative	accusative

Table 3: An abstract pattern for a form which is nominative instead of accusative

A different type of error is shown in (6). Unlike *táta* in (3), *babičkem* is a non-word. However, it can be interpreted as consisting of the feminine stem *babičk-* and the masculine singular instrumental suffix *-em*, compatible with the preposition but incompatible with the gender of the stem.[9]

(6)   Byl jsem doma s   ***babičkem** → babičkou.
       was AUX at home with granny
       'I was at home with Grannie.'

The pattern is shown in 4. A more abstract pattern could include only the location and morphemics rows.

	original	target
formal	replacement of two characters	
location	inflectional suffix	
orthography	*em*	*ou*
morphemics	feminine stem + masculine suffix	feminine stem + feminine suffix
morphology	instrumental noun (?)	instrumental noun

Table 4: A pattern for *babičkem* in (6)

Tags referring to such patterns can be used as a powerful indicator of the type of interlanguage and the language learner's competence, and can help to build models of interlanguage by machine learning methods. The scheme will be evaluated in trial annotation, including inter-annotator agreement, and tested in machine learning experiments.

4   Identifying non-standard language in a corpus

Except for individual word forms (colloquial, dialectal or non-words) in mainstream corpora and error annotation in learner corpora, corpus annotation rarely distinguishes regular, expected or "standard" expressions on the one hand from less predictable evidence of language use on the other.

Non-standard usage defies general rules of grammar: non-standard language may involve performance errors, creative coinages, or emerging phenomena. Most of these phenomena are still not random, even though it is far from trivial to discover the underlying patterns. In this section, we show an attempt to detect and annotate these phenomena in a treebank/parsebank of Czech.

The theoretical assumption is that linguistic annotation of a corpus represents the meeting point of the empirical evidence (parole) and the theory (langue), in the sense of Saussurean *sign* (de Saussure, 1916). Moreover, the annotation is also where multiple levels of analysis and linguistic theories may meet and

---

[9]The suffix may also be interpreted in other ways, e.g. as the first person plural ending in the present tense of some verbal paradigms (*nesem*). However, rather than multiplying alternatives, which do not appear as likely candidates given the context, we give the author the benefit of the doubt and choose the instrumental interpretation. For the same reason, we refrain from suggesting the hypothesis that the author was at home with her grandpa (*s dědečkem*) rather than her granny (*s babičkou*).

be explicit about any, even irregular phenomena. An annotation scheme defined as a formal grammar can help to identify the difference between the regular and irregular, between the language as a system and the use of language.

This is the motivation behind the project of a corpus annotated by standard stochastic tools[10] and checked by a rule-based grammar and valency lexicon, which are also used to infer additional linguistic information about the annotated data.[11] After some detail about the grammar and the lexicon, their current coverage will be presented in terms of statistical results, based on the share of expressions that satisfy the definition of "correctness" as stated by the grammar and the lexicon.

The grammar is used as a watchdog: to check stochastic parses for both formal and linguistic correctness and consistency. Compliant parses receive additional information: relevant properties of lexical categories are projected to phrasal nodes and lexical categories including lemmas matching lexical entries receive valency frames to be saturated by complements in the parse. The grammar is thus supposed to define standard, 'canonical' language in the 'technical' sense of Hirschmann et al. (2007) (see § 2 above). However, this is an idealized picture: the grammar both overgenerates, leaving some non-standard utterances undetected, and undergenerates, falsely deciding that some utterances are not correct – see below for more on this topic.

The grammar consists of a lexical module, providing candidate lexical entries to supply valency frames for verbal lexemes in the data, and a syntactic module, checking the parse and making it more informative by projecting information in the leaf nodes of the constituency tree along the phrasal projections and to the complement sister nodes (dependents). The lexical module operates on lexical entries derived from external valency lexica. The module is responsible for generating a list of entries specific to available diatheses of verbal lexemes. The syntactic module matches the generated lexical entries with the data. The categorial information about words and phrases in the data and in the lexicon follow the cross-classifying taxonomy, used for the learner corpus. The taxonomy captures all distinctions present in a standard Czech tagset used in the stochastic parse and opens the option to use the multi-level scheme to represent non-standard forms in a way it is used in the learner corpus.[12]

The grammar is implemented in Trale,[13] a formalism designed for grammars based on HPSG,[14] a linguistic theory modeling linguistic expressions as typed feature structures. Formally, the grammar consists of two parts: (i) *signature*, i.e. a definition of types of linguistic objects, ordered in a type hierarchy, including their attributes and values; and (ii) *theory*, i.e. a set of constraints on the types and their properties. The parses and lexical entries are in a format compatible with the grammar formalism. The fewer constraints a *constraint-based* grammar includes, the more it *overgenerates*, i.e. the more permissive it is. This is viewed as a welcome property in the development of a grammar that is used primarily for checking existing parses.

There are several important points in which the grammar differs from a standard HPSG grammar, or – more specifically – from a grammar implemented in Trale:

- Rather than parsing or generating strings of word forms, the grammar operates on structures produced by a stochastic parser. As a result, it does not include any syntactic rules of the context-free type. The syntactic backbone, often assumed to be a necessary component of a context-free grammar, is present in the data rather than in the grammar.

- The grammar is run in the mode of a constraint solver, rather than a parser or generator. The constraints come from three sources: the data, the lexicon, and the grammar proper.

- The data are unambiguous in the sense of including a single parse for each sentence. Ambiguities or (preferably) underspecifications may arise only due to the more detailed taxonomy in the treebank format and/or an uncertainty about the choice of a valency frame.

---

[10]See Jelínek (2016).

[11]For more detail about the project see, e.g., Petkevič et al. (2015a).

[12]See also Petkevič et al. (2015b) for a description of the annotation of periphrastic verb forms using an additional analytical dimension.

[13]http://www.ale.cs.toronto.edu/docs/

[14]See, e.g., Pollard and Sag (1994) or Levine and Meurers (2006).

The lexical module uses two external sources of lexical knowledge, both are available and down-loadable valency lexicons: VALLEX[15] and PDT-VALLEX,[16] including about 5,000 and 10,000 verbs, respectively, with their deep valency frames and information about the forms of the syntactic arguments (case, verbal form, etc.). The frames reflect the Praguian valency theory of the Functional Generative Description (Panevová, 1994) and are used to check whether valency requirements of the verbs in the parsed sentence are met. The lexical module provides the mapping of the frames to their instantiations in specific verbal diatheses and morphological forms, using the same signature and formalism as the syntactic component.

The syntactic module is responsible for checking the parse using the lexical specifications and con-straints of the module. The grammar may decide that the parse complies in all respects and provide all available information in the resulting structure. If, however, not all relevant lexical entries are found for the sentence, predicates without valency frames cannot check completeness and coherence of the argu-ment structure in the data, but they can still check grammatical agreement. A valency frame may also cause failure of the check. If so, the sentence is checked also without that frame. A sentence may also fail due to the constraints of the syntactic module. The last remaining and the weakest test is then to apply only the data format definition without constraints (the signature, i.e. the definition of objects and their properties as feature structures representing constituents and their parts).

In most of the above levels of checking, a failure can occur due to non-standard linguistic phenomenon in the data, an incorrect decision of the parser or the tagger, or an error in the grammar or lexicon. An efficient and powerful diagnostics is an important task for the future. One option is to make use of the constraint-based architecture by successively relaxing constraints to find the grammatical or lexical constraint and the part of the input responsible for the failure. Another possibility is to use constraints targeting specific non-standard structures or lexical specifications, the so-called mal-rules.[17]

The examples below illustrate the role of the grammar. In (7-a) and (7-b) the possessive form agrees in gender and case (and number) with the head noun. Examples (7-c) and (7-d) are different: in (7-c) the possessive form does not agree with the head noun in case, in (7-d) in case and gender. Note that the possessive form in (7-c), which is the same as in (7-a), does not strike many speakers as incorrect. In the SYN2015 corpus, the share of these non-standard forms is about 4% in the total number of masculine dative singular NPs preceded by the preposition k. Example (7-d) has a similar status, but it is acceptable only to speakers of a dialect of Czech.

(7)   a.   Přitiskl se   k otcově   noze.
            clung   RFLX to father's$_{\text{FEM,DAT}}$ leg$_{\text{FEM,DAT}}$
            'He pressed against his father's leg.'

     b.   Přistoupil   k otcovu   stolu.
            approached to father's$_{\text{MASC,DAT}}$ desk$_{\text{MASC,DAT}}$
            'He approached his father's desk.'

     c.   Přistoupil   k **?otcově**   stolu.
            approached to father's$_{\text{MASC,LOC}}$ desk$_{\text{MASC,DAT}}$

     d.   Přistoupil   k **?otcovo**   stolu.
            approached to father's$_{\text{NEUT,NOM/ACC}}$ desk$_{\text{MASC,DAT}}$

The stochastic parser ignores the agreement mismatch and builds a correct tree. On the other hand, the grammar does not accept the parse. Like every rule-based grammar, the grammar does not have an optimal coverage. In our case it is not a fatal flaw: in most cases a missing account of a phenomenon only means that the grammar is more permissive than it should be (i.e. it overgenerates). The filling of gaps in the coverage is another priority for the future.

The syntactic module includes constraints found in other HPSG-like grammars, such as Head Fea-

---

[15]See http://ufal.mff.cuni.cz/vallex, Lopatková et al. (2008; Žabokrtský and Lopatková (2007)

[16]See Hajič et al. (2003)

[17]Mal-rules have been used in the context of CALL (computer-assisted language learning) at least by Schneider and McCoy (1998) (for users of American Sign Language learning English as their L2), Bender et al. (2004), and Flickinger and Yu (2013) (both implemented in HPSG).

ture Principle, making sure that the head daughter shares appropriate features with its mother, Valency Principle, matching complements and adjuncts with a surface valency frame produced by the lexical component, and other more specific constraints targeting individual types of constructions. The constraints operate mostly on words, such as those specifying morphological categories relevant for agreement within the valency slots of subjects (for subject-predicate agreement) or within a slots for the head (for attribute-noun agreement). The rest is the task of Valency Principle. A special set of constraints is concerned with analytic verb forms, which are treated with respect to their dual status, i.e. from the paradigmatic perspective as forms of the content verb, and from the syntagmatic perspective as constructions.

A grammar of linguistic competence can never fit the corpus as the evidence of linguistic performance completely. In fact, this may be seen as a benefit: the unexpected or non-standard phenomena in the data can be detected in this way. To distinguish the cases of truly non-standard language from the problems of the syntactic and lexical specifications of the grammar component (useful for the grammar development) on the one hand and to identify and diagnose the types of nonstandard language on the other, the diagnostic part of the tool will be extended to find which specific constraints are violated by which specific words or constructions in the data.

The grammar and lexicon has been developed and tested on a set of 876 sentences, extracted from the manual for the annotation of the Prague Dependency Treebank (Hajič et al., 1997), representing a wide range of linguistic phenomena. Currently, for 592 sentences a valency frame from the lexicon was found. The number of sentences verified by the grammar is 560. This includes 301 sentences with a valency frame. A more extensive testing is under way, using a 100M corpus.

For more extensive testing, the SYN2015 corpus was used, including about 100 million words, i.e. 7.2 million sentences. For 77% sentences at least one valency frame was found and 55% sentences passed the grammar, 16% including a valency frame, 23% without any valency frame, and 16% after the valency frame was dropped.

The next step will be to categorize the failures and build a corpus showing the results, including the grammar flags, in a user-friendly way.

5   Discussion and conclusion

We have shown two ways how to approach non-standard languages, with a stress on its proper detection and diagnosis. We see this effort as an attempt to tackle a domain of growing importance, one in which the methods and tools available for standard language have only limited usability. Admittedly, this is very much work in progress, but we hope to have achieved some promising results already.

Acknowledgements

This work has been supported by the Grant Agency of the Czech Republic, grant no. 16-10185S. The author is grateful to Hana Skoumalová and Jiří Znamenáček for their generous help with the data and to anonymous reviewers for their very useful comments.

References

Katsiaryna Aharodnik, Marco Chang, Anna Feldman, and Jirka Hana. 2013. Automatic identification of learners' language background based on their writing in Czech. In *Proceedings of the 6th International Joint Conference on Natural Language Processing (IJNCLP 2013), Nagoya, Japan, October 2013*, pages 1428–1436.

Emily M. Bender, Dan Flickinger, Stephan Oepen, Annemarie Walsh, and Tim Baldwin. 2004. Arboretum: Using a precision grammar for grammar checking in CALL. In *Proceedings of the InSTIL/ICALL Symposium: NLP and Speech Technologies in Advanced Language Learning Systems*, Venice, Italy.

Yevgeni Berzak, Jessica Kenney, Carolyn Spadine, Jing Xian Wang, Lucia Lam, Keiko Sophie Mori, Sebastian Garza, and Boris Katz. 2016. Universal dependencies for learner English. *CoRR*, abs/1605.04278.

Anne L. Bezuidenhout. 2006. Nonstandard language use. In Keith Brown, editor, *Encyclopedia of Language and Linguistics. Second Edition*, pages 686–689. Elsevier, Oxford.

Viggo Brøndal. 1928. *Ordklasserne. Partes Orationis*. G. E. C. Gad, København.

Aoife Cahill. 2015. Parsing learner text: to shoehorn or not to shoehorn. In *Proceedings of The 9th Linguistic Annotation Workshop*, pages 144–147, Denver, Colorado, USA, June. Association for Computational Linguistics.

Noam Chomsky. 1970. Remarks on nominalization. In R. Jacobs and P. Rosenbaum, editors, *Reading in English Transformational Grammar*, pages 184–221. Ginn and Co., Waltham.

Pitt Corder. 1981. *Error Analysis and Interlanguage*. Oxford University Press, Oxford.

Ferdinand de Saussure. 1916. *Cours de linguistique générale*. Paris. Publié par Ch. Bally et A. Sechehay avec la collaboration de A Riedlinger.

Rose-Marie Anne Dechaine. 1993. *Predicates across categories: Towards a category-neutral syntax*. Ph.D. thesis, University of Massachusetts, Amherst.

Markus Dickinson and Marwa Ragheb. 2015. On grammaticality in the syntactic annotation of learner language. In *Proceedings of The 9th Linguistic Annotation Workshop*, pages 158–167, Denver, CO, June.

Jakub Dotlačil. 2016. Shoda podmětu s přísudkem, pravopis a iluze gramatičnosti. A talk presented at the conference Linguistics and Literary Studies: Paths and Perspectives, Liberec, 22–23 September 2016, September.

Ana Díaz-Negrillo, Detmar Meurers, Salvador Valera, and Holger Wunsch. 2010. Towards interlanguage POS annotation for effective learner corpora in SLA and FLT. *Language Forum*, 36(1–2):139–154. Special Issue on Corpus Linguistics for Teaching and Learning. In Honour of John Sinclair.

Jacob Eisenstein. 2013. What to do about bad language on the internet. In *Proceedings of the North American Chapter of the Association for Computational Linguistics (NAACL)*, pages 359–369, Stroudsburg, Pennsylvania. Association for Computational Linguistics.

Dan Flickinger and Jiye Yu. 2013. Toward more precision in correction of grammatical errors. In *Proceedings of the Seventeenth Conference on Computational Natural Language Learning: Shared Task*, pages 68–73, Sofia, Bulgaria. Association for Computational Linguistics.

Renata Grzegorczykowa, Roman Laskowski, and Henryk Wróbel, editors. 1998. *Gramatyka współczesnego języka polskiego – Morfologia*, volume 1. Wydawniczwo Naukowe PWN.

Jan Hajič, Jarmila Panevová, Eva Buránová, Zdenka Urešová, and Alla Bémová. 1997. A manual for analytic layer tagging of the Prague Dependency Treebank. Technical Report TR-1997-03, ÚFAL MFF UK, Prague, Czech Republic. in Czech.

Jan Hajič, Jarmila Panevová, Zdeňka Urešová, Alevtina Bémová, and Petr Pajas. 2003. PDT-VALLEX: Creating a large-coverage valency lexicon for treebank annotation. In *Proceedings of The Second Workshop on Treebanks and Linguistic Theories*, pages 57–68. Växjö University Press.

Hagen Hirschmann, Seanna Doolittle, and Anke Lüdeling. 2007. Syntactic annotation of non-canonical linguistics structures. In *Proceedings of Corpus Linguistics 2007*, Birmingham.

Ray S. Jackendoff. 1977. *X-bar syntax: A study of phrase structure*. MIT Press, Camebridge, Massachusetts.

Tomáš Jelínek. 2016. Combining dependency parsers using error rates. In *Text, Speech and Dialogue – Proceedings of the 19th International Conference TSD 2016*, pages 82–92. Springer.

Miroslav Komárek. 1999. Autosemantic Parts of Speech in Czech. In *Travaux du Cercle linguistique de Prague*, volume 3, pages 195–210. Benjamins, Amsterdam.

Steven G. Lapointe. 1999. Dual lexical categories vs. phrasal conversion in the analysis of gerund phrases. In Paul de Lacy and Anita Nowak, editors, *University of Massachusetts Occasional Papers in Linguistics*, number 24, page 157–189. University of Massachusetts.

Robert D. Levine and Walt Detmar Meurers. 2006. Head-Driven Phrase Structure Grammar: Linguistic approach, formal foundations, and computational realization. In Keith Brown, editor, *Encyclopedia of Language and Linguistics. Second Edition*. Elsevier, Oxford.

Markéta Lopatková, Zdeněk Žabokrtský, and Václava Kettnerová. 2008. *Valenční slovník českých sloves*. Univerzita Karlova v Praze, Nakladatelství Karolinum, Praha.

Jarmila Panevová. 1994. Valency frames and the meaning of the sentence. In P. A. Luelsdorff, editor, *The Prague School of structural and functional linguistics. A short introduction*, pages 223–243. John Benjamins, Amsterdam – Philadelphia.

Vladimír Petkevič, Alexandr Rosen, and Hana Skoumalová. 2015a. The grammarian is opening a treebank account. *Prace Filologiczne*, LXVII:239–260.

Vladimír Petkevič, Alexandr Rosen, Hana Skoumalová, and Přemysl Vítovec. 2015b. Analytic morphology – merging the paradigmatic and syntagmatic perspective in a treebank. In Jakub Piskorski, Lidia Pivovarova, Jan Šnajder, Hristo Tanev, and Roman Yangarber, editors, *The 5th Workshop on Balto-Slavic Natural Language Processing (BSNLP 2015)*, pages 9–16, Hissar, Bulgaria.

Slav Petrov and Ryan McDonald. 2012. Overview of the 2012 shared task on parsing the web. In *Notes of the First Workshop on Syntactic Analysis of Non-Canonical Language (SANCL)*, volume 59.

Barbara Plank, Hector Martinez Alonso, and Anders Søgaard. 2015. Non-canonical language is not harder to annotate than canonical language. In *The 9th Linguistic Annotation Workshop (held in conjuncion with NAACL 2015)*, pages 148–151. Association for Computational Linguistics.

Barbara Plank. 2016. What to do about non-standard (or non-canonical) language in NLP. In *KONVENS 2016*.

Carl J. Pollard and Ivan A. Sag. 1994. *Head-Driven Phrase Structure Grammar*. University of Chicago Press, Chicago.

Loganathan Ramasamy, Alexandr Rosen, and Pavel Straňák. 2015. Improvements to Korektor: A case study with native and non-native Czech. In Jakub Yaghob, editor, *ITAT 2015: Information technologies – Applications and Theory / SloNLP 2015*, pages 73–80, Prague. Charles University in Prague.

Alexandr Rosen, Jirka Hana, Barbora Štindlová, and Anna Feldman. 2014. Evaluating and automating the annotation of a learner corpus. *Language Resources and Evaluation – Special Issue: Resources for language learning*, 48(1):65–92, March.

Alexandr Rosen. 2014. A 3D taxonomy of word classes at work. In Ludmila Veselovská and Markéta Janebová, editors, *Complex Visibles Out There. Proceedings of the Olomouc Linguistics Colloquium 2014: Language Use and Linguistic Structure*, volume 4 of *Olomouc Modern Language Series*, pages 575–590, Olomouc. Palacký University.

Zygmunt Saloni and Marek Świdziński. 1985. *Składnia współczesnego języka polskiego*. Państwowe Wydawnictwo Naukowe, Warszawa.

David Schneider and Kathleen F. McCoy. 1998. Recognizing syntactic errors in the writing of second language learners. In *Proceedings of the 36th Annual Meeting of the Association for Computational Linguistics and 17th International Conference on Computational Linguistics - Volume 2*, ACL '98, pages 1198–1204, Stroudsburg, PA, USA. Association for Computational Linguistics.

Larry Selinker. 1983. Interlanguage. In *Second Language Learning: Contrastive analysis, error analysis, and related aspects*, pages 173–196. The University of Michigan Press, Ann Arbor, MI.

Petr Sgall and Jiří Hronek. 1992. *Čeština bez příkras*. H&H, Praha.

Mark Steedman and Jason Baldridge. 2011. Combinatory Categorial Grammar. In Robert Borsley and Kersti Börjars, editors, *Non-Transformational Syntax*, pages 181–224. Blackwell.

Zdeněk Žabokrtský and Markéta Lopatková. 2007. Valency information in VALLEX 2.0: Logical structure of the lexicon. *The Prague Bulletin of Mathematical Linguistics*, (87):41–60.

Author Index

Association for Computational Linguistics
209 N. Eighth Street
Stroudsburg, Pennsylvania 18360

ISBN 978-1-5108-3318-0